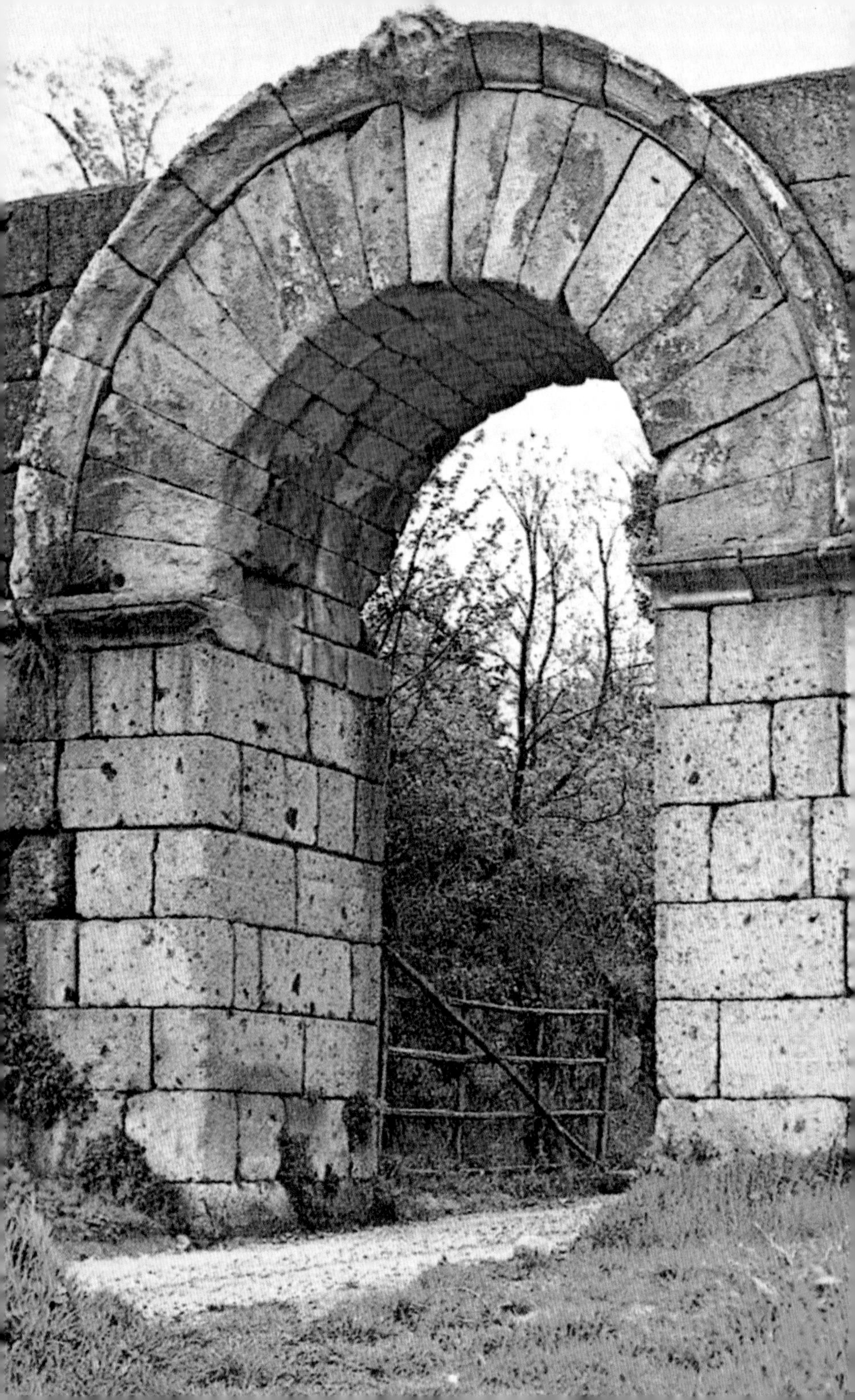

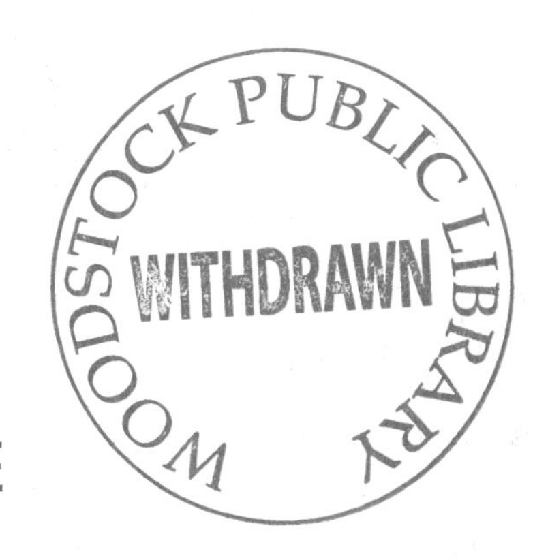

THE ETRUSCANS

Art, Architecture, and History

Federica Borrelli
Maria Cristina Targia

Edited by Stefano Peccatori
and Stefano Zuffi

Translated by Thomas Michael Hartmann

THE J. PAUL GETTY MUSEUM
LOS ANGELES

Browsing Guide

The pages in this series are color-coded into three categories so that the reader might access information easily and enjoyably. Yellow tabs mark pages dedicated to art and architecture, blue denotes historical and artistic background, and pink identifies analyses of specific masterpieces of art. Each two-page spread treats a single subject, with an introduction and commentary on the illustrations and photos. The reader can freely choose how and in what order to browse this book, by either leafing through the chapters in order or taking a more personal approach.
Maps, a glossary, and indexes of museums and historical places complete the volume. These too are illustrated in order that the reader might immediately identify various artworks, historical figures, and geographic locations.

■ *On page 2,* The Porta di Giove, third century B.C., Falerii Novi

Contents

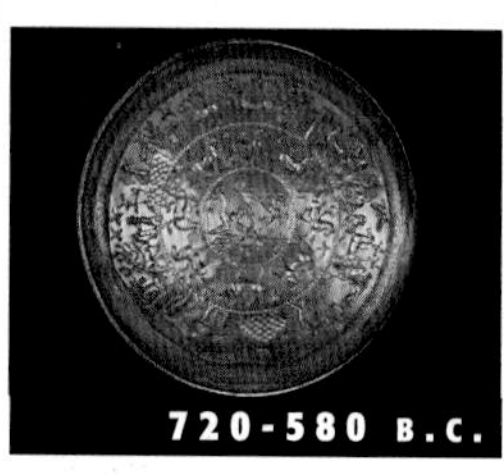

720-580 B.C.

The Orientalizing Period

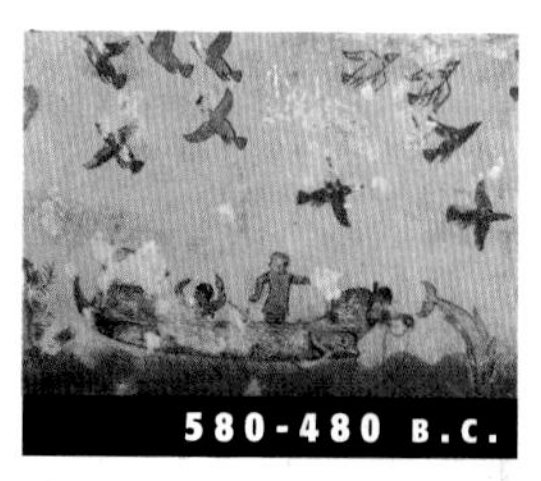

580-480 B.C.

The Archaic Period

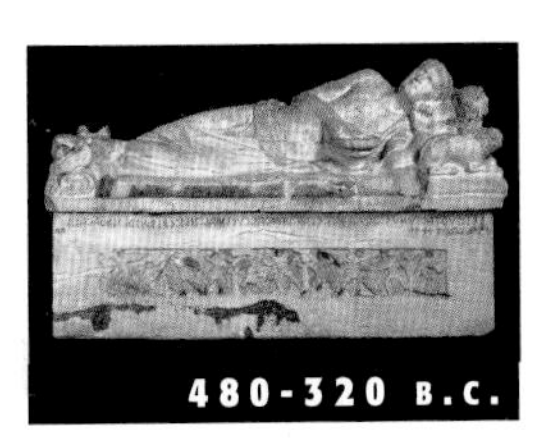

The Classical Period

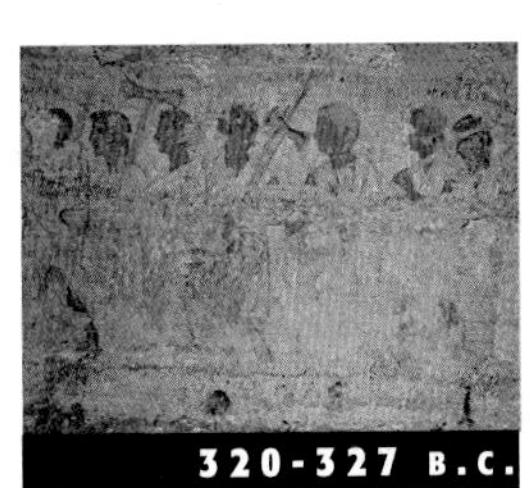

Hellenism and Romanization

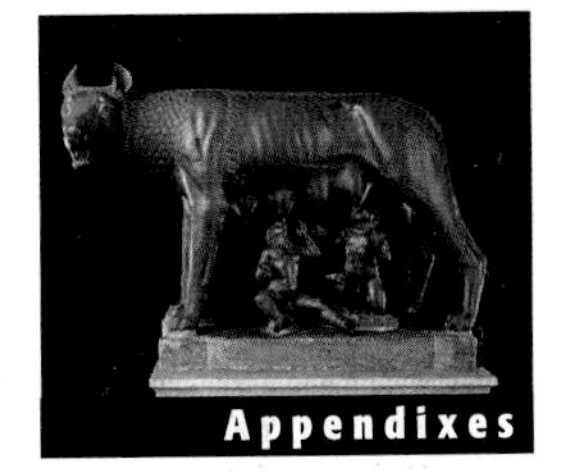

Etruscan Origins and the Villanovan Civilization

Both ancient and modern scholars have debated the Etruscans' origins, approaching the subject with a variety of motives and methods. Three theories have emerged. The first, originally proposed by the historian Herodotus, held that they were the descendants of sailors who arrived from the East. A second saw them as part of migratory movements from the Alpine regions, and the third, put forward by Dionysius of Halikarnassos, placed the ancestors of the Etruscans among the ancient inhabitants of Etruria. It is, in any case, indisputable that Etruscan culture emerged from the fusion of diverse elements in an environment—the area of central Italy that faced the Tyrrhenian Sea—that was particularly receptive. The oldest signs of this fusion can be found in the so-called Villanovan culture at the city of Villanova near Bologna, where the earliest archaeological evidence has been uncovered. Cinerary urns containing the ashes of the deceased were placed in trench tombs along with personal objects that indicate clear differences between male and female belongings. Agricultural activity and the utilization of mineral resources favored the economic and cultural development of the Villanovan villages, which sprang up at the sites of future Etruscan cities.

▶ Hut urn reproducing the dwelling of the deceased. Tarquinia, Museo Archeologico. The hut was oval in shape and its roof was made of a framework of beams covered with straw, with openings for smoke to escape. The walls were made of reeds or branches covered with clay.

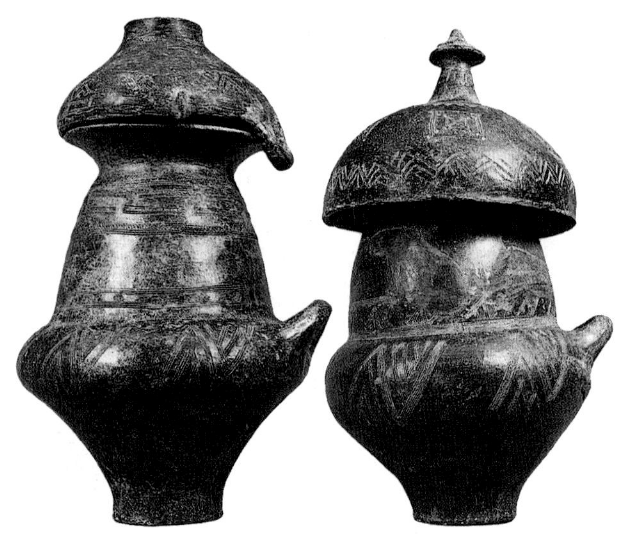

◀ Cinerary urn from the Villanovan period. Tarquinia, Monterozzi necropolis. These ceramic urns are biconical and feature Geometric decoration that was stamped or cut into the body and cover. The lid varied according to the sex of the deceased: usually an inverted bowl for a woman and a helmet for a man. The simplicity of these early grave goods does not provide evidence of any social differentiation within the group, an element that would appear later.

▶ Bronze helmet with an embossed decoration, found in a necropolis in Tarquinia, 800–750 B.C. Florence, Museo Archeologico. It was used as the lid for the cinerary urn of a person of high social status, perhaps a warrior. Typical of grave goods in southern Etruria, this helmet is comparable to others unearthed in urn fields in northern Europe.

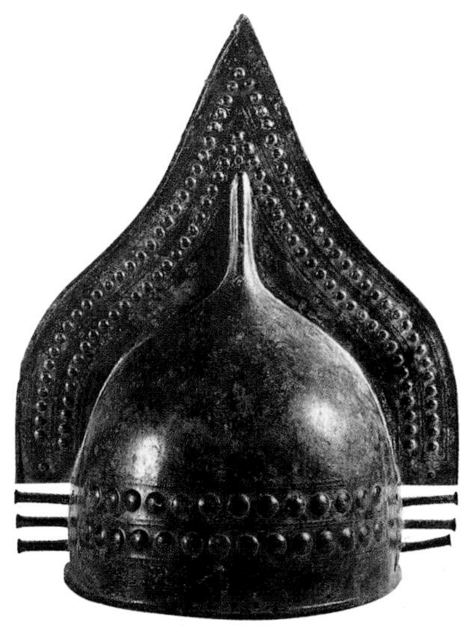

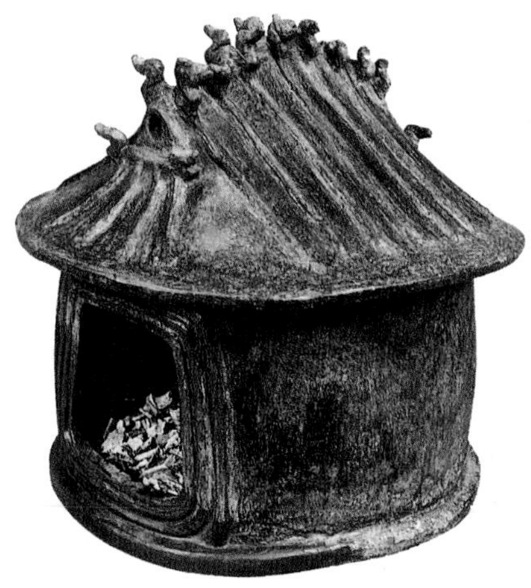

▼ Ceremonial incense burner from Bisenzio, 750–700 B.C. Rome, Museo di Villa Giulia. This extraordinary masterpiece of Etruscan bronzework from the late Villanovan period offers a mixture of indigenous features—the crowd of human and animal figurines—with Eastern elements in the object's shape.

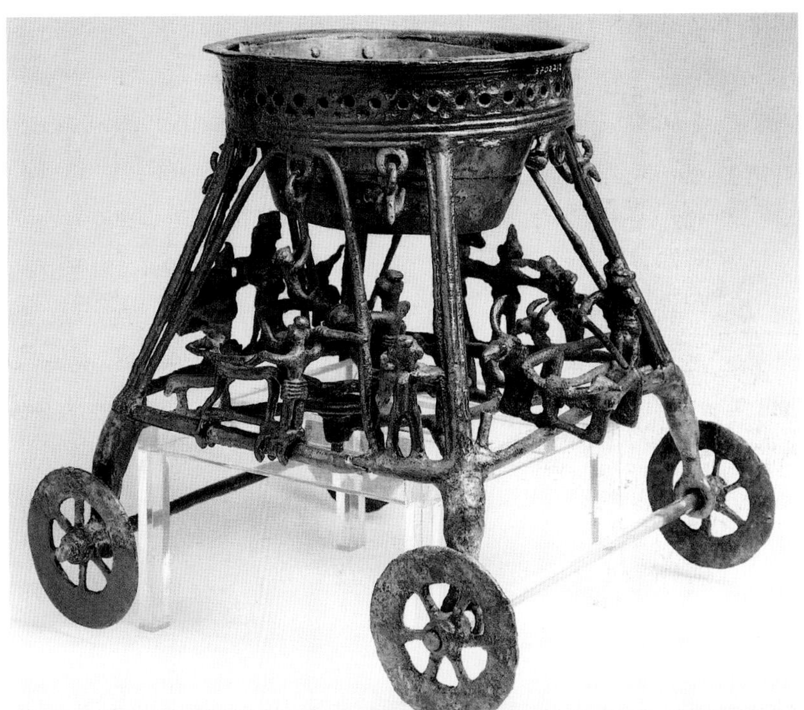

Economic Activity in the Etruscan World

The Etruscan economy first developed within several specialized spheres: farming, animal breeding, metalworking, and the production and exchange of manufactured goods. The relationships among these activities varied throughout the centuries, as did their qualitative and quantitative impacts on the structure of the regional economy. From the villages of the late Bronze Age to the urban center of the Classical and Hellenistic periods and their surrounding areas, a few families were able to achieve hegemony through two main activities: agriculture and metallurgy. The rise of an aristocratic class marked the passage from a collective economy to an individual one. Southern cities rose thanks to their mines and proximity to the sea, and a homogeneous class of free individuals emerged, intermediaries who oversaw agriculture and craftsmanship. This economic system would gradually produce a society with an unbridgeable social gap between masters and servants. Subjugation by Rome and the removal of the aristocracy eventually dismantled the system of production and altered the city–country relationship. The decadence of the second century B.C., halted in the north by a policy of apportioning and redistributing land to the population's lower classes, would signal their definitive decline.

◀ The Palm Painter (attributed), an Italian Geometric *oinochoe* (wine jug) with a depiction of fish and boats, 700–675 B.C. Columbia (Mo.), Museum of Art and Archaeology, University of Missouri. The boats recall the ships with rudders and curved keels that plowed the Tyrrhenian Sea.

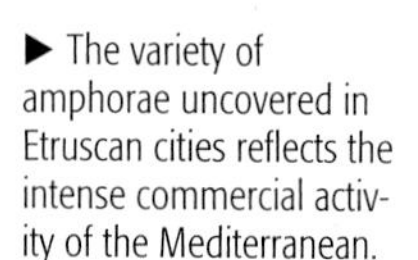

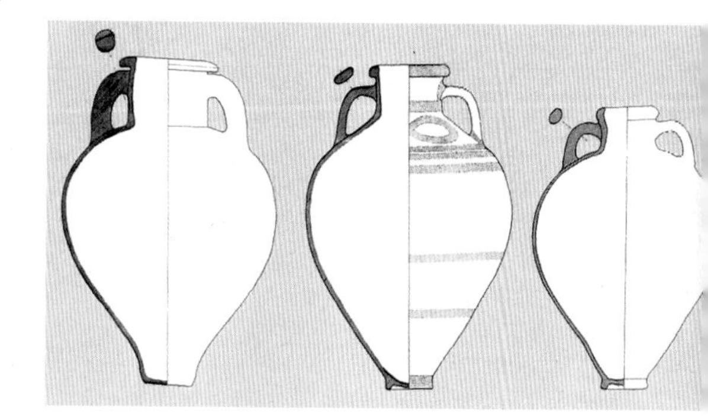

▶ The variety of amphorae uncovered in Etruscan cities reflects the intense commercial activity of the Mediterranean.

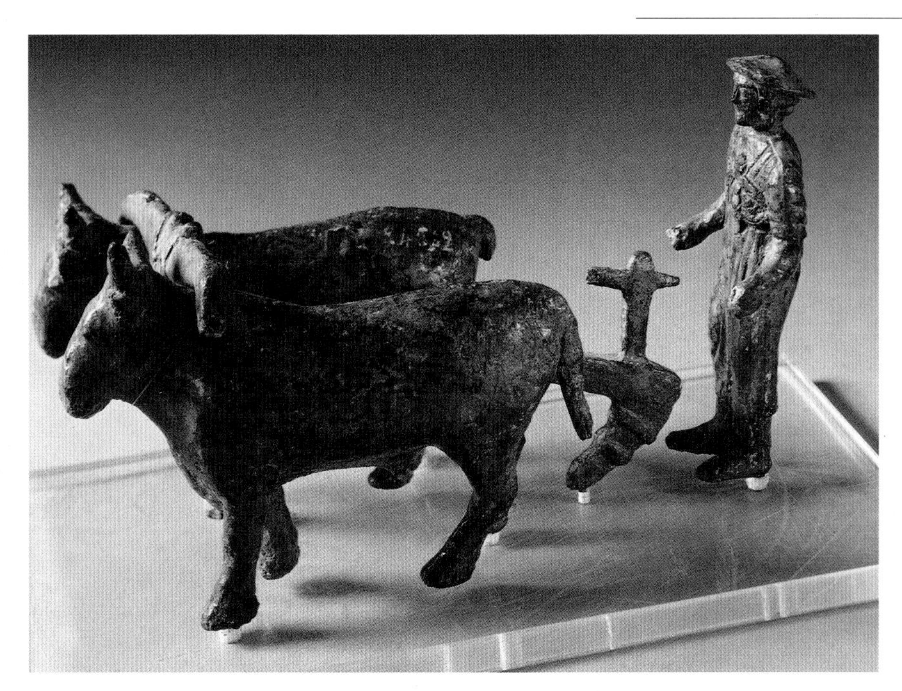

▲ Bronze Group of the Ploughman, produced in a northern Etrurian workshop, from Arezzo, 400–700 B.C. Rome, Museo di Villa Giulia. The group comprises a pair of oxen and a farmer guiding a plow, which includes a plowshare, handle, and tiller.

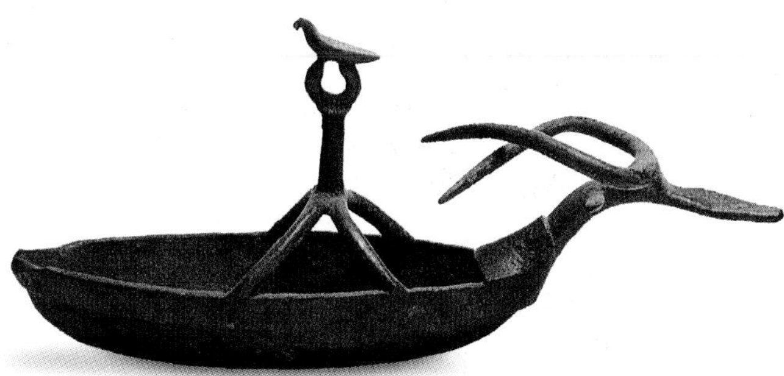

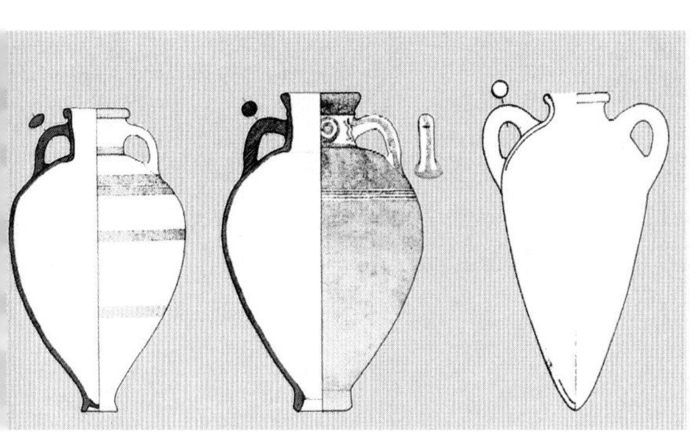

▲ Bronze lamp in the shape of a small ship, with a bovine protome on its prow and a bird facing the stern, from the sanctuary of Gravisca, 600 B.C. Tarquinia, Museo Archeologico. A number of Sardinian bronzes discovered in Etruria provide evidence of Etruscan relations with Sardinia.

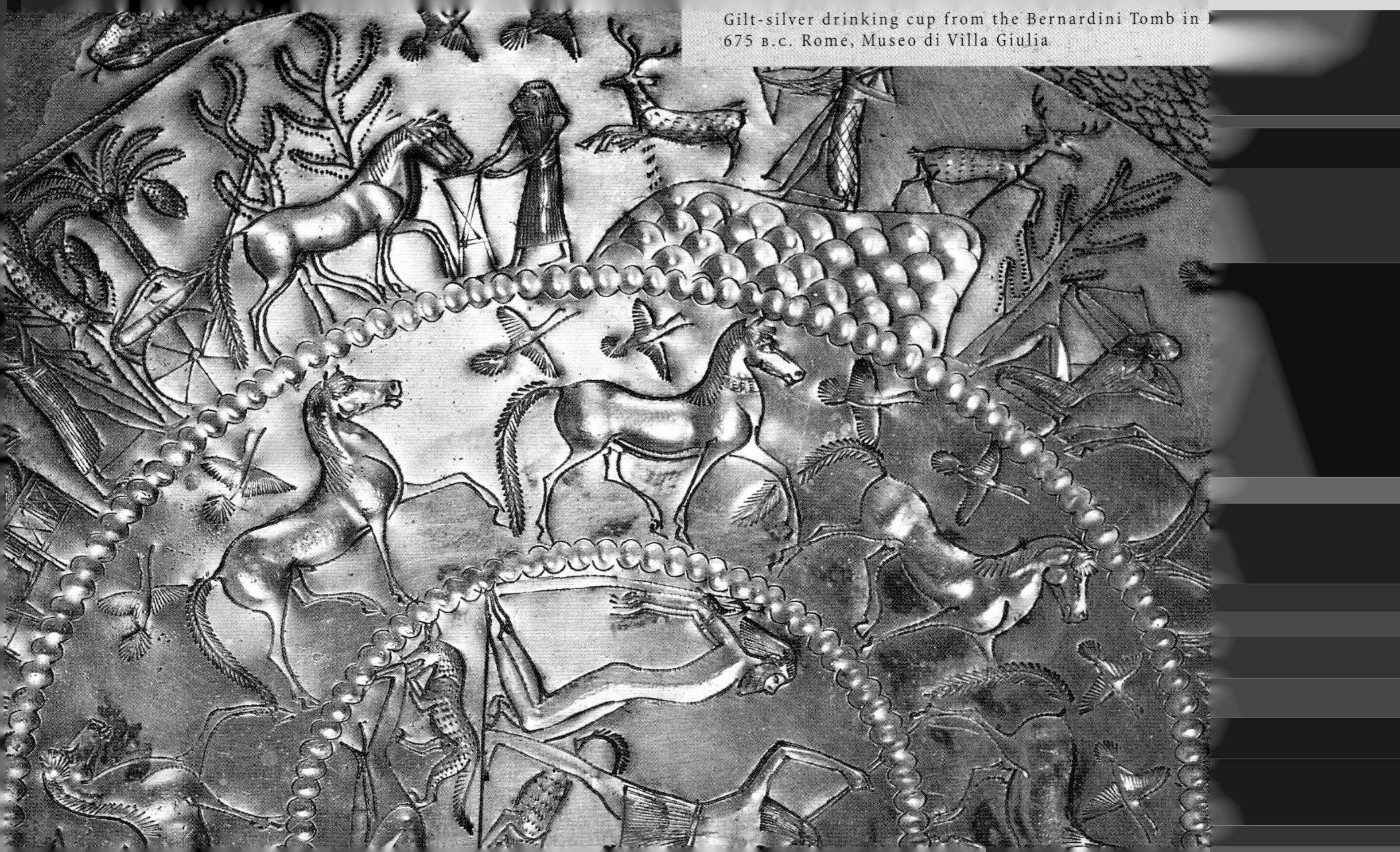

Gilt-silver drinking cup from the Bernardini Tomb in
675 B.C. Rome, Museo di Villa Giulia

The Orientalizing Period

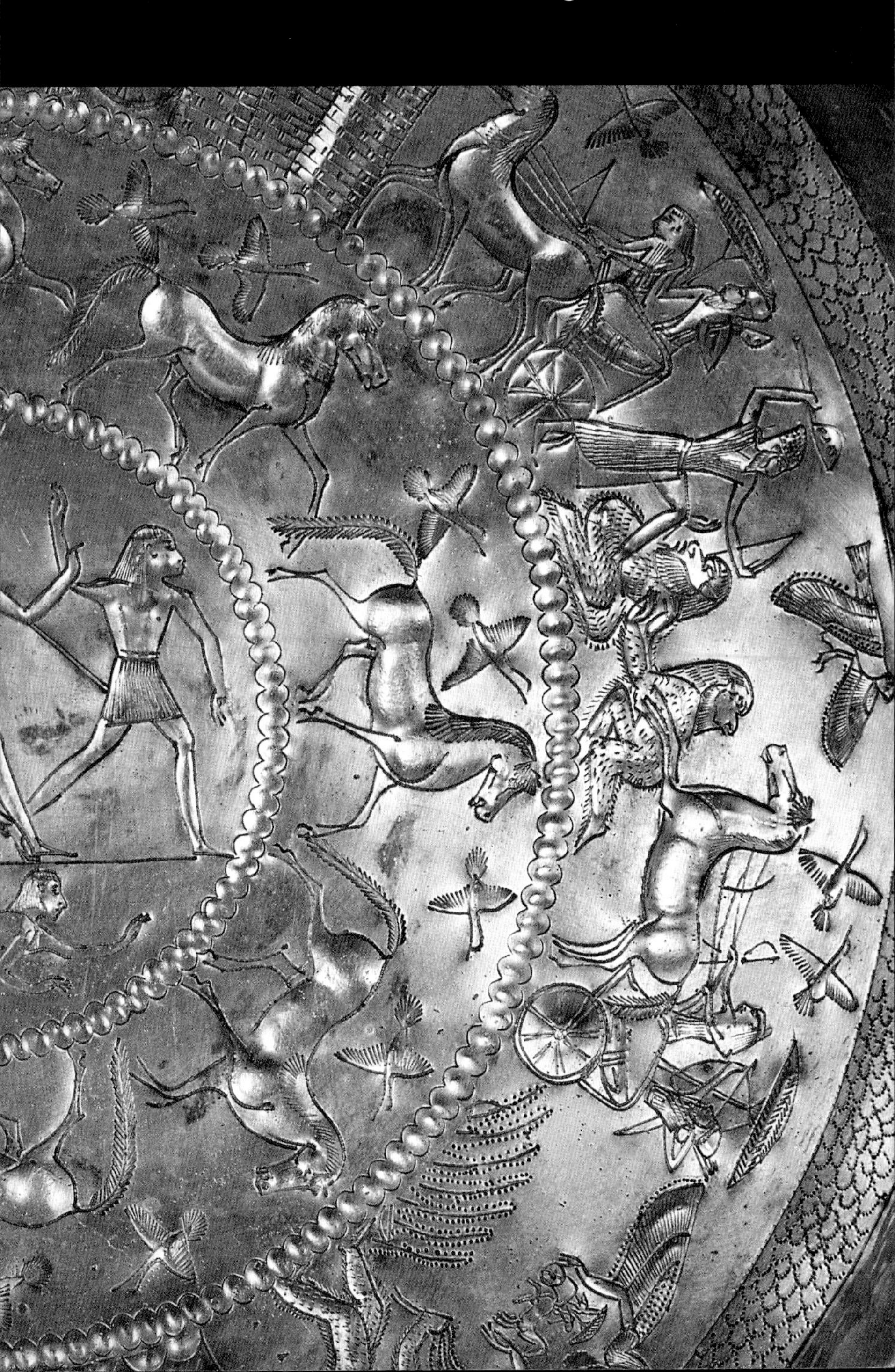

Etruria and the East

In the eighth century B.C., Greek and Phoenician navigators followed the routes that the Mycenaeans had pioneered across the Mediterranean Sea. The need to acquire metals, slaves, and other goods spurred Eastern merchants and Greeks to sail the Tyrrhenian Sea with cargoes of their own: precious goods that apparently found favor with the Etruscan aristocracies. With the founding of the Euboean colony of Pithecusae (Ischia) during the first half of the eighth century B.C., relations between the Italic peoples and those of the eastern Mediterranean became more intense and important for the development of local cultures. The Etruscan elites, who legitimized their power over the community by acquiring luxury goods, looked to the Assyrian sovereigns and the magnificence of their courts as models. The demand for gold, silver, and ivory objects was so great that it became necessary to create local workshops. There, craftsmen improvised on the techniques and iconography that had been imported from the eastern Greek world.

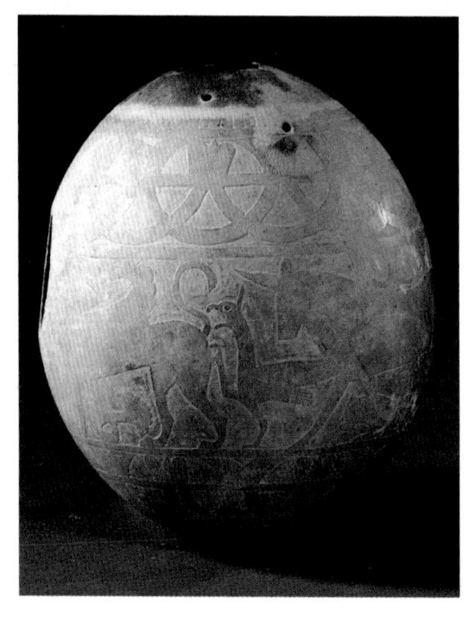

◀ Ostrich egg discovered at the Tomb of Isis in Vulci, 625–600 B.C. London, The British Museum. An able craftsman, knowledgeable in Protocorinthian and Eastern iconography and in the luxury goods of the Near East, created this decoration of imaginary animals.

▲ Phoenician-made cup in gilt-silver leaf from the Regolini-Galassi Tomb in Cerveteri, 675–650 B.C. Vatican City, Museo Gregoriano Etrusco. Scenes of a lion hunt and the procession of warriors recall the iconography of Egyptian works and Assyrian reliefs.

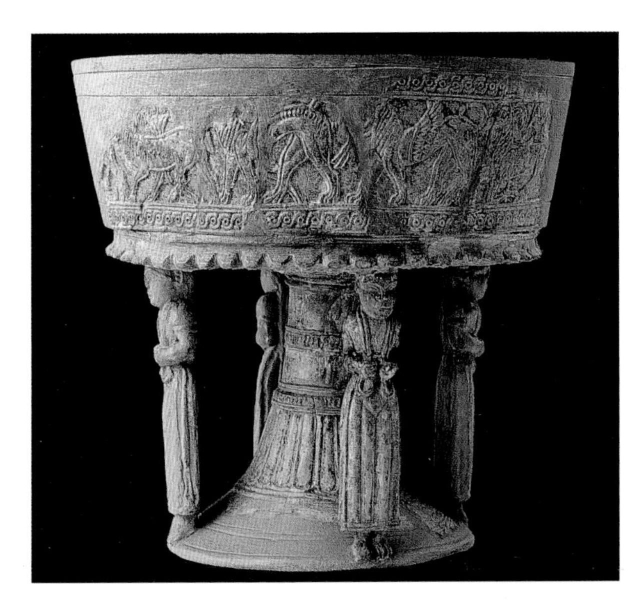

◀ Ivory chalice from the Barberini Tomb in Palestrina, 675 B.C. Rome, Museo di Villa Giulia. In this refined object, which belonged to the grave goods of a high-ranking warrior buried in one of the richest Orientalizing tombs, four caryatids in full-length chitons support a cup decorated with a procession of animals. The same shape can be found in bronze and bucchero vessels.

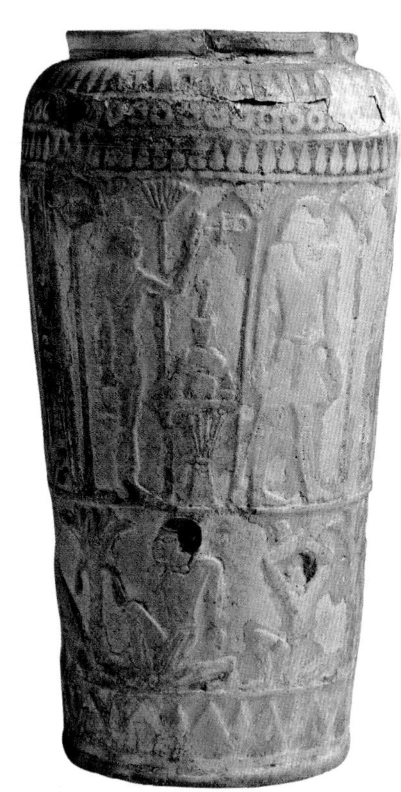

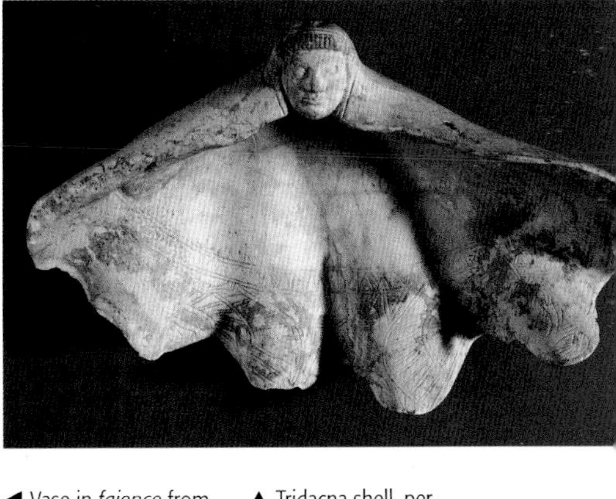

◀ Vase in *faience* from Tarquinia bearing a cartouche of the pharaoh Bocchoris, who reigned between 720 and 715 B.C. Tarquinia, Museo Archeologico. This is important evidence for dating the grave goods belonging to the interred female and for the chronology of the Etruscan Orientalizing phase.

▲ Tridacna shell, perhaps from Vulci, seventh century B.C. London, The British Museum. Decorated with sphinxes and lotus flowers. It originated in the Syrian or Palestinian regions and was used as a container for cosmetics. Other examples of its kind are known from the eastern and southern Mediterranean.

The Etruscan Aristocracy

Beginning in the first decades of the eighth century B.C., archaeological records show an increase in costly grave goods, an indication of stratification within a social structure that had not shown profound differences in status up to that point. Wealth, accumulated through a variety of economic activities, allowed the Etruscan elites to mold their images after the rulers of the Near East. The precious grave goods from the monumental tombs of Cerveteri from the Orientalizing phase show a preference for those luxury goods that echo the magnificence and majesty of Eastern aristocracies. Complete suits of armor made of precious metals, the property of high-ranking warriors, are found in tombs from this period. We see similarly clad warriors depicted on vases and reliefs, fully armed and mounted on chariots like the heroes of the Greek world. Attributes of royalty and power—silver scepters, bronze fans, carriages, ceremonial axes, shields, and the *lituus* (a curved ceremonial staff)—brought the Etruscan elites ever closer to the Eastern sovereigns and the Homeric idols. Etruscan aristocrats adopted the banquet, a traditional Eastern ceremony, as attested by ceramic tableware discovered among the grave goods. It demonstrates their desire to adopt Eastern lifestyles that would affirm and exalt their noble status, as well as Eastern ideological attitudes.

▼ Gold garment clasp from the Bernardini Tomb in Palestrina, 680–660 B.C. Rome, Museo di Villa Giulia. Decorated with 131 animal figures fashioned by filigree and granulation techniques, it is the work of capable local artisans who were trained in the Orientalizing style.

▲ Biga from Populonia. Florence, Museo Archeologico. This two-horse chariot was used to transport aristocrats into battle or during a triumphal parade.

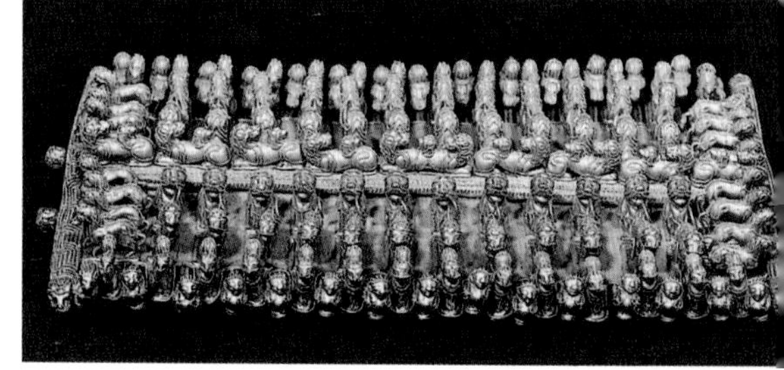

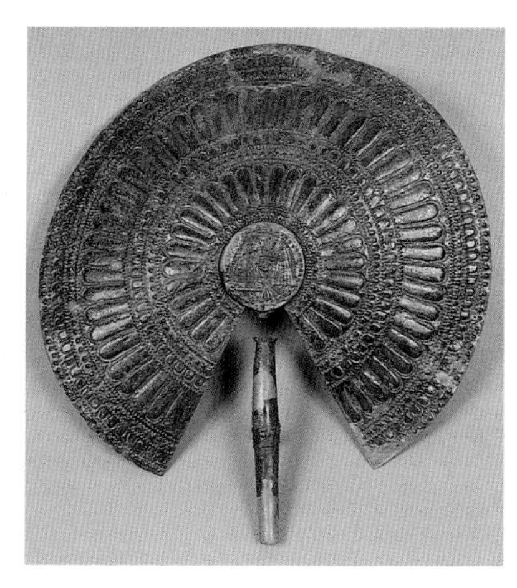

◀ Fan in sheet bronze, northern Etruscan work from Populonia, 675–625 B.C. Florence, Museo Archeologico. A figure making an offering before another of larger size is recognizable at the disc's center. Fans are recorded in the banquet scenes of Assyrian reliefs and in bronzes of various shapes from the Etruscan world.

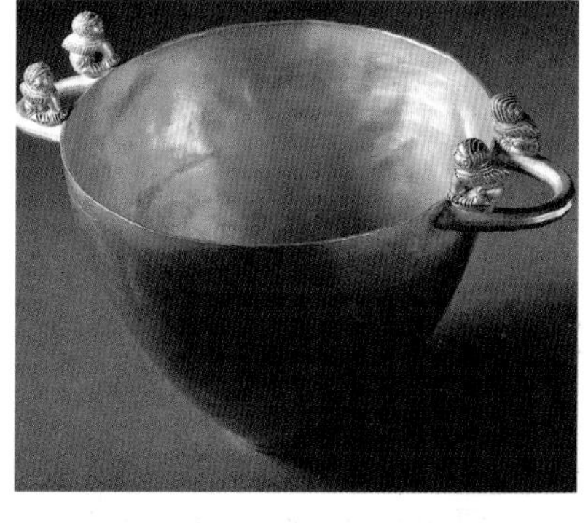

▼ Ax with Villanovan ornamentation, 700–675 B.C. Tarquinia, Museo Archeologico. It was placed together with the shield (*right*) and the trumpet-*lituus* (*below*) in a votive depository at the entrance to Civita's sacred enclosure.

▶ Gold *kotyle* from the Bernardini Tomb in Palestrina, about 675 B.C. Rome, Museo di Villa Giulia. The shape of this two-handled cup recalls the Protocorinthian *kotylai,* while the sphinxes on the handles, which have been decorated using the granulation technique, can be found on jewelry from other tombs at Palestrina.

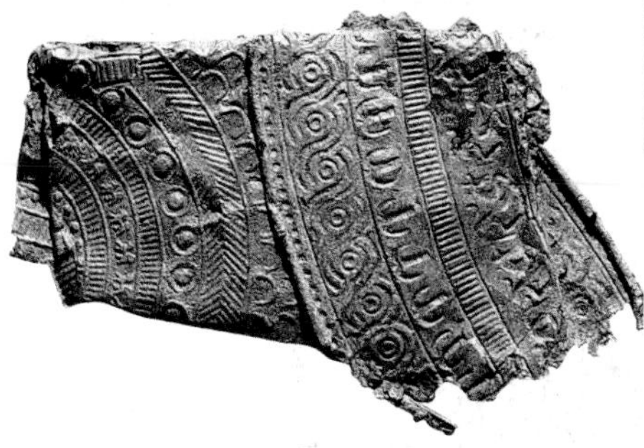

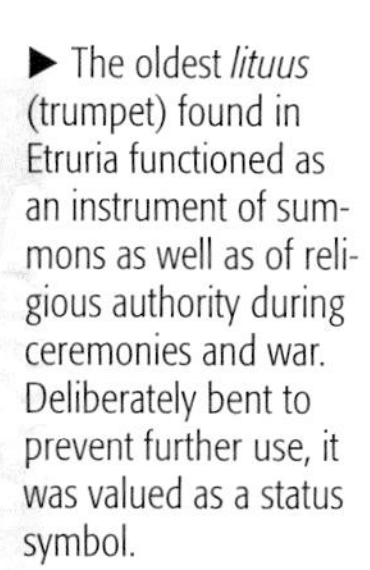

▲ This shield of sheet bronze has been stripped of any functionality. It is comparable to the parade shields used to decorate the atrium walls in aristocratic households, as seen in the Tomb of the Shields and Seats at Cerveteri.

▶ The oldest *lituus* (trumpet) found in Etruria functioned as an instrument of summons as well as of religious authority during ceremonies and war. Deliberately bent to prevent further use, it was valued as a status symbol.

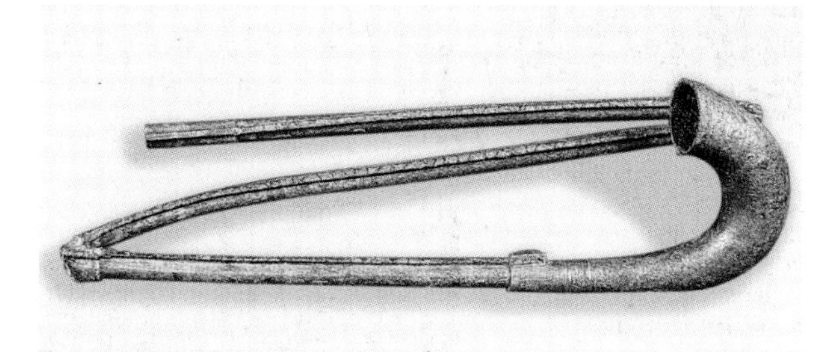

The Silver-Gilt *Lebes* from Palestrina

Silver-gilt *lebes* from the Bernardini Tomb in Palestrina, 675 B.C. Rome, Museo di Villa Giulia. This tiny embossed *lebes* stands out among the rich vessels of Eastern origin that formed part of the grave goods of a high-ranking warrior. The work may have been that of artisans native to the isle of Cyprus. This can be inferred from the hunting and fighting scenes and the processions of warriors and animals, which were derived from the iconographic repertory of the Near East, Egypt, and Greece. Its shape and the serpentine protomes placed around its rim most nearly recall the huge bronze cauldrons that were once used in banquets, a ceremony that spread from the East to many regions of the Mediterranean basin.

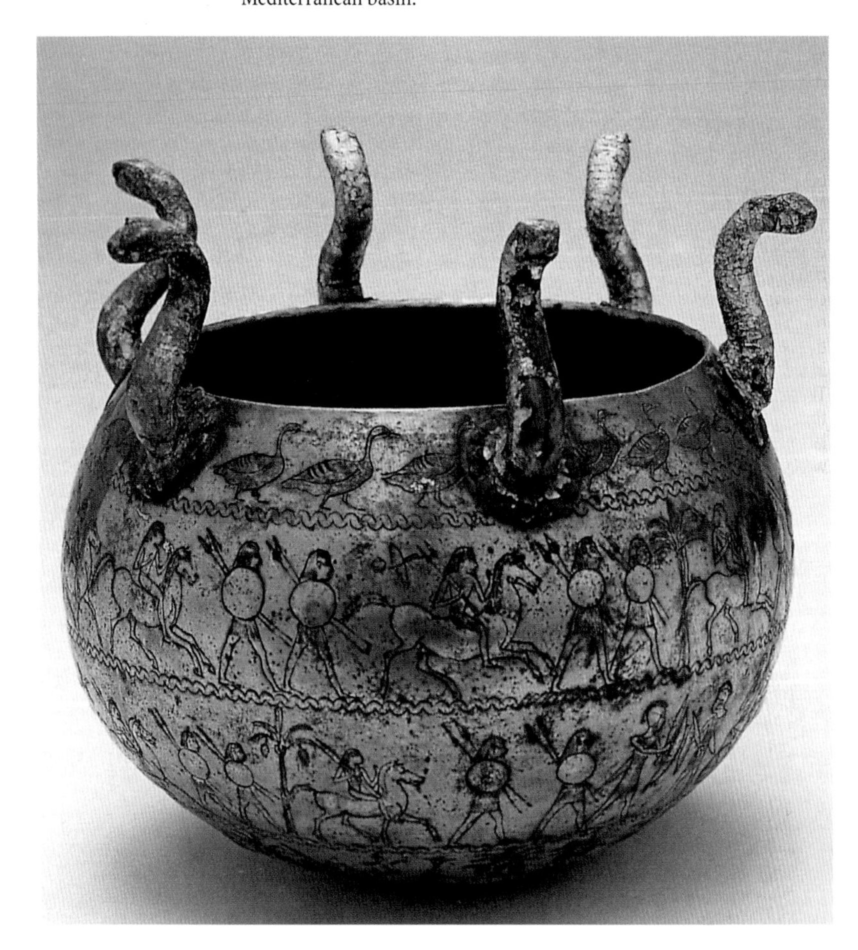

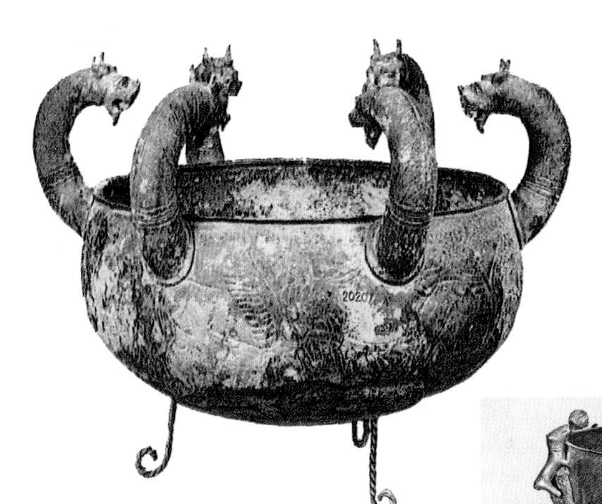

◀ Bronze *lebes* from Cerveteri, seventh century B.C. Vatican City, Museo Gregoriano Etrusco. *Lebes* typically display *protomes,* or decorative heads, of griffins, snakes, or sphinxes. This item, however, features lions, which face toward the vessel's center.

▼ Four protomes of cast-bronze griffins employed as ornaments around the mouth of a cauldron, from Tarquinia, 600–575 B.C. Tarquinia, Museo Archeologico. The large metal cauldrons were imported from the Near East. After crossing Greece, they reached Italy, where they were later imitated in bronze and impasto. These examples are thought to have been late products of the workshops of Sarno.

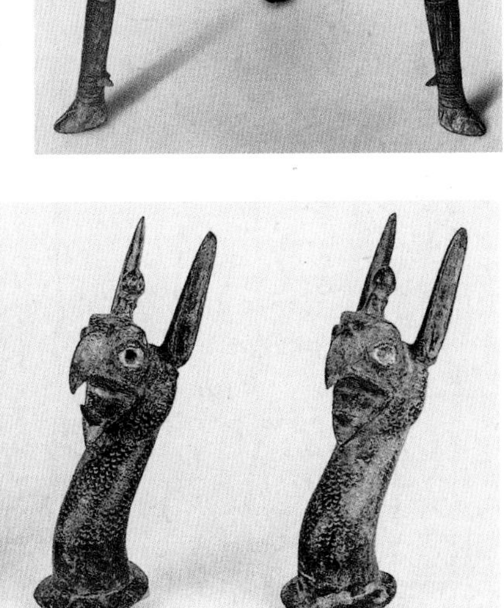

▶ Bronze *lebes* (bowl) on a tripod, also from the Bernardini Tomb. Rome, Museo di Villa Giulia. Its shape recalls foreign prototypes and, in its modeled ornamentation, Villanovan artifacts. The figures of dogs and animals facing toward the vessel's center have the same decorative function as the griffins or sirens in Eastern examples that were uncovered in Etruria and in this same Orientalizing tomb.

Women's Grave Goods

From the Villanovan era onward, women's grave goods featured objects connected to women's activities within the community and the roles they played. The impasto spools and spindle whorls found in tombs, together with personal ornaments and containers of various usage, are proof of Etruscan women's main occupation at home: wool-working. Like the high-class female figures of the Homeric poems, the lady of the Etruscan house oversaw the work of maidservants shearing sheep and winding the coarse wool, and weaving. But rich Etruscan women also led an active public life. The precious goldwork and the sumptuous fabric work by noblewomen record not only the sophistication achieved by artisan goldsmiths but also the wealth and majesty of the aristocratic class. Besides necklaces, fibulae, bracelets, and ivory fans, there were also objects that typically belong to males, such as shields hung as decorations on the walls of the house-shaped tombs, thrones, and two-wheeled carts used to transport the *domina* to public events.

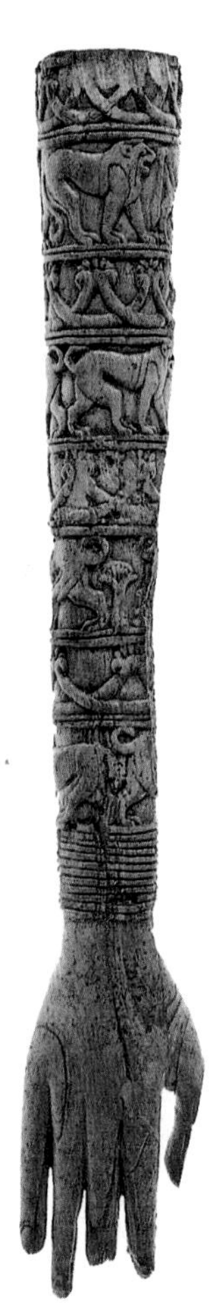

▼ Ivory fan handle from Palestrina, 675–650 B.C. Rome, Museo di Villa Giulia. This represents one of the many carved-ivory works made by local artisans in imitation of Eastern models. The passion of the local aristocracy for these goods led to imported works from the East being copied and replaced by the Etruscan workshops.

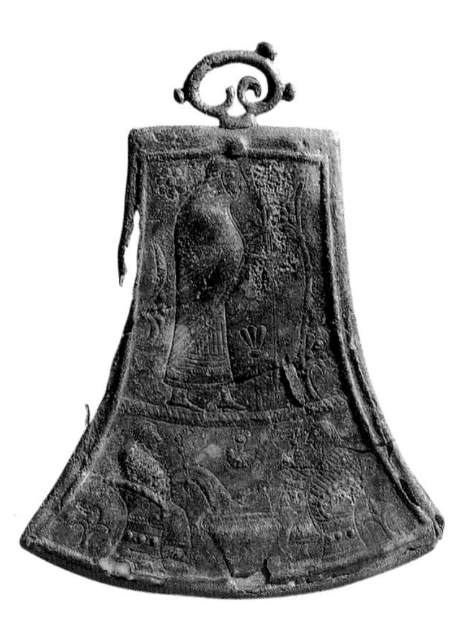

▶ Embossed bronze *tintinnabulum,* 625–600 B.C. Bologna, Museo Civico Archeologico. Orientalizing works from Bologna are of particular interest for the scenes they portray. Here we can discern two seated women, intent on preparing distaffs for the spinner in the frame above. Technical and stylistic elements allow this work to be attributed to an expert artisan from northern Etruria.

▶ A variety of decorated impasto whorls and spools from Populonia. Florence, Museo Archeologico. Along with spindles of amber, bronze, or glass paste, these objects record the Etruscan woman's activity within the home. They were found in women's tombs dating between the seventh and sixth centuries B.C.

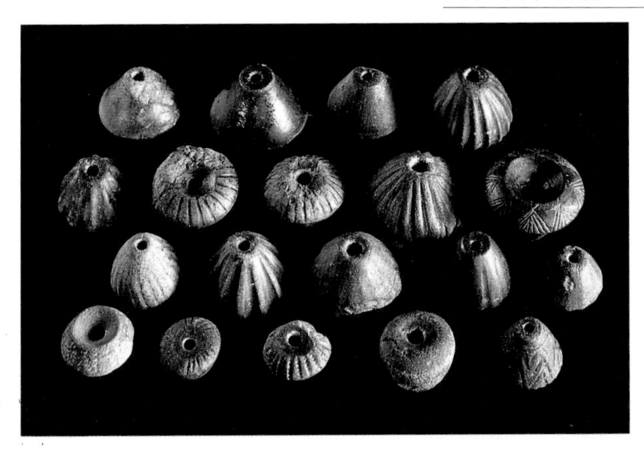

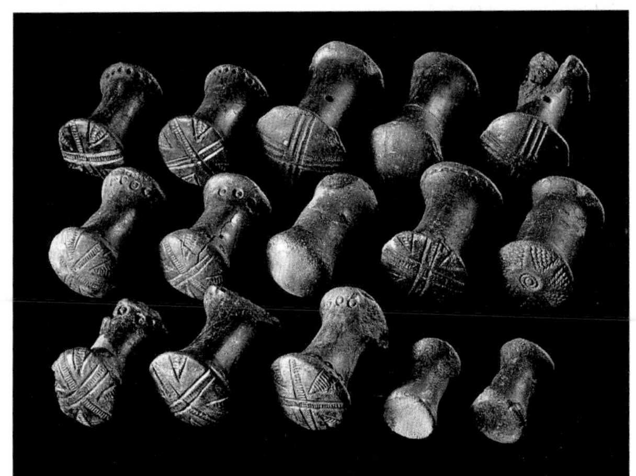

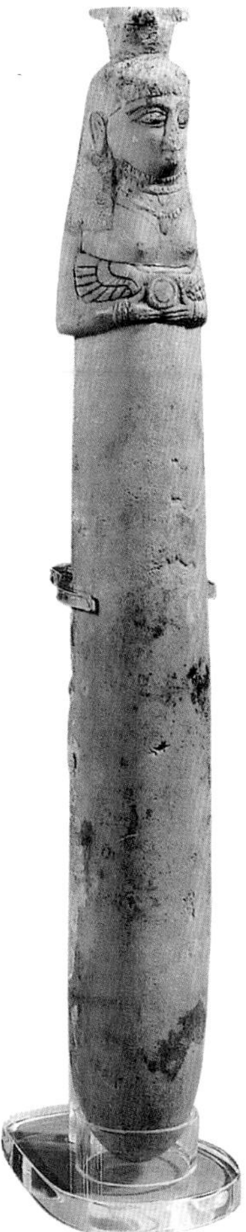

◀ Vase in gypsum for perfumed oils, from Vulci. London, The British Museum. The female figure with the winged solar disc in her hands could be an Eastern goddess.

▶ Ivory comb from Marsiliana d'Albegna, 675–650 B.C. Grosseto, Museo Archeologico. The extraordinary intaglio work and the object's fragility suggest that it was used for ritual purposes.

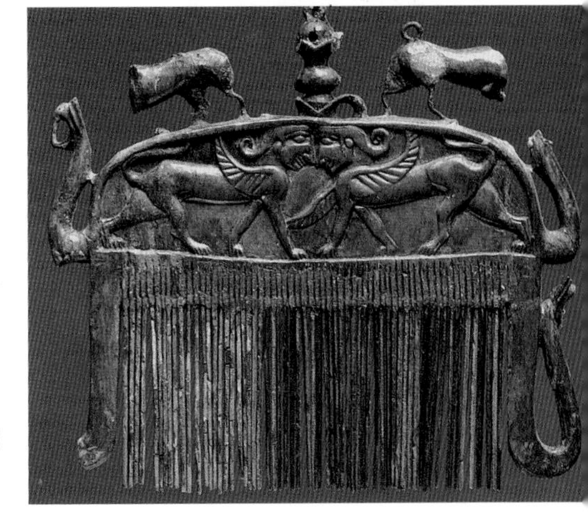

Etruria and Greece

Beginning in the ninth century B.C., relations intensified between the navigators of Euboea and the peoples of Southern Italy, Sicily, and Etruria. From a material and cultural point of view, these associations introduced important innovations and led to the founding of the first Greek colony on the island of Pithecusae (Istria). Interest in Etruria's mineral resources made the Tyrrhenian region commercially quite active: The Etruscan aristocracy took a leading role in this trade and, as a result, gained new models from Greece and the Near East for their lifestyle, technology, and iconography. Vases for banquets and symposia, which were originally Greek and Eastern traditions, feature scenes from everyday life and from the Homeric epics, which show the Etruscan elites' assimilation of the values of Greek civilization. The acquisition of an alphabet, which reached Etruria through the Campanian colonies during the second half of the eighth century B.C., proved fundamentally important. The aristocratic classes adapted it to the needs of Etruscan phonetics, thereby making it an instrument of local power.

▼ Krater from Cerveteri signed by Aristonothos, 650 B.C. Rome, Musei Capitolini. This side features the episode of Odysseus blinding the cyclops. The narrative scheme reveals different elements of the Greek painter's artistic culture and his familiarity with figurative works from eastern Sicily.

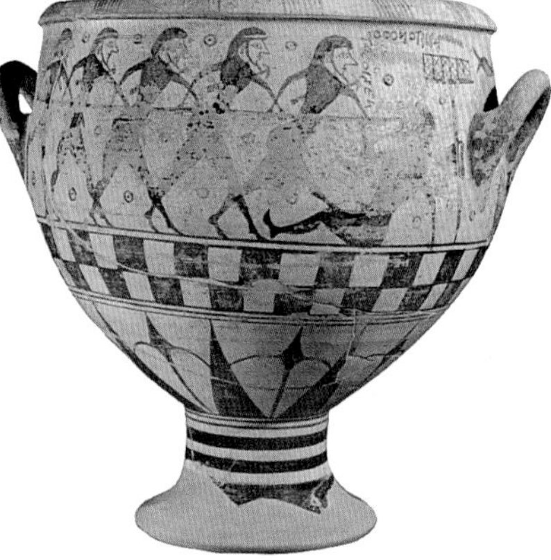

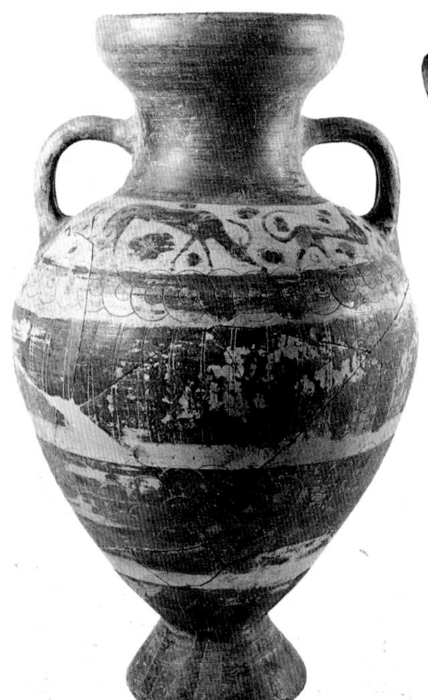

◀ Large amphora with grazing animals. Milan, Civiche Raccolte Archeologiche. According to tradition, the arrival of the Corinthian Damaratos in Italy marked the beginning of the production of Etrusco-Corinthian artifacts such as this.

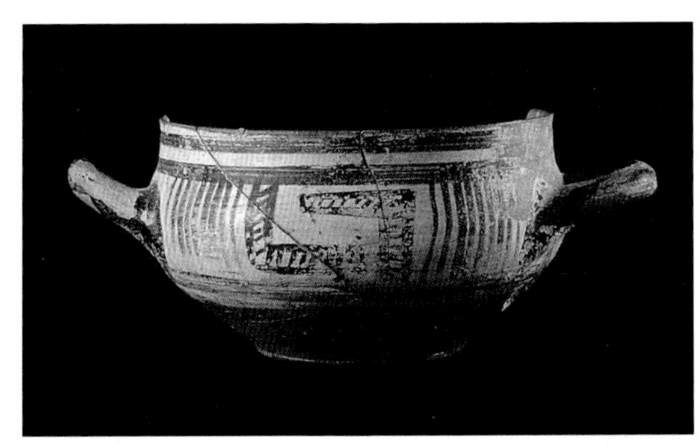

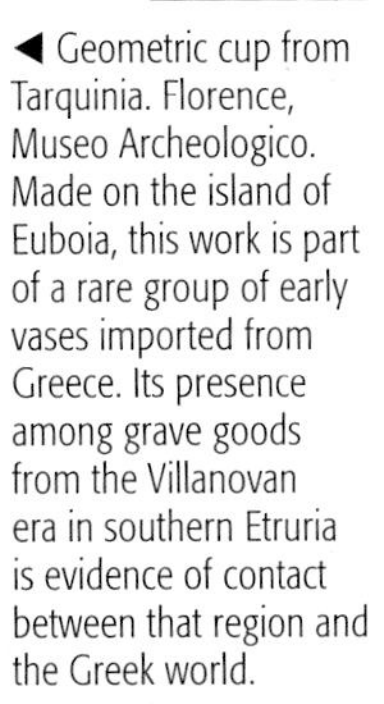

◀ Geometric cup from Tarquinia. Florence, Museo Archeologico. Made on the island of Euboia, this work is part of a rare group of early vases imported from Greece. Its presence among grave goods from the Villanovan era in southern Etruria is evidence of contact between that region and the Greek world.

▼ Corinthian krater from Cerveteri, called "of Eurystheus" after the character from the Hercules myth that is depicted on it, about 600 B.C. Paris, Musée du Louvre. This is an extraordinary work, both for its dimensions and iconography. Vases of large size were used in banquets and symposia to mix wine with water.

▶ Olla with a typical Geometric decoration in red and black paint from a Bisenzio workshop, from the beginning of the seventh century B.C. Florence, Museo Archeologico. The workshops of Vulci and its surrounding area specialized in the production of huge vases for wine that were decorated with Geometric motifs, derived from the Euboean and Cycladic traditions.

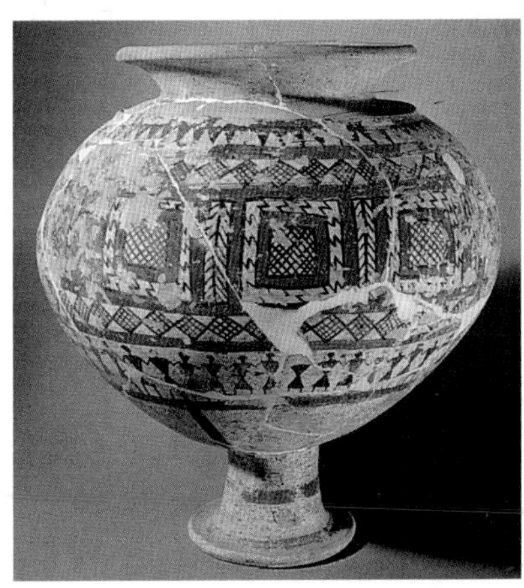

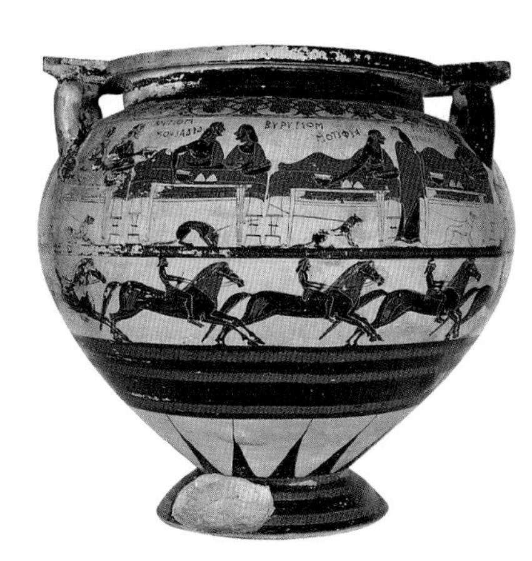

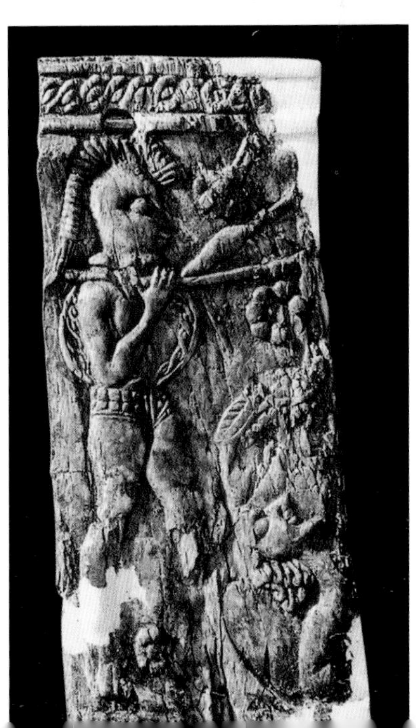

▶ Small, ivory plaque from the tumulus of Montefortini, 640–580 B.C. Florence, Museo Archeologico. The Etruscan use of hoplite armor is evidenced by this warrior with a Corinthian helmet.

The Ivory Pyxis from the Pania Necropolis

This pyxis in ivory from the necropolis at Pania, which is preserved at the Museo Archeologico in Florence, is one of the Orientalizing works from Chiusi. Part of the grave goods of a woman buried during the third quarter of the seventh century B.C., the object is of particular interest for its decorative rendering of warriors, horsemen, and real and imaginary animals, and for the episodes of the legend of Odysseus that are depicted.

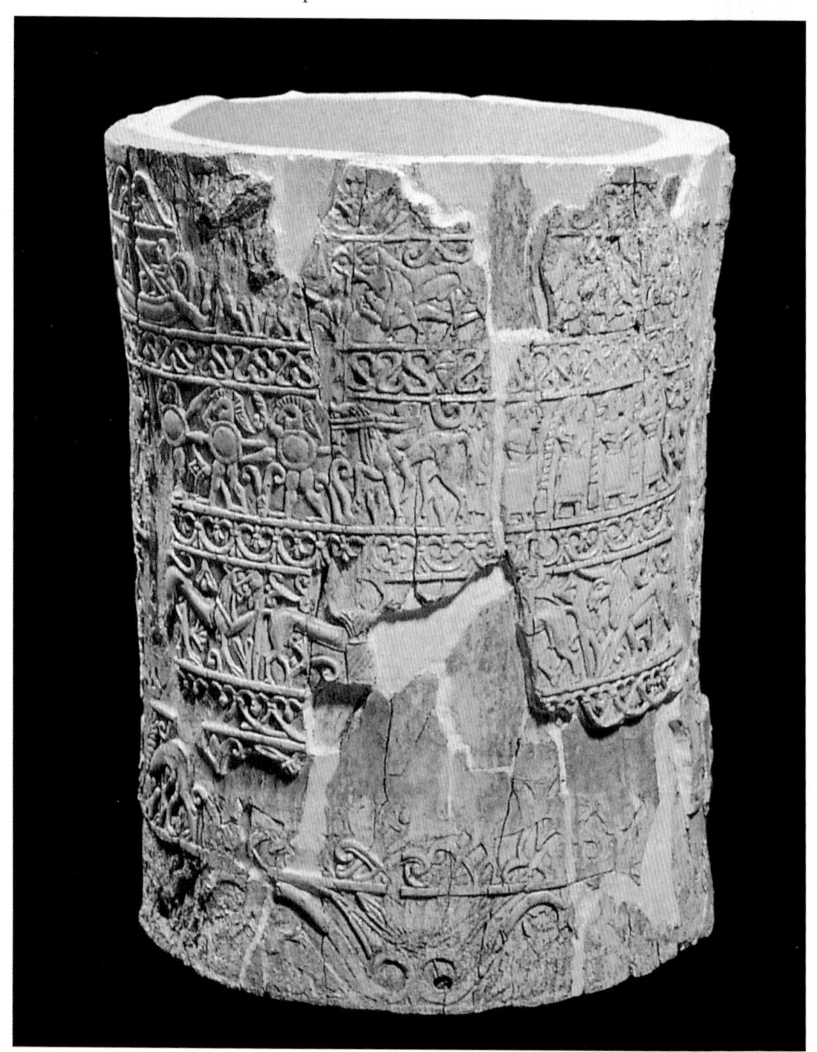

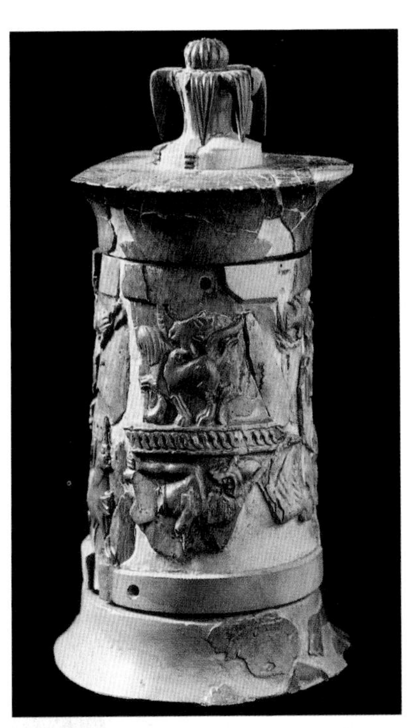

◀ Ivory pyxis from the Circle of the Ivories in Marsiliana d'Albegna, from the second quarter of the seventh century B.C. Grosseto, Museo Archeologico. It belongs to some of the richest grave goods from the Etruscan Orientalizing stage. It was carved from a single piece of elephant tusk and decorated with scenes of combat between men and animals and among animals. Produced in Vetulonia, it seems to be the work of an able carver who was an expert in Eastern techniques and iconography.

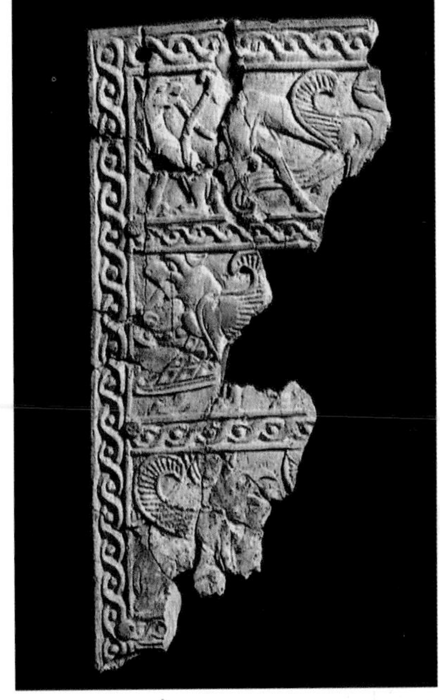

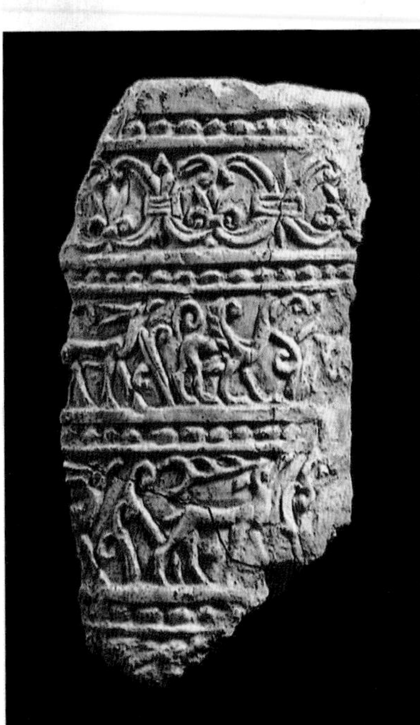

◀ Ivory fragment from the tumulus of Calzaiolo in San Casciano Val di Pesa, dating from the late seventh century B.C. Florence, Museo Archeologico. From an earlier period, though in the same style as the pyxis from Chiusi, this work features three bands of decoration with processions of real and imaginary animals and vegetal motifs.

▲ Ivory plaque, perhaps belonging to a piece of furniture, from San Casciano Val di Pesa. Florence, Museo Archeologico. Lines of imaginary animals recur once again in this example, whose refined execution reveals the work of an expert artist. Its iconography and style recall the pyxis from Pania.

Architecture and Urban Planning

Recent archaeological excavations at the sites of city settlements have contributed to a wider knowledge of Etruscan planning and architecture, which had previously been based solely on the most famous monumental necropolises. Beginning in the ninth century B.C., built-up areas seem to have had common features: They developed on hilly plateaus at the convergence of two watercourses in naturally protected positions, with the necropolises set apart upon neighboring rises. From the second half of the eighth century on, due to an increase in the population, larger settlements were formed by consolidating scattered Villanovan villages. The diverse functions of buildings, the creation of fortifications, and the overall solidity of the habitations signal the beginning of an urbanization process in the Etruscan cities. The custom of burying cremated remains in hut-shaped urns has made it possible to reconstruct the early dwellings: They were laid out according to an oval or rectangular plan and had frames of posts and reeds or branches covered with clay, and roofs thatched with straw. Beginning in the second half of the seventh century, the roofs became more complex. They were composed of terra-cotta elements whose workmanship suggests the presence of artists specialized in the art of modeling. According to Pliny, this expertise had reached Etruria via the Corinthian merchant Damaratos.

▲ A group of roof tiles with animal protomes stands out among the architectural terra-cottas from Etruscan dwellings in Acquarossa. The figures of lions and griffins derive from ornamentation on Orientalizing bronze cauldrons and their ceramic imitations. The "white-on-red" technique was applied to the terra-cottas and vases in the same workshops at Cerveteri.

◀ Bronze cinerary urn, reproducing the type of dwelling in use during the first half of the eighth century B.C. in the Vulci area. Rome, Museo di Villa Giulia.

▶ The oldest examples of Etruscan funerary architecture included models of dwellings used during the seventh century B.C. The Tomb of the Hut in Cerveteri represents a house type with a rectangular plan that derived from the longhouses of the Bronze Age, but with one innovation: its interior partition. The funerary architecture of that century shows that the Cerveteran aristocracy had adopted this style of residence.

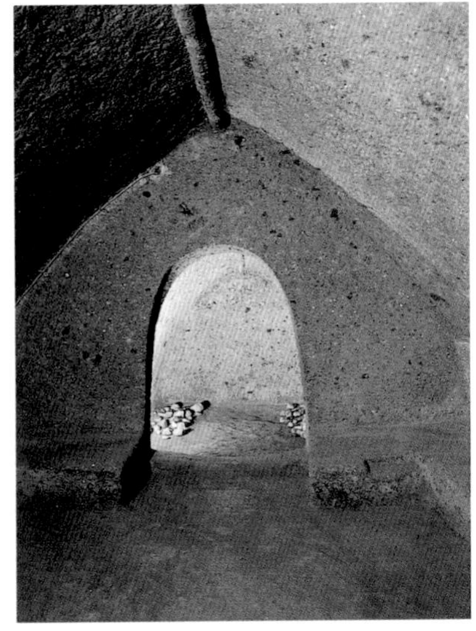

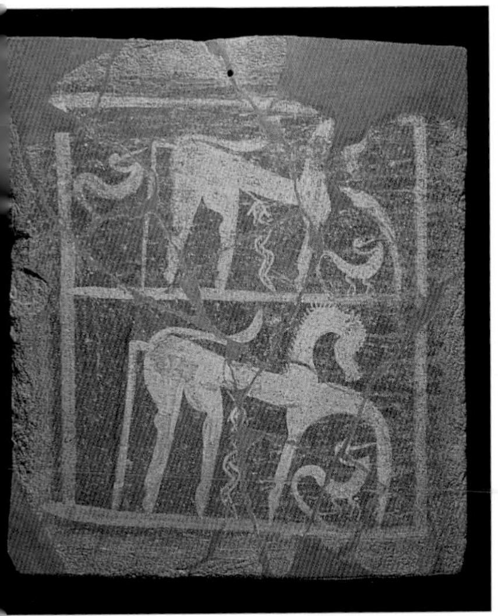

◀ Painted tile from Acquarossa, from the late seventh to the early sixth centuries B.C. The horses, snakes, and herons show the close relationship between architectural terra-cottas and contemporary pottery production.

▼ The Calabresi Urn, 650–625 B.C. Vatican City, Museo Gregoriano Etrusco. Even the rich ornamentation of this house-shaped urn recalls the Orientalizing repertory of pottery from Cerveteri.

◀ Model of an acroterion with horse and rider, derived from Protocorinthian pottery, dating to the last quarter of the seventh century B.C. Murlo, Antiquarium di Poggio Civitate. Acroteria in openwork first appeared in Etruria and seem to be distinctively Etruscan. These objects were cut from a flat slab of clay and then attached to a roof tile using a support.

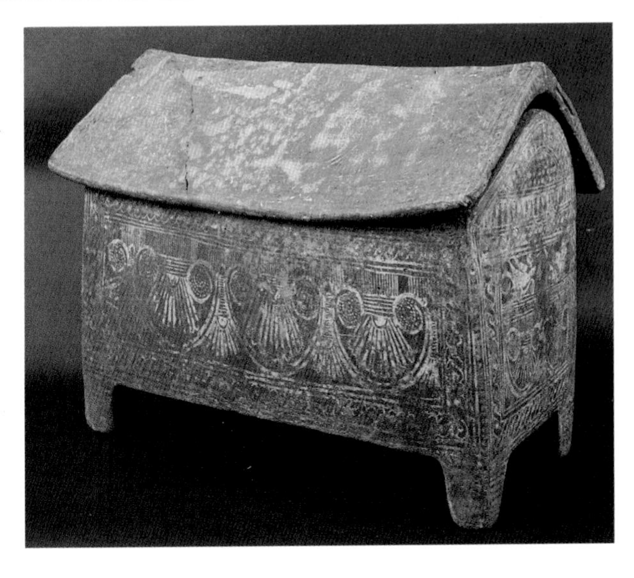

Gold from the Regolini-Galassi Tomb

Vatican City, Museo Gregoriano Etrusco. The extraordinary goldwork at the Regolini-Galassi Tomb was discovered in Cerveteri in 1836. It belonged to the grave goods of an Etruscan noblewoman who lived during the first half of the seventh century B.C.

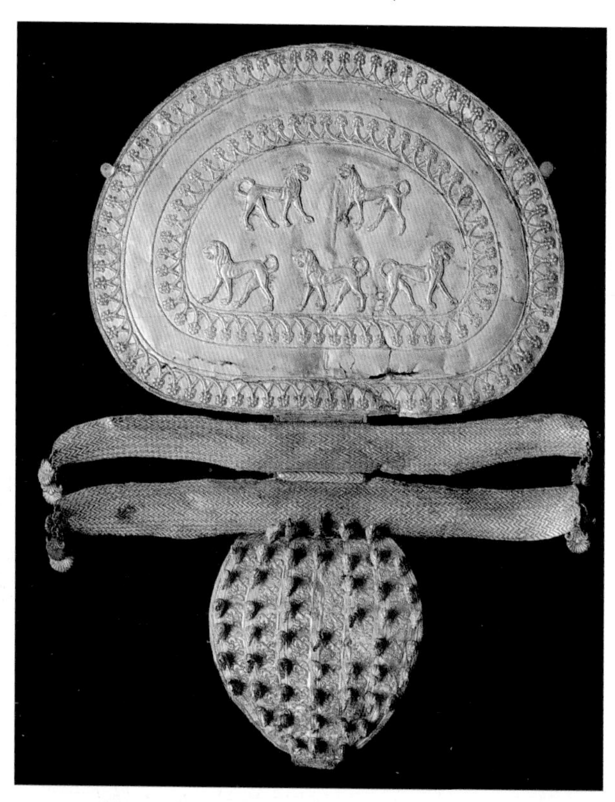

◀ These masterpieces of goldwork were among the rich Orientalizing grave goods from the tombs of southern Etruria, where a number of gold artisans had workshops. With the experience and knowledge gained from the new Eastern technologies, they produced exceptional pieces for the Etruscan elites. This large disk fibula, in a shape already in use during the earlier Iron Age, bears an elaborate decoration with animal motifs rendered in the refined technique of granulation: the soldering of tiny balls to a base of gold design.

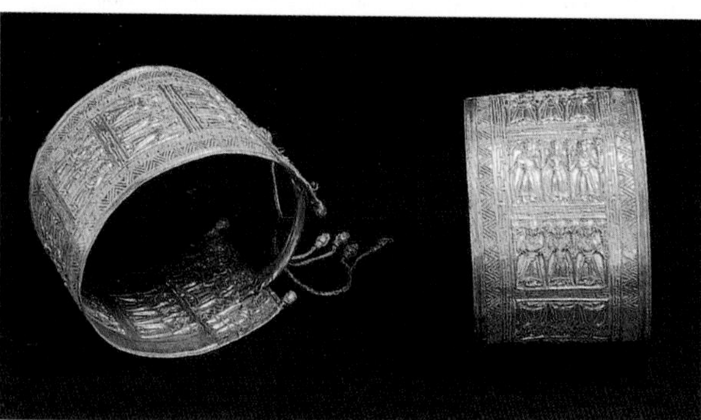

◀ The talent of the Etruscan goldsmiths is also evident in this pair of gold bracelets with embossed ornamentation enhanced by granulation. For most of the decorative elements, the artisan drew on the iconographic repertory of Phoenician ivory reliefs.

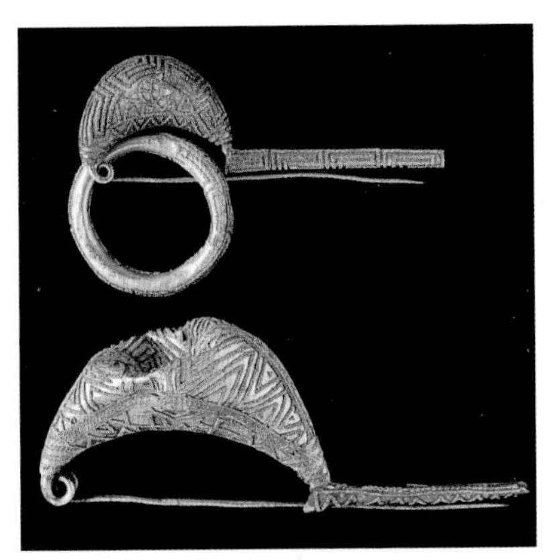

◀ The fibula was a personal decorative object used since the Iron Age to fasten men's and women's clothing. These examples taken from the tomb have a leech-shaped arch decorated with Geometric patterns formed by granulation. The smaller of the two shows a tubular ring decorated with a meander, a motif common to both examples.

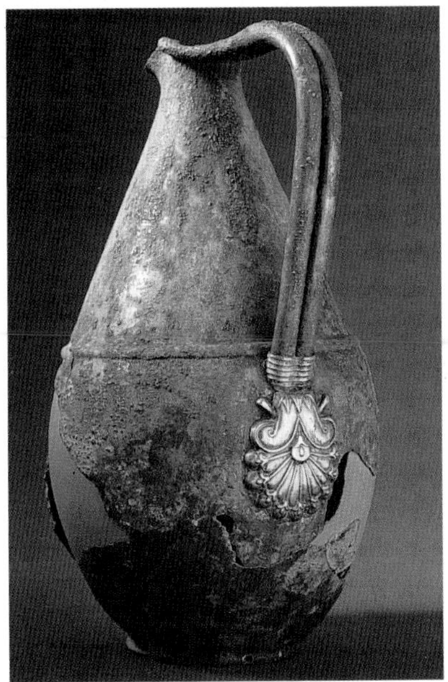

▲ This silver *oinochoe* is similar to those uncovered among the royal grave-goods in Cumae, Pontecagnano, Vetulonia, and Palestrina, which date between 700 and 650 B.C. In the workshops of Cerveteri and Veii, this shape was copied in impasto and bucchero and was used in bronze examples from Cyprus and Spain.

▶ The reconstruction of this *situla* was possible owing to the discovery of numerous stamped and cut silver laminates that must have once wrapped a container, probably made of wood. Its technique and style recall the Castellani *cista* from Palestrina and Cervetaran goldwork.

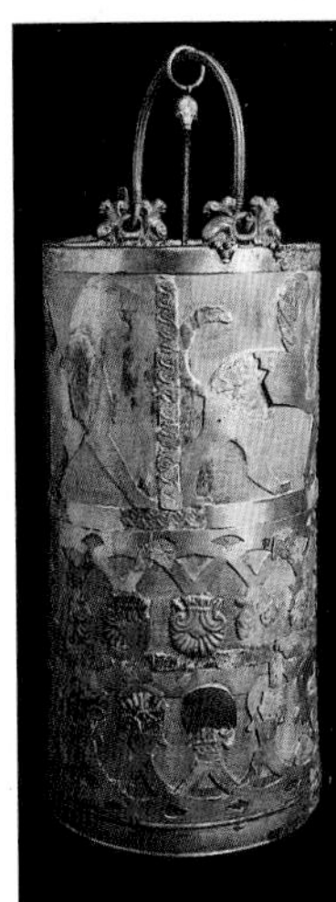

▲ A noblewoman once wore this magnificent breastplate of embossed gold laminate, which features a mixture of Greek and Eastern iconographic motifs. The object's great worth and the refined technique of the stamped decoration show the importance that the Etruscan aristocracy bestowed on personal ornament as signs of affluence and power.

Images of Ancestors

Ancient sources confirm the importance of ancestor images in ancient Rome, where they were carried in procession during funeral ceremonies. These *imagines maiorum* were kept in the atriums of Archaic Roman homes in order to protect the family. Statues representing the ancestors of the deceased also have been found in the halls and atriums of Etrurian tombs. The enthroned male figures at the Tomb of the Statues in Cerveteri, for example, dating to the middle decades of the seventh century B.C., were sculpted in high relief along the lateral walls of the vestibule. In Cerveteri, the placement of sculptures has led to the theory that northern Syrian artists introduced monumental statues into the repertoire of funerary portraiture in that city. The five clay figures from the Tomb of the Five Chairs in Cerveteri illustrate that the Etruscan elites sought to maintain solidarity within the family. This same focus is obvious in their practice of holding ceremonies in honor of ancestors in the *regia* courtyard at Poggio Civitate, or in placing huge statues on its roof, which emphasized the power of the noble clan and the ancestors' protection of the inhabitants of the palace complex.

▼ Biconic cinerary urn from Montescudaio, middle of the seventh century B.C. Florence, Museo Archeologico. Its modeled ornamentation is intriguing; a figure is depicted in front of a small table pouring libations with the help of an attendant. A huge jar for wine and other furnishings suggest the scene's meaning: the deceased is attending a banquet in the Homeric tradition.

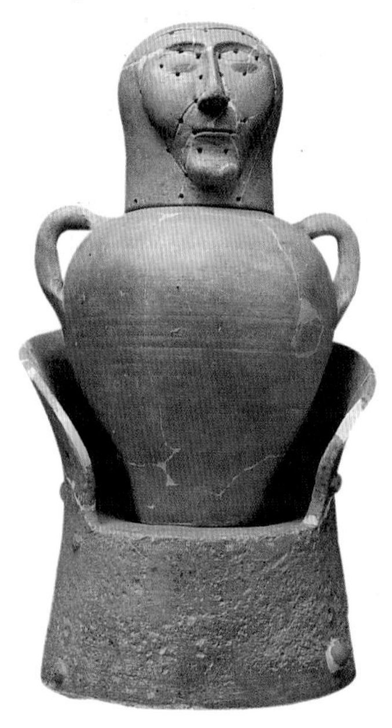

◀ Impasto canopic urn made in Chiusi, from Cetona, 650–600 B.C. Florence, Museo Archeologico. The prominent status of the deceased is emphasized by his placement on a throne. Holes for a mask can be seen on his face.

▼ Funerary vase, 630–600 B.C. Chiusi, Museo Archeologico Nazionale. The dimensions of the statue on the lid point to the elevated status of the deceased. He is shown standing, encircled by smaller figures of mourners and large griffin-head protomes attached to the body of the vessel.

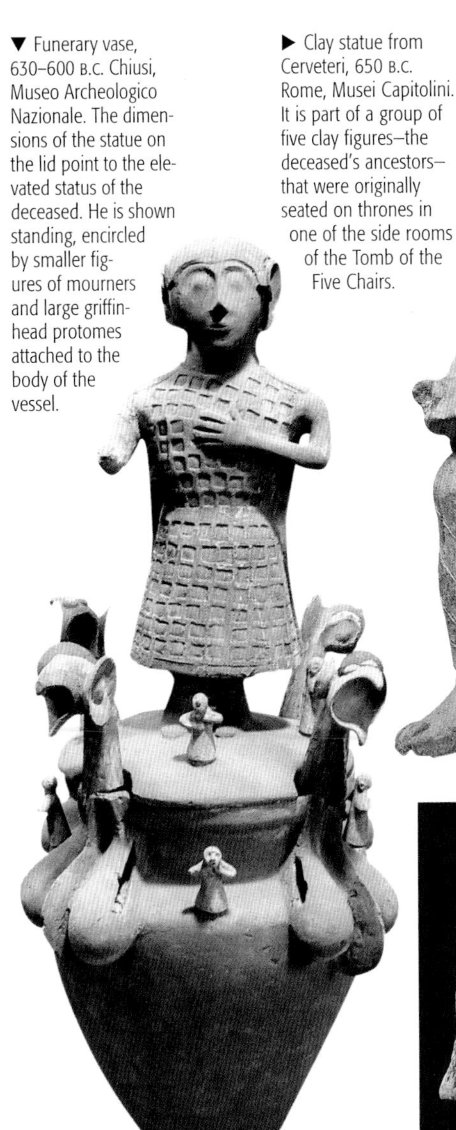

▶ Clay statue from Cerveteri, 650 B.C. Rome, Musei Capitolini. It is part of a group of five clay figures—the deceased's ancestors—that were originally seated on thrones in one of the side rooms of the Tomb of the Five Chairs.

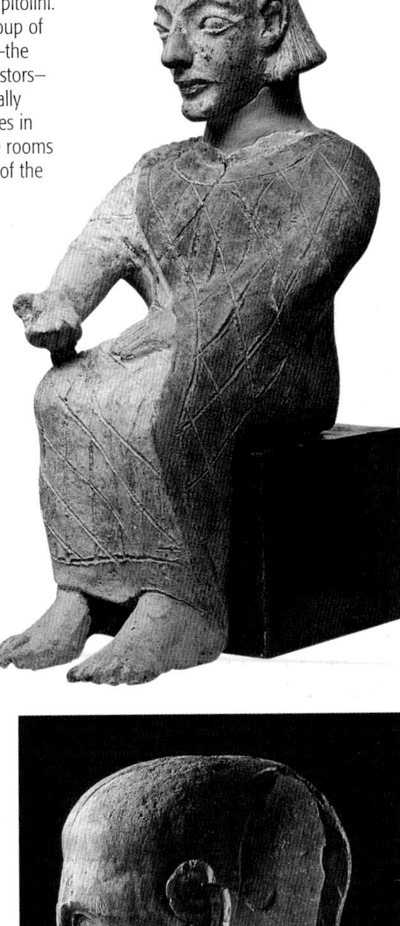

▶ Wooden head of a male, perhaps from Vulci, from the middle of the seventh century B.C. Milan, Civiche Raccolte Archeologiche. It was recently identified as being part of a statue or a *cippus* with a human head. Traces of the gold sheet that once covered the face and holes in the earlobes for earrings can still be seen.

Pottery in Impasto and Bucchero

In the eighth century B.C., the introduction of the pottery wheel favored the rise of workshops of potters. They specialized in producing handmade works for different uses with an impasto whose quality gradually became more refined. Besides biconical or hut-shaped urns, the most common shapes during the tenth and ninth centuries were vases used for symposia or banquets with motifs from the Geometric tradition. In the course of the seventh century, vases were made in more evolved shapes, which in some cases were derived from metal examples of Eastern origin. Impasto production, which continued until the Roman era for household earthenware, was eventually joined by bucchero. This term refers to a type of impasto that is purified and blackish gray due to being fired in a reduced-oxygen environment. While the elegance and refined nature of the oldest vases leads us to believe that they were based on metal models, many bucchero shapes recall the impasto tradition from the end of the eighth century, such as small amphorae with spirals, *kantharoi,* and chalices widely produced during the entire seventh and sixth centuries.

▼ Small amphora in bucchero. Cerveteri, Museo Cerite. The oldest tomb where bucchero was discovered is Tomb 2 in Casaletti di Cerveteri. Bucchero is represented in the tomb by this small amphora as well as a pail and a cup. It is datable, thanks to the presence of Greek pottery among the grave goods, to the second quarter of the seventh century B.C. This amphora, whose impasto prototype is from the eighth century, is quite refined.

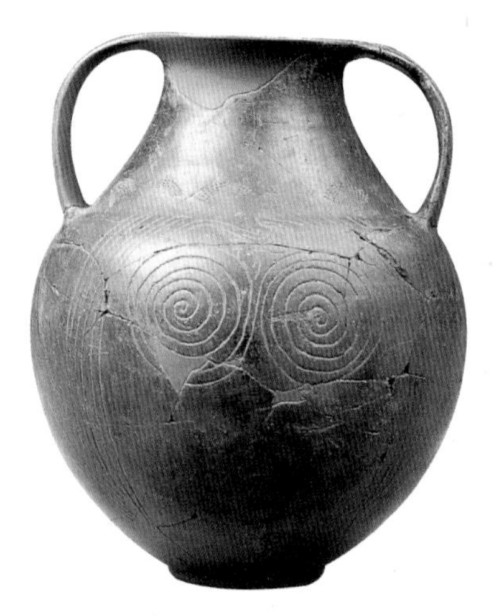

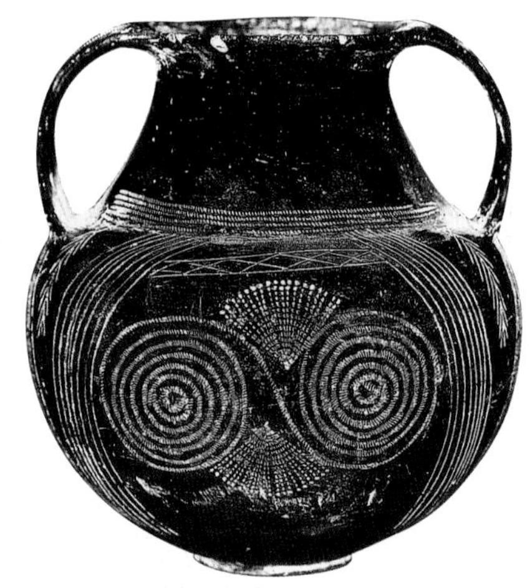

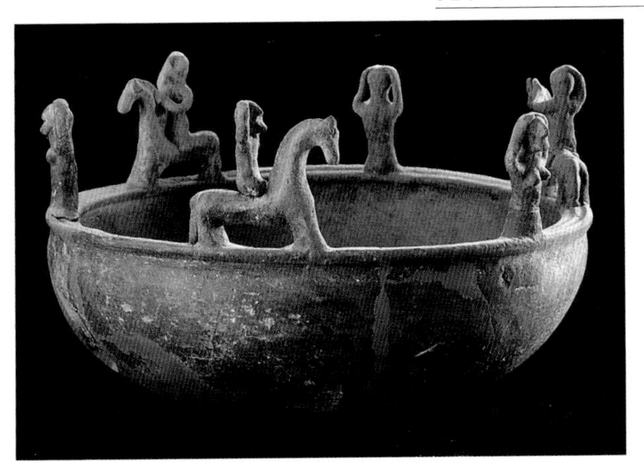

▶ Impasto *lebes* with modeled decorations, from a tomb near Pitigliano, 650–600 B.C. Florence, Museo Archeologico. The figures of horsemen and mourners place this *lebes* within the same late Villanovan tradition as the funerary vase of Montescudaio. They make reference to the social status of the deceased and to funerary rituals.

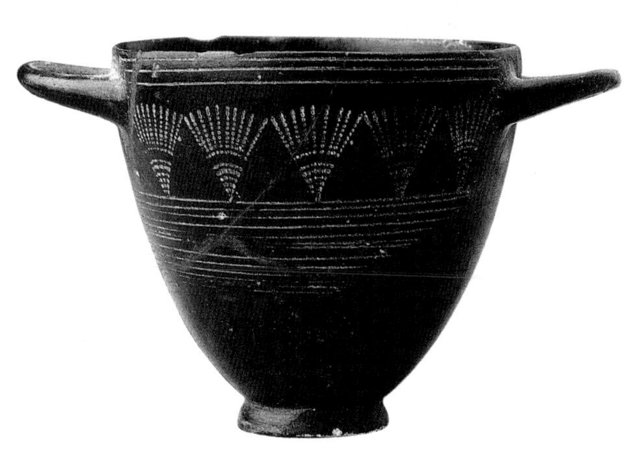

◀ Bucchero *kotyle* from Cerveteri, 650 B.C. Rome, Museo di Villa Giulia. Beginning in the first decades of the seventh century B.C., Corinthian pottery was imported into Etruria, where its shape and decoration were imitated. There are notable gold and silver *kotylai* that postdate the first examples in bucchero, and others in impasto and potter's clay.

◀ Small impasto amphora from Tomb 89 in the Monte Abetone necropolis, Cerveteri. Milan, Civiche Raccolte Archeologiche. The tiny fans in the decoration allow the piece to be dated to the second half of the seventh century B.C. The spirals imprinted on the two sides characterize this type of vase, which was duplicated in metal and more often in bucchero.

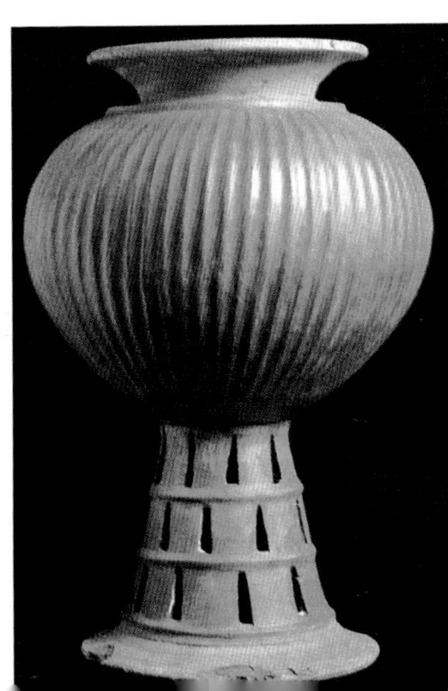

◀ This olla made of reddish impasto with a red-glazed neck seems to have been a favorite creation of workshops in Tarquinia during the Orientalizing era. Its shape derives from rough impasto prototypes that were often painted with Geometric patterns in the late Villanovan tradition. The vase's perforated base recalls the supports for impasto *lebetes* that imitated metal ones and were widespread during the second half of the seventh century B.C.

Writing

The oldest Etruscan inscriptions date back to the beginning of the seventh century B.C. Despite their simplicity, they furnish fundamental data for the understanding of this facet of Etruscan culture. The first signs and letters of a written or painted alphabet on pottery, which was more commonly found among women's possessions, can be traced back to the Greek Euboean alphabet, which spread throughout the Tyrrhenian region via the colonies of Pithecusae and Cumae. Enriched by contributions from other Greek areas, this alphabet was adapted to the requirements of the local Etruscan language and utilized by the Etruscan aristocracy, who played a determining role in the acquisition and promotion of the written word. The letters engraved on small tablets, vases, and precious objects recorded dedications of ownership. Found among the grave goods in tombs of the nobility, they demonstrate that writing was considered a mark of social distinction. It was also a means of affirming ownership of goods, which were often obtained as gifts or trades and buried beside the deceased. The inclusion of the family name, or *gens* (*nomen gentilicum*) from this point on illustrates the importance that the noble families ascribed to the transfer of lineage and the material goods connected to it. Other inscriptions contain information on the practice of giving and exchanging between members of the same family or representatives of other *gentes,* with the goal of either establishing relations or strengthening bonds of friendship.

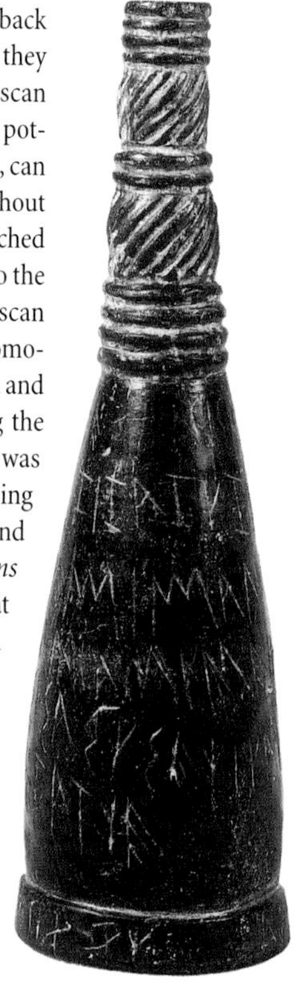

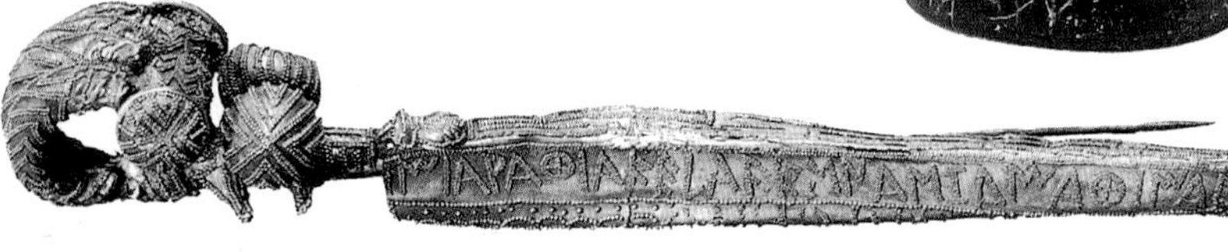

▲ Dragon-shaped fibula from Casteluccio di Pienza, 625–600 B.C. Paris, Musée du Louvre. This inscription, written in an alphabet from Chiusi, illustrates the aristocracy's practice of gift-giving. The granulation technique and the inscription itself can be traced to goldsmiths in southern Etruria.

► Ivory tablet from the Circle of the Ivories in Marsiliana d'Albegna, 675–650 B.C. Grosseto, Museo Archeologico. This was part of a set of writing instruments. The twenty-six left-facing letters of the archaic Greek alphabet engraved along the border confirm that the object was used for learning. Etruscan was often written from right to left.

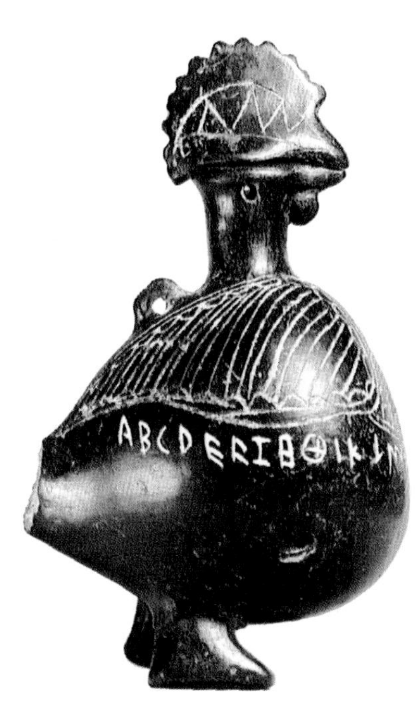

◀ Bucchero vase in the shape of a rooster, dating to the second half of the seventh century B.C., from Viterbo. New York, The Metropolitan Museum of Art. This vase, which was probably used as a container, has the twenty-six letters of the Etruscan alphabet engraved across it.

▼ Small amphora of thin bucchero from Monte Acuto, Formello, from the last quarter of the seventh century B.C. Rome, Museo di Villa Giulia. Along its neck and body, next to a series of letters and a right-handed inscription, are meaningless letters and syllables.

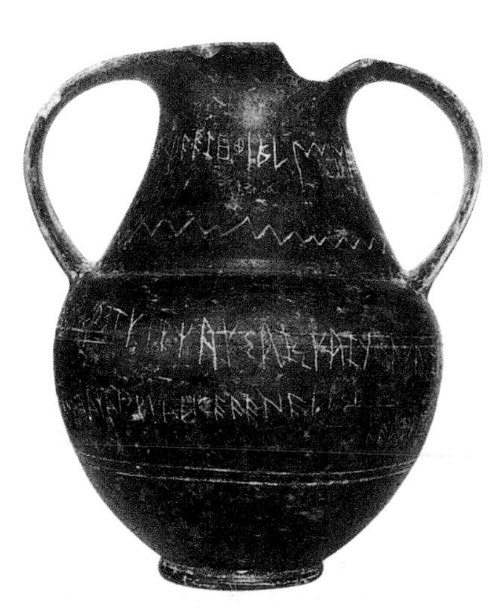

◀ Bucchero inkwell from Cerveteri, 650–600 B.C. Vatican City, Museo Gregoriano Etrusco. The alphabet is engraved around the ring of the base, while a spelling text covers the body. A number of errors in the alphabet reveal this to be the work of someone who was inexperienced at writing.

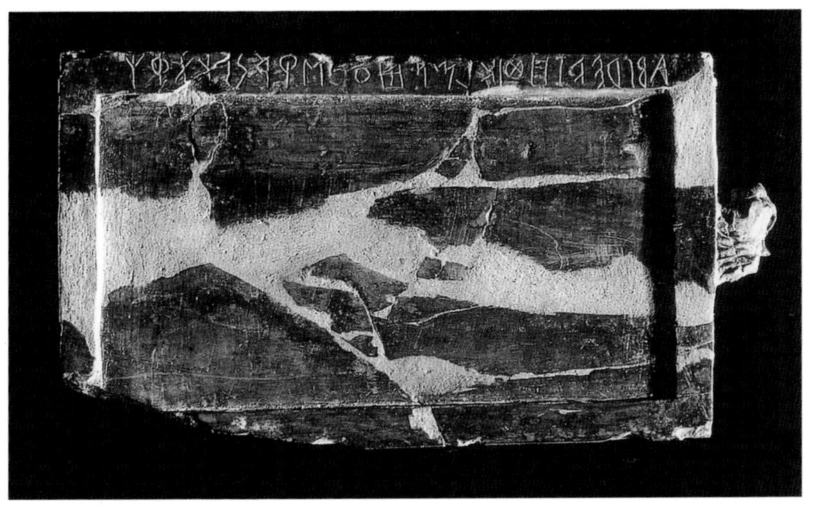

580–480 B.C.

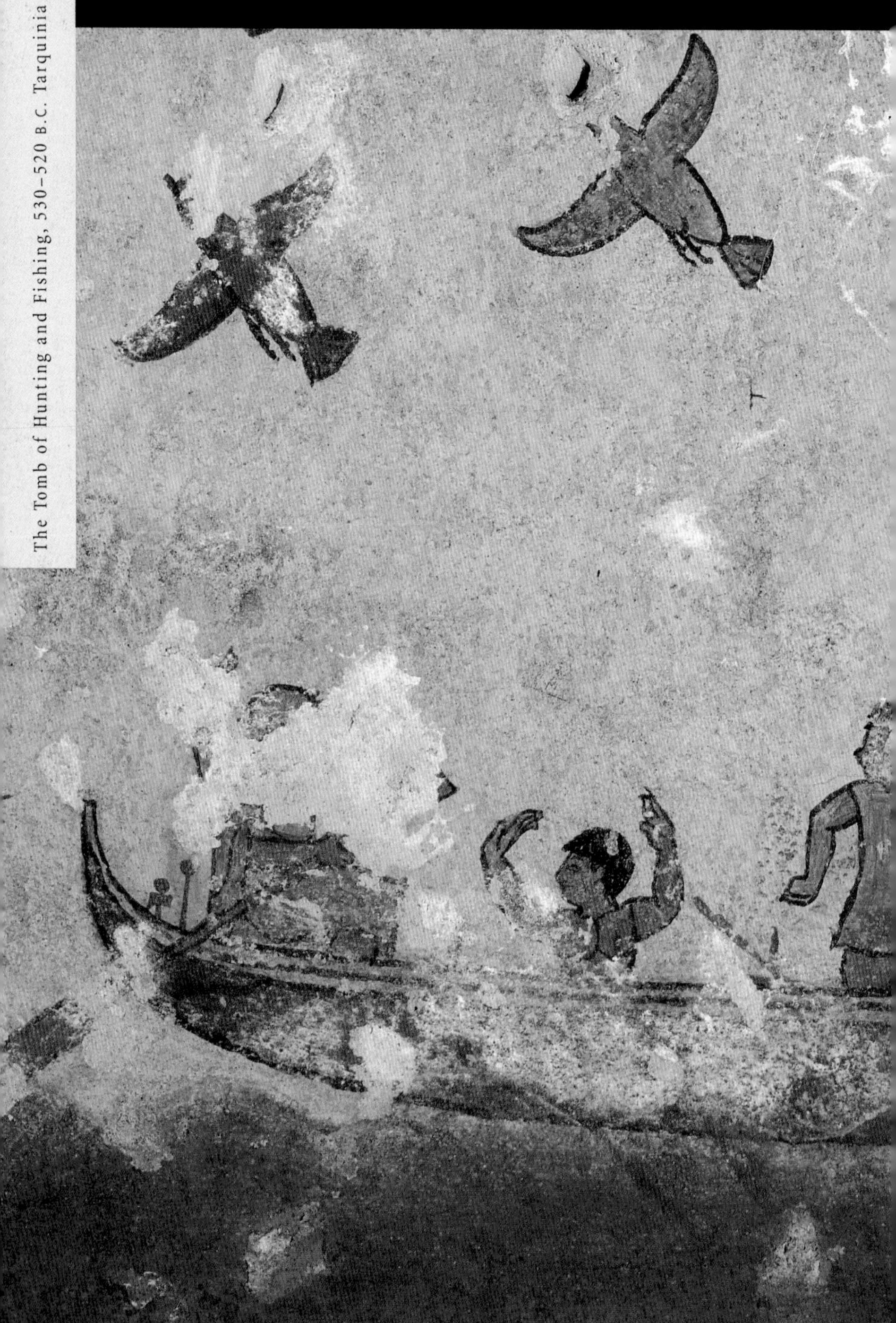

The Tomb of Hunting and Fishing, 530–520 B.C. Tarquinia

The Archaic Period

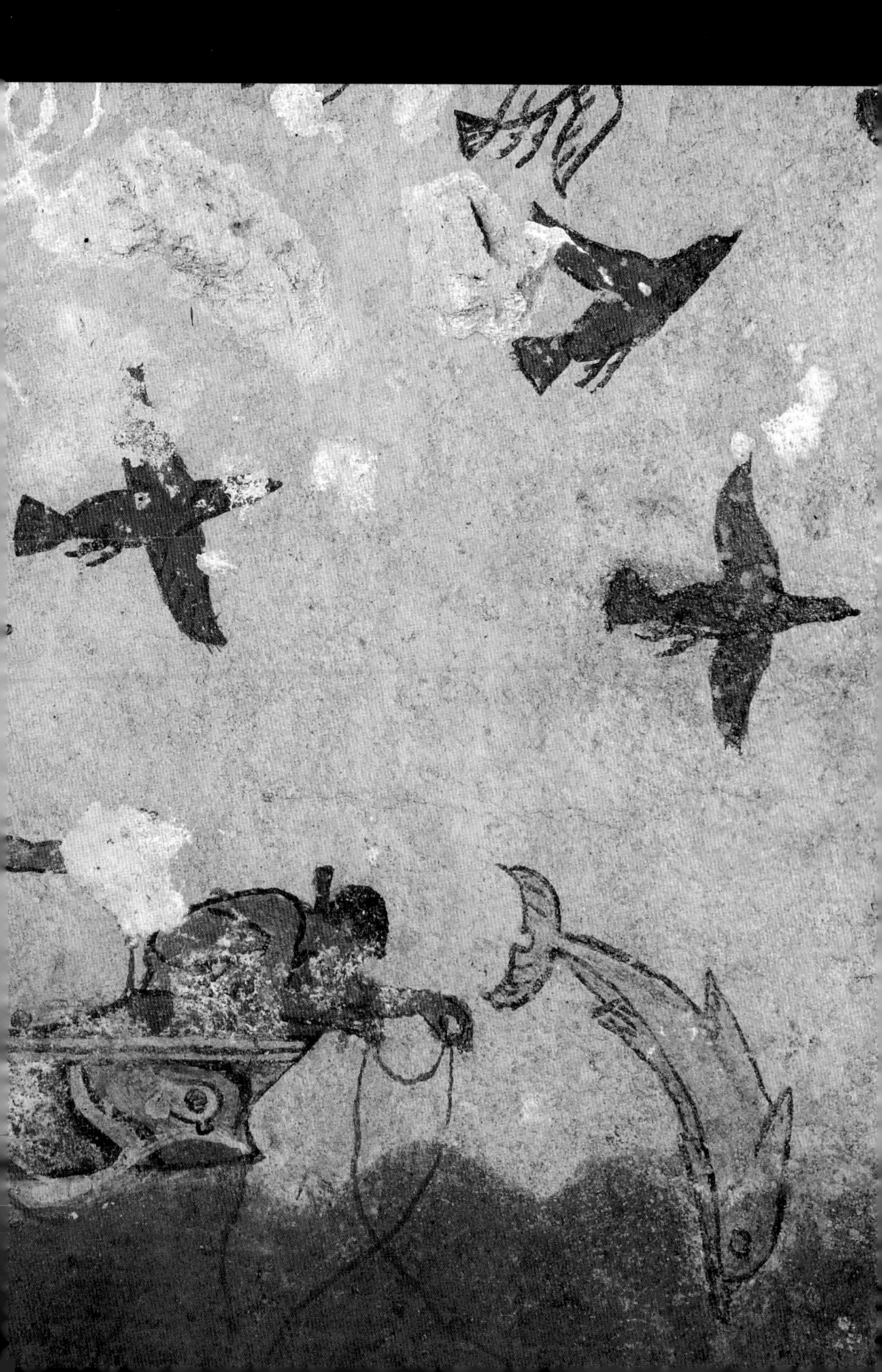

Houses and Palaces

▶ Terra-cotta friezes that decorated the walls of the palace courtyard at Poggio Civitate. Murlo, Antiquarium di Poggio Civitate. These plaques illustrated the ceremonial pursuits of aristocratic life, including horse races.

The middle of the seventh century B.C. saw the introduction of new construction techniques. Rectangular-shaped houses became more solid, with brick walls and roofs covered with tiles. Between the end of the seventh century and the beginning of the sixth, houses underwent a "latitudinal" development: Their main entrances were now located at the center of their long sides, which led to the interior space being subdivided into three sections. This layout had originated in the East and was reproduced in the Etruscan world in palaces at Poggio Civitate and Acquarossa. In the former, the most ancient section has been identified as being built around 650 B.C.; it was destroyed by fire just before 600 B.C. and rebuilt a short time later. The characteristics of the palace structures—a central courtyard enclosed by four wings and complex architectural decorations composed of modeled slabs and impressive acroteria—demonstrate the important cultural function attributed to them by the aristocratic community. The palace at Acquarossa from the Archaic period, which was preceded by an older building, seems less developed and has some architectural and decorative features that illustrate the religious and ideological transformation that lay behind the decline of the palace structure. Toward the end of the sixth century, both palaces were destroyed when a new social order was instated.

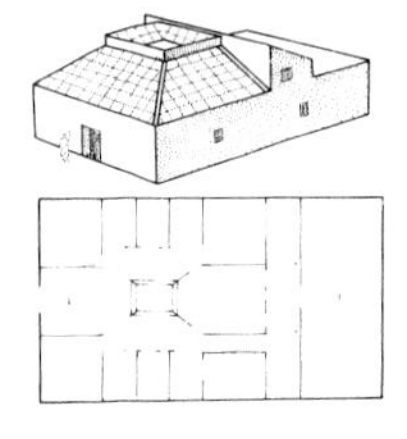

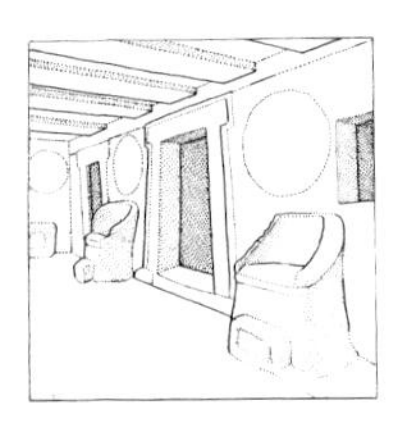

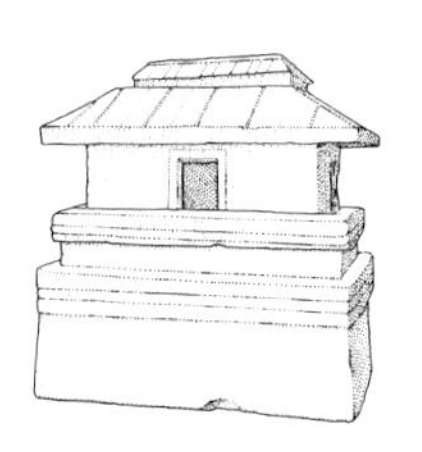

▲ *From the top:* An Etruscan house at Pompeii with a roof opening to gather rainwater; the reproduction of a house interior from the Tomb of the Shields and Chairs in Cerveteri from the sixth century B.C., with thrones and shields along the walls; and a funerary urn from Chiusi. Berlin, Staatliche Museen.

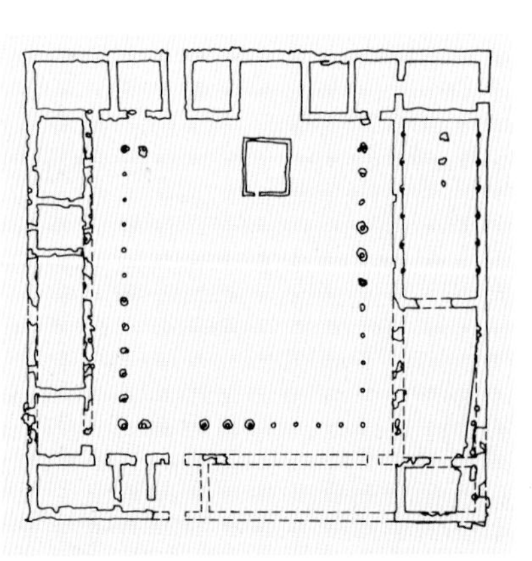

▶ A central courtyard measuring about forty meters (130 ft.) can be seen in the plan of the Archaic palace at Poggio Civitate, together with wide porticoes and four corner structures that were probably watchtowers. In front of the palace hall, where the owner and his family lived, is a tiny rectangular structure thought to have been used for worship by the noble family.

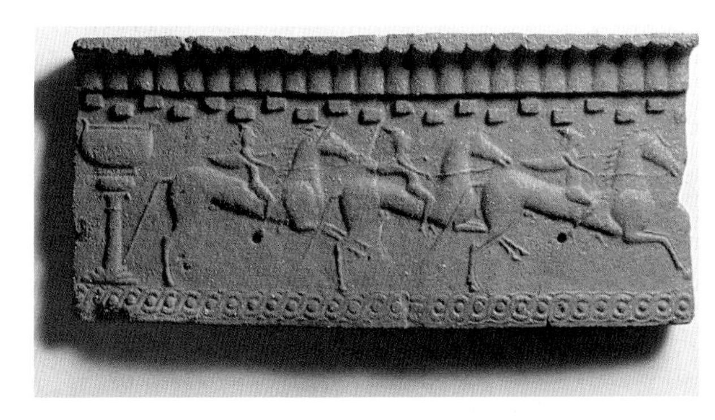

▼ Among a group of plaques from Poggio Civitate, modeled and painted by local artisans, is one portraying an assembly of figures who have been variously interpreted as divinities, members of aristocratic families, and magistrates.

▼ A terra-cotta plaque that lined the interior porticoes of the *regia* (palace) at Acquarossa, 650–625 B.C. Viterbo, Museo Archeologico. Hercules celebrates his victory over the Cretan bull. This depiction of the myth represents an innovation for the narrative repertory of the Etruscan *regiae*.

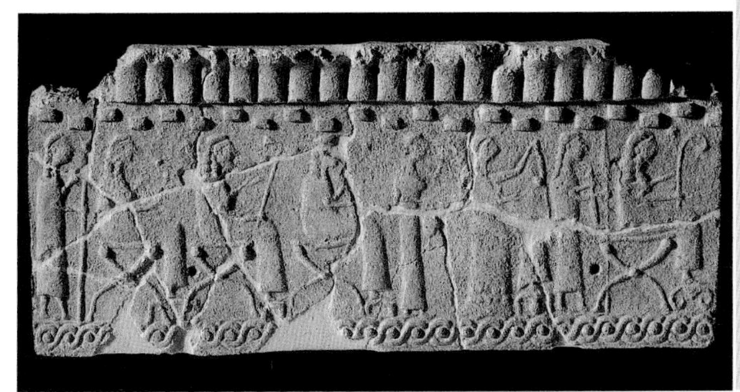

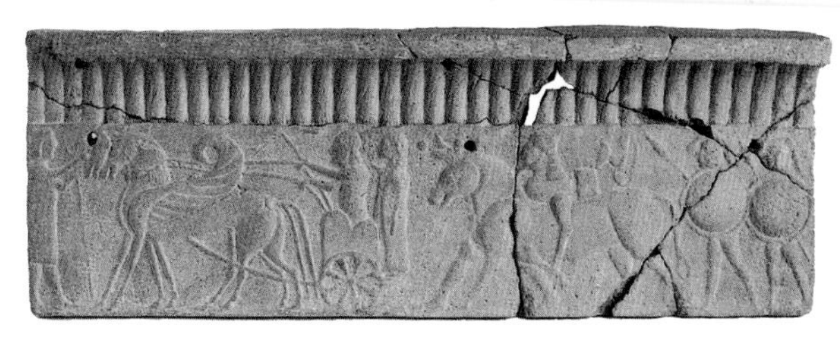

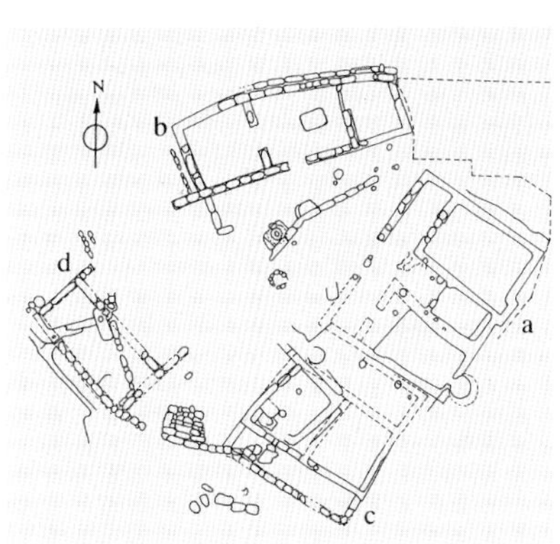

◀ A map of a residential area at Acquarossa with houses placed around a triangular courtyard.

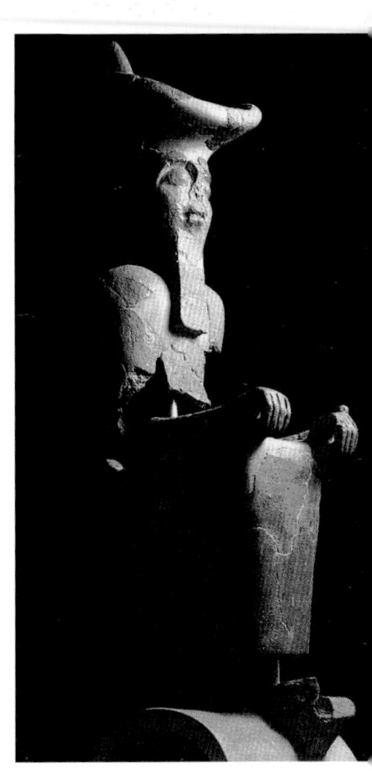

▶ This acroterion in the shape of a male figure represents the ancestor of the clan that resided in the palace at Poggio Civitate. Its function was to protect the building and its inhabitants.

Trading Centers

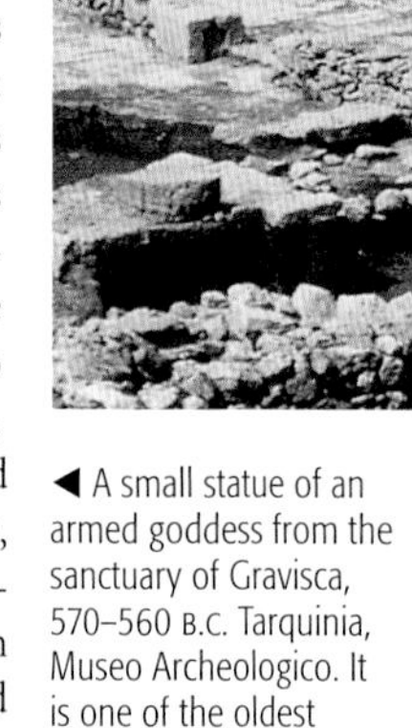

The Etruscans had always taken a leading role in commercial activities in the Mediterranean, and, along with the Greeks, they controlled the sea routes and the most important trading centers. Up until the final decades of the seventh century B.C., control over trade had remained in the hands of the aristocracy, whose wealth was mainly in property. Now, however, there was a management change: Professional sailors took charge of trade, and Etruscan cities such as Cerveteri and Tarquinia organized and supplied trading posts. Such was the origin of the trading center of Gravisca, where the presence of a sanctuary fostered relations between the local community and foreigners who came to exchange their goods. With the arrival of merchants, artisans, and goods from the eastern Greek world came the introduction of new technologies, lifestyles, and cultural models. Beginning in the sixth century, it was mainly merchants from eastern Greece who frequented the port of Gravisca, and the local community even provided them with a sacred space to practice their own religion and rituals. A sanctuary to Aphrodite was erected, and, during the second half of the sixth century, two more were added that were dedicated to other originally Greek divinities: Hera and Demeter. At this point sanctuary life became increasingly intense until the first decades of the fifth century, when relations with the Greek world ended and the sanctuary was restructured to suit the needs of the local Etruscan community.

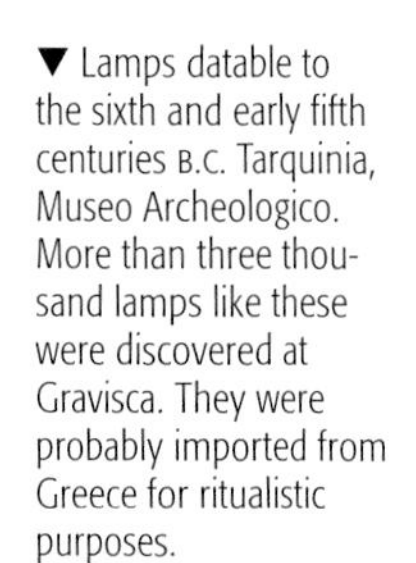

◀ A small statue of an armed goddess from the sanctuary of Gravisca, 570–560 B.C. Tarquinia, Museo Archeologico. It is one of the oldest bronze votive images of a deity known in Etruria.

▼ Lamps datable to the sixth and early fifth centuries B.C. Tarquinia, Museo Archeologico. More than three thousand lamps like these were discovered at Gravisca. They were probably imported from Greece for ritualistic purposes.

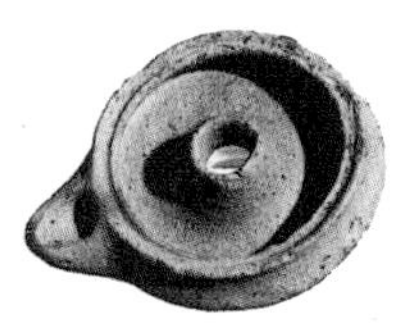

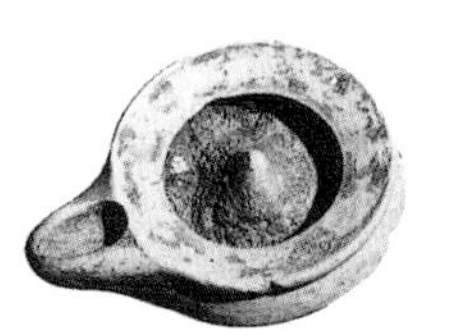

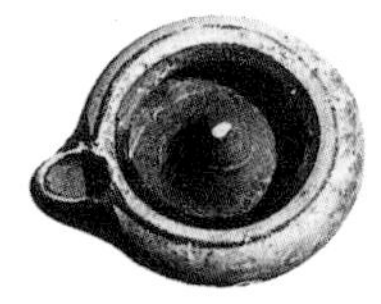

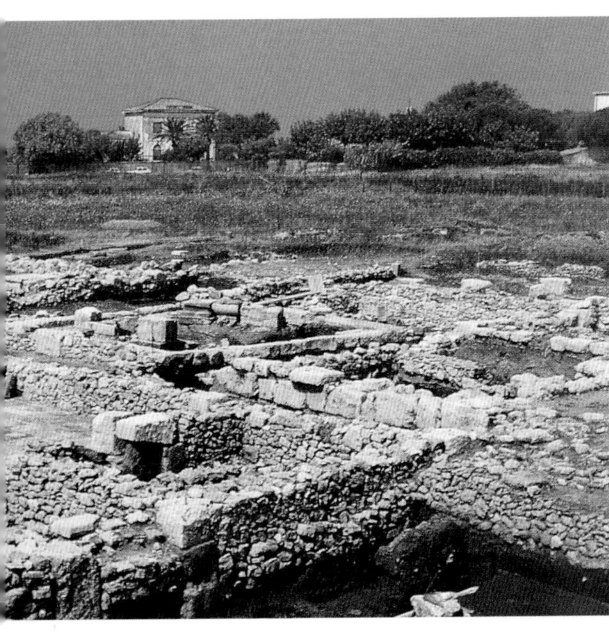

◀ Ruins at the site of Gravisca, the Etruscan port of Tarquinia. A complex of sacred buildings dedicated to female gods from the Greek pantheon has been identified in this area. The buildings were in use from the beginning of the sixth century B.C.

▼ Aerial view of the Gravisca area. Ex-votos, amphorae, dedicatory inscriptions, and figurative pottery discovered during excavation demonstrate that sailors from different areas of Greece frequented this site.

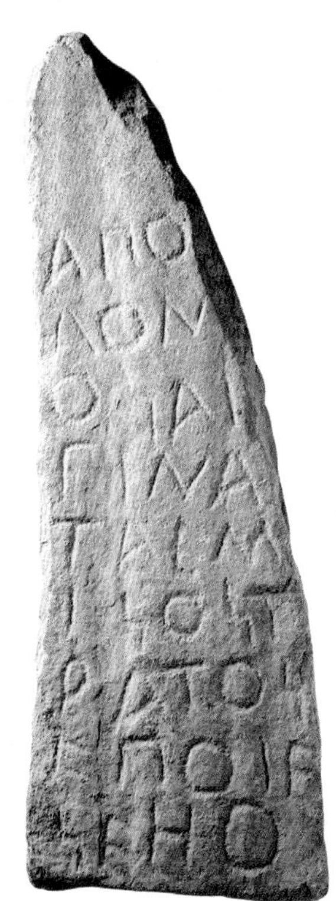

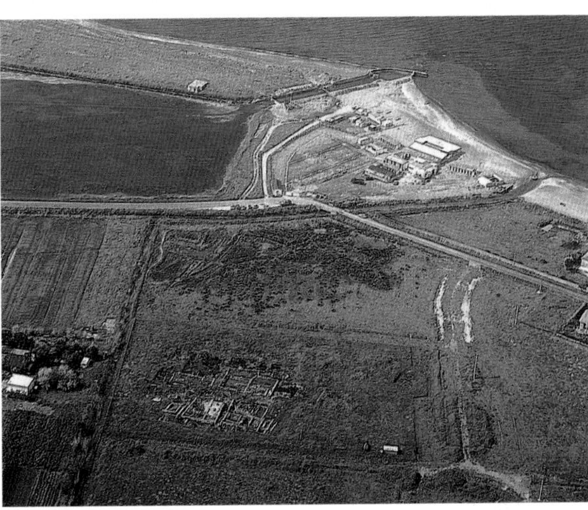

◀ Anchor stock from the end of the sixth century B.C. Tarquinia, Museo Archeologico. This item is part of a group of stocks bearing dedications to divinities that were unearthed at the sanctuary of Gravisca and in other regions of the Mediterranean. The inscription, which is in the Doric dialect using an alphabet from Aegina, bears the name Sostratos, an Aeginetan merchant. It is proof of commercial relations between Tyrrhenian merchants and Aeginetans at the end of the sixth century.

Temples

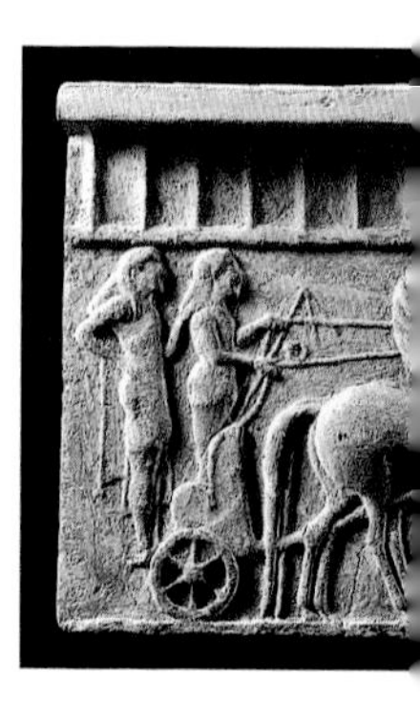

Sacred buildings in the Archaic cities needed to be immediately recognizable through distinctive architectural characteristics. The standard plan for a temple was almost square, erected on a podium foundation designed to elevate the building, and with a front entrance accessible by means of stairs. The front section was open with a wide colonnade while the rear section was subdivided into three rooms. Other features of this type of Etruscan temple, which was defined as "Tuscan" in Vitruvius's *De Architectura,* were a wooden roof, terra-cotta revetments, an open gable, and post-and-lintel construction antefixes. The oldest example of this type is the Temple of Mater Matuta in Rome, which was built by Servius Tullius around 570 B.C. with just one *cella* (chamber) flanked by two aisles (wings) and two stone columns in front. Perhaps the most impressive temple, dedicated to Jupiter and located on Capitoline Hill, was begun by Tarquinius Priscus and inaugurated in 501. It was embellished with fine terra-cotta decorations by Etruscan artists. Here the Tuscan temple with three *cellae* was enriched by a colonnade in front and one on each side, a feature also found in sanctuaries with a single *cella,* such as Temple B of Pyrgi and Satricum. Both Roman colonies and municipalities would adopt this model of sacred architecture, which developed over the course of the seventh century.

▼ Reconstruction of Temple A in Pyrgi. This monumental temple was part of Etruria's largest sanctuary, whose construction began around 510 B.C. The elements of the Tuscan order were applied freely, as is evident, for example, in the addition of four columns to the facade in front of the pronaos.

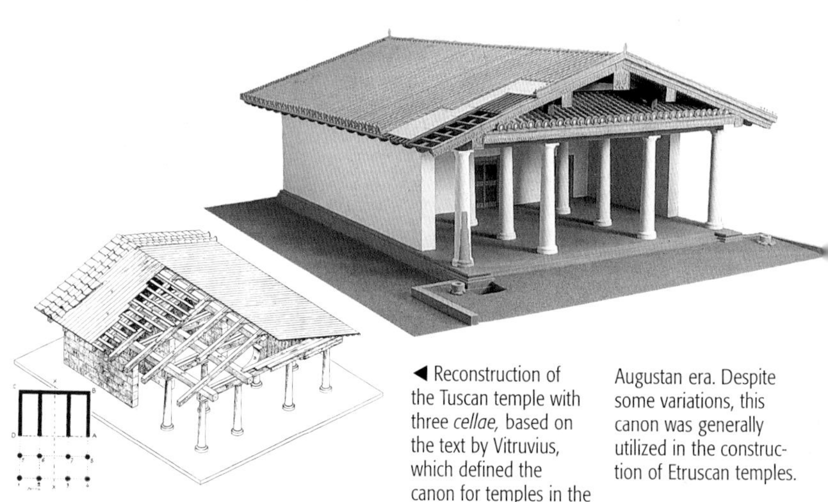

◀ Reconstruction of the Tuscan temple with three *cellae,* based on the text by Vitruvius, which defined the canon for temples in the Augustan era. Despite some variations, this canon was generally utilized in the construction of Etruscan temples.

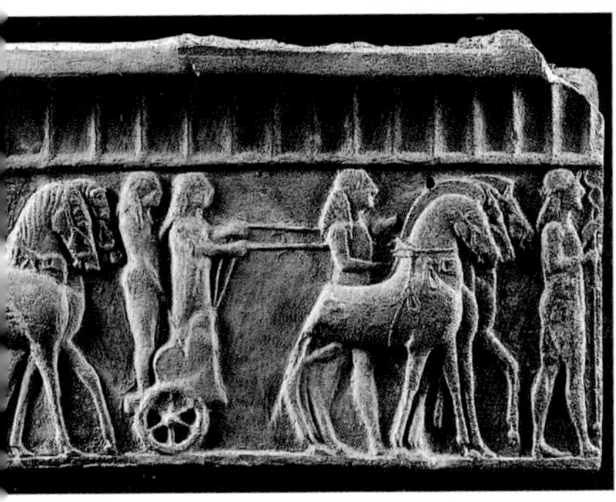

▲ A group of terra-cotta plaques that decorated the temple discovered under the church of Santa Maria delle Stimmate, 525–500 B.C. Naples, Museo Nazionale. Its scenes, like this one of a procession, recall those of the friezes at Poggio Civitate depicting the most significant events of aristocratic life.

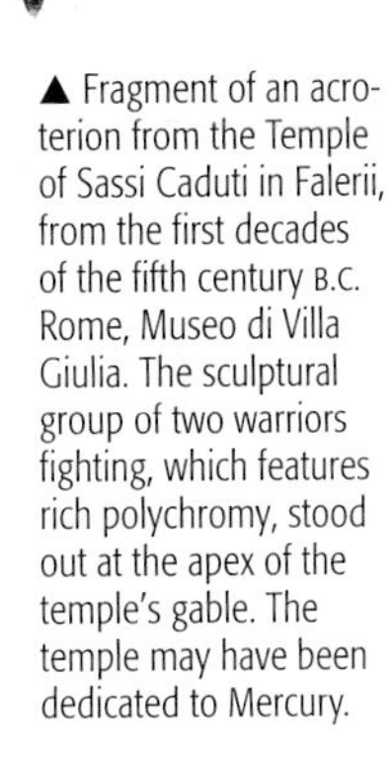

▲ Fragment of an acroterion from the Temple of Sassi Caduti in Falerii, from the first decades of the fifth century B.C. Rome, Museo di Villa Giulia. The sculptural group of two warriors fighting, which features rich polychromy, stood out at the apex of the temple's gable. The temple may have been dedicated to Mercury.

◀ Antefix with a maenad and a silenus from the Temple at Satricum, which was built between 490 and 480 B.C. Rome, Museo di Villa Giulia. Antefixes decorated the eaves of the temple. These subjects, which were common in other cities of Etruria as well, belonged to the cult of Dionysus.

The Etruscan Kings in Rome

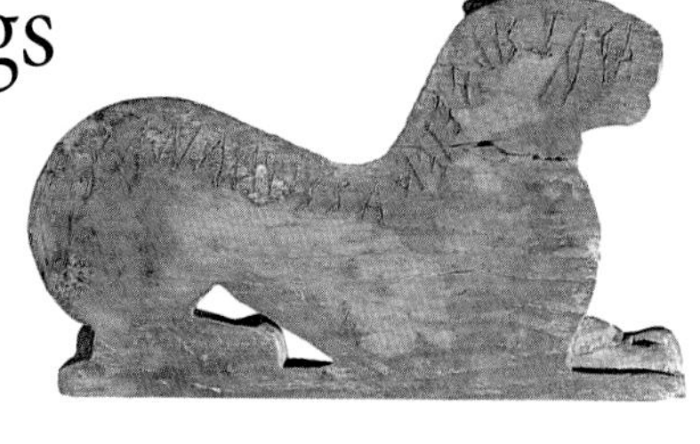

▲ A tiny ivory plaque shaped as a crouching lion from the sacred area of Sant'Omobono, from the middle of the sixth century B.C. Rome, Antiquarium Comunale. This artifact was one of two linking plaques. A right-to-left Etruscan inscription from the middle of the sixth century is engraved on its reverse side and confirms the presence of Etruscan aristocrats in Rome during the era of the monarchy.

Like Etruria and Campania, Lazio was influenced by the cultural and artistic climate of the Orientalizing phase, as illustrated by the rich grave goods of princes and princesses in tombs at Palestrina. The presence of goldwork and ivory from Cerveteri in tombs at Lazio during this period shows an Etruscan influence, which was also typical of grave goods from the end of the seventh century B.C. It remains uncertain, however, whether this corresponded to political dominance by the Etruscans. According to ancient historiography, the period of Etruscan rule in Rome falls between the end of the seventh and the end of the sixth centuries, when the Tarquin kings were in Rome. The kings undertook important and innovative social and urban-planning projects. Among the public works attributed to Tarquinius Priscus are the development of the Roman Forum and the creation of the Circus Maximus; Servius Tullius expanded the city to the Seven Hills and built a city wall; and Tarquinius Superbus completed the Temple of Jupiter on Capitoline Hill. The votive deposits in the Roman Forum and in Sant'Omobono provide good evidence of this period in Roman history, which featured reforms in the social and economic spheres by Servius Tullius. This king was called Mastarna and depicted in Etruscan paintings in the François Tomb in Vulci.

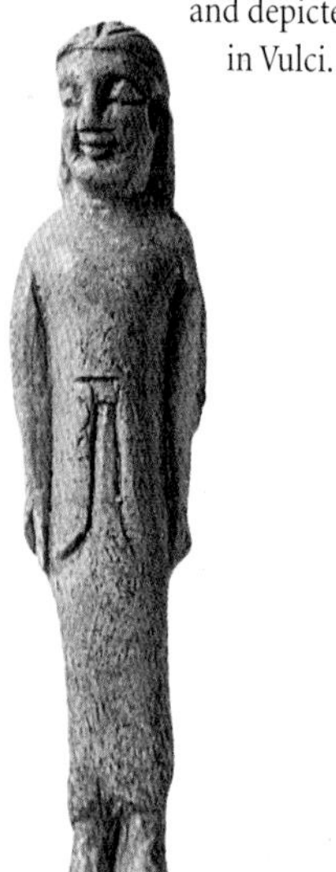

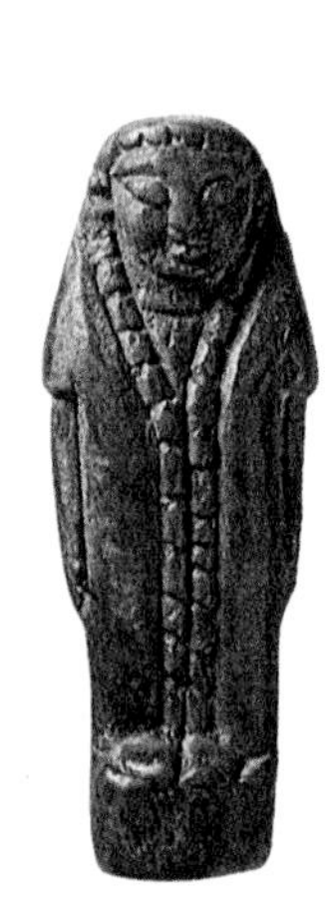

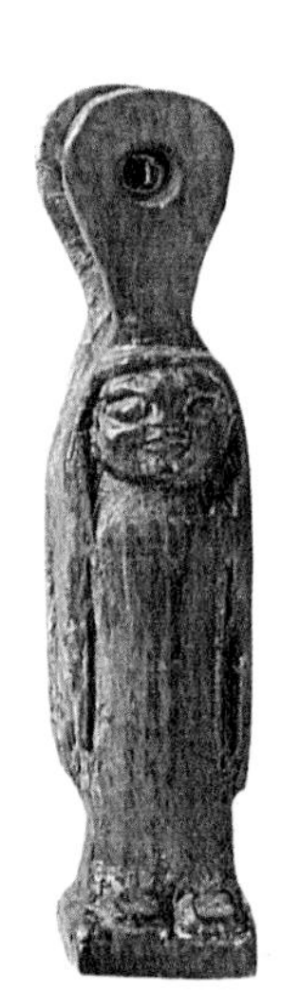

◀ Bone pendants of female figures from votive deposits at Sant'Omobono, dating to the middle of the sixth century B.C. Rome, Antiquarium Comunale. Here, stylistic and iconographic elements recall the northern Etruscan and eastern Greek worlds.

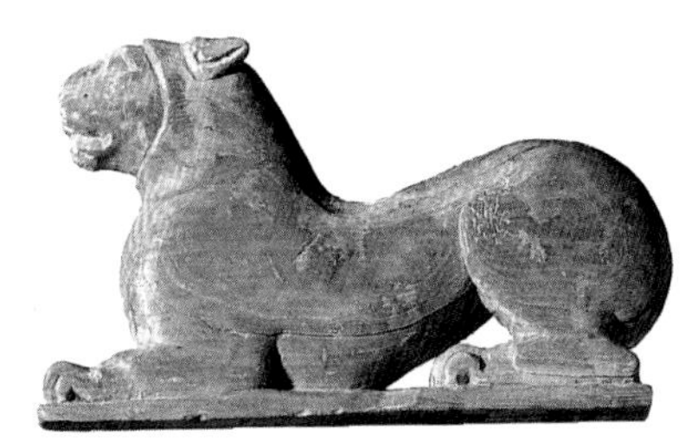

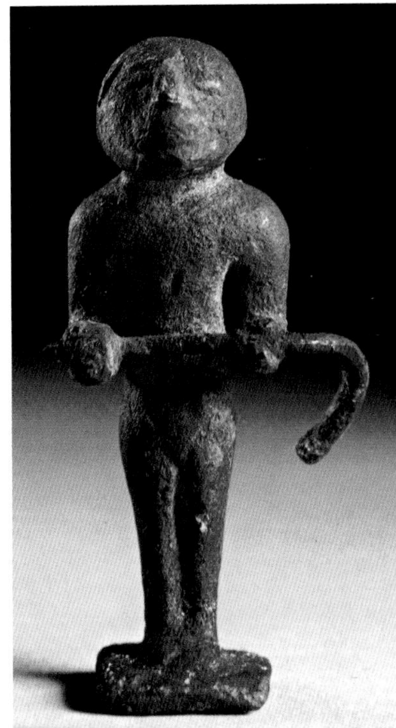

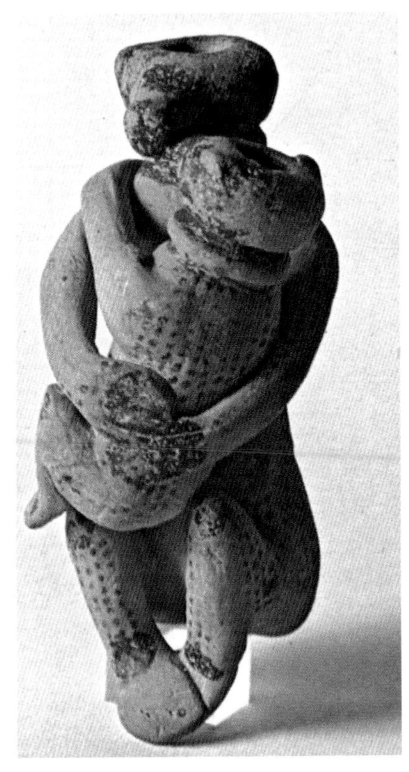

◀ Ointment jar shaped like a monkey with her offspring, from votive deposits at Sant'Omobono. Rome, Antiquarium Comunale. This object belongs with works from Etruscan workshops that imitate handmade goods in the Corinthian tradition.

▲ Bronze statue from votive deposits at Lapis Niger, 550 B.C. Rome, Museo del Foro. An augur, a priest who had the power to read divine signs, holds a *lituus,* an attribute of his position.

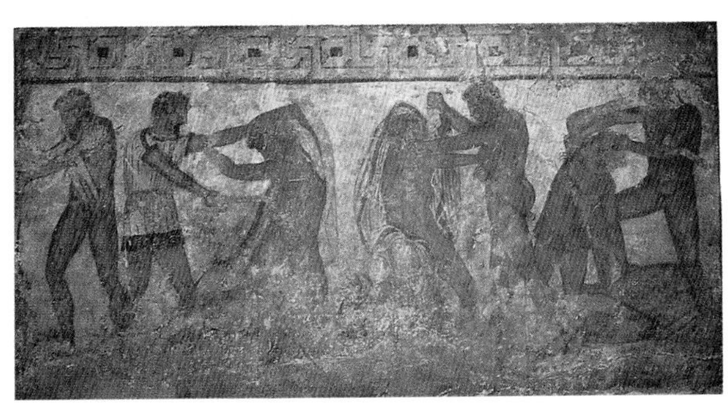

◀ A painting of the Vulcian heroes Caelius and Aulus Vibenna from the François Tomb in Vulci. Rome, Villa Albani Torlonia. A figure named Mastarna, who according to Emperor Claudius was the future king Servius Tullius, is shown naked and facing left as he frees Aulus.

The Temple at Portonaccio in Veii

The sanctuary of Portonaccio in Veii was part of a sacred area enclosed within a wall, the *temenos*. It was dedicated to Minerva and other divinities, including Apollo: The statues that crowned the pediment illustrate the god's activities. The complex terra-cotta ornamentation was the product of a workshop of extremely talented artisans, whose master was a famous artist of Veii named Vulca. The latter was called to Rome by Tarquinius Priscus to create a statue for the Temple of Jupiter on Capitoline Hill.

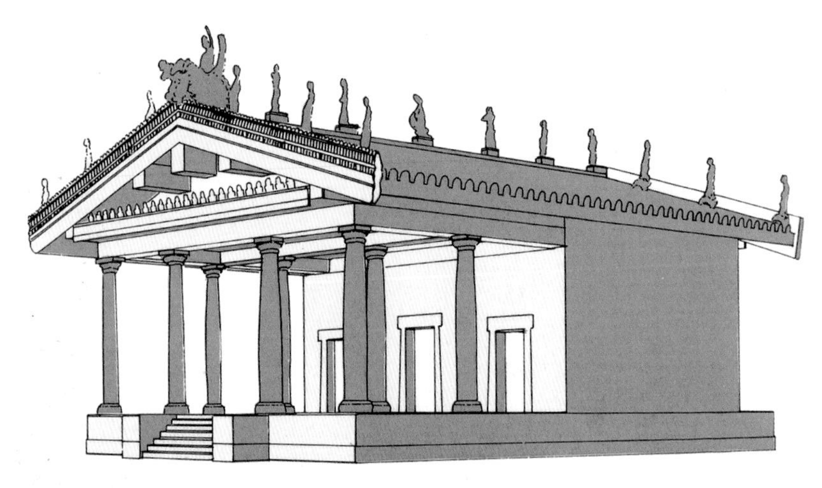

▲ The temple had a square plan that was 18.5 meters (60 ft.) long on each side. The interior was subdivided into three *cellae* while the pronaos was fitted with columns. The roof was decorated with antefixes and a series of acroteria, statues placed along the ridge.

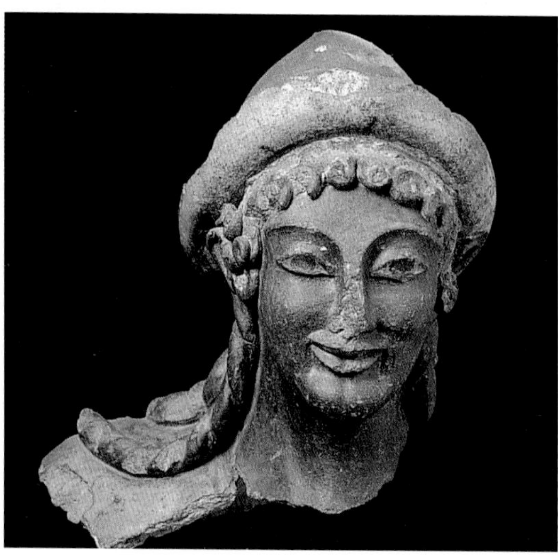

◀ The head of a statue of Hermes wearing a pileus. Rome, Museo di Villa Giulia. This head belonged to an acroterion of the greater temple, which dates between 510 and 500 B.C.

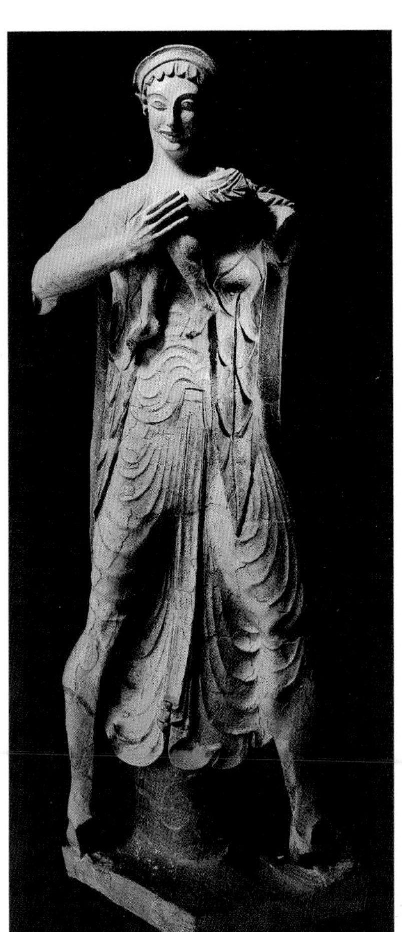

◀ A sculptural group of Leto carrying the tiny Apollo, who slays the serpent Python. Despite being the work of different hands, these acroteria present a number of common stylistic traits, such as the rigid drapery that wraps the bodies, the stiff movement of the figures, and the faces fashioned in the late Greek Archaic style.

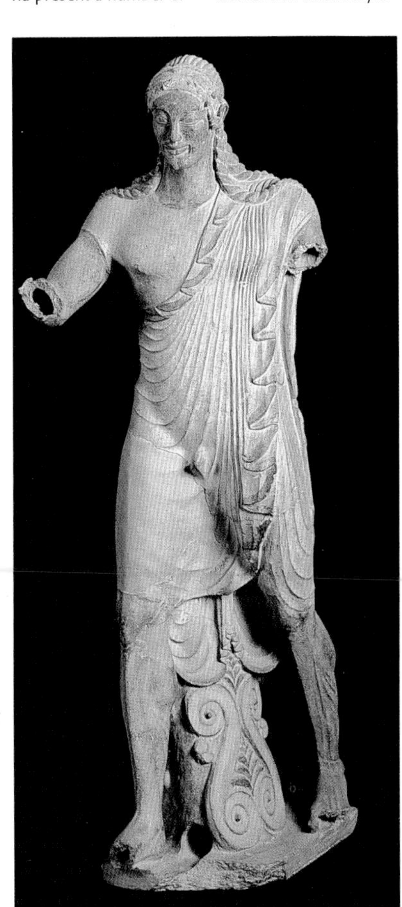

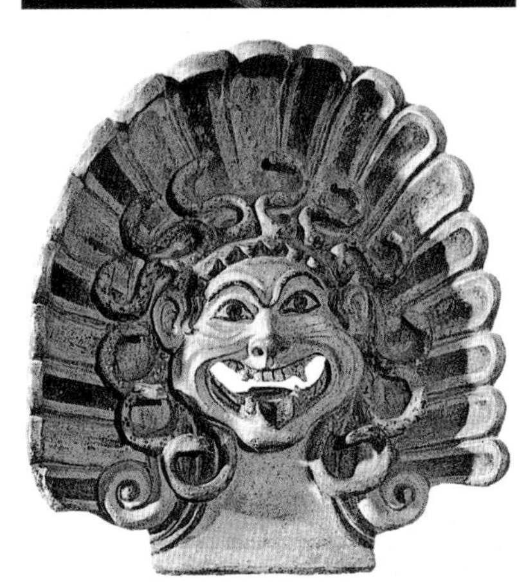

◀ Antefix with the head of Medusa circled by a crown of serpents, 510–500 B.C. Antefixes from the temple are characterized by lively polychromy, which here highlights Medusa's terrifying grimace.

▲ The famous "Apollo of Veii," a masterpiece of Etruscan terra-cotta work from the late Archaic period. Together with Hercules and Hermes, it was part of a group portraying the struggle to capture the Cerynitian stag, a subject linked to the cult of Pythian Apollo at Delphi.

Banquets

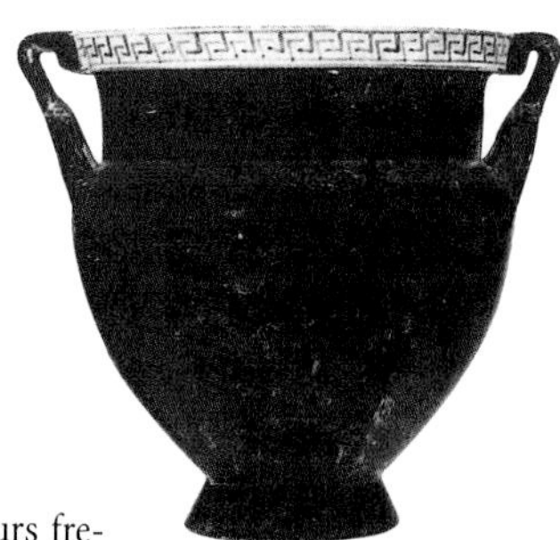

▲ Black painted krater, made in Laconia, from the grave goods of a Cerveteri tomb from the first half of the sixth century B.C. Cerveteri, Museo Archeologico. During symposia, wine was poured from an *oinochoe* into kraters, where it was mixed with water and then served in bowls.

The subject of banquets recurs frequently in a variety of Etruscan works. The ancient sources, referring to the final stages of Etruscan culture, emphasize an inclination toward feasts, banquets, and lives of luxury and pleasure. However, the best evidence of the lifestyle that these people enjoyed comes from archaeology. The oldest depiction of a banquet can be found on a cinerary urn from Montescudaio. Its biconic shape recalls the Villanovan urns, but because of its context it can be dated to the second half of the seventh century B.C. The position of the main figure, which stands before a small table, recalls a type of Homeric banquet, with a few variations derived from the Eastern world. The custom of feasting while reclining on *klinai* began in the Eastern courts around the eighth century and was adopted by the Greek and Etruscan aristocracies at the end of the seventh, as the Corinthian krater of Eurystheus uncovered at Cerveteri from the year 600 shows. From the fifth century on, banquet scenes became common in Etruscan art, with one important innovation with regard to the Greek tradition. Wives of the guests also attended and were shown lying next to their husbands, reclining under the same cover. The painted tombs of Tarquinia, the terra-cotta plaques of Poggio Civitate, Acquarossa, and Velletri, the elegant table services from grave goods, and the urns of Chiusi all show the banquet ceremony—cheered by music, dances, games, and conversation—as being a significant part of the Etruscan aristocratic ideology.

▼ Details of a banquet in the pediment of the back wall of the Tomb of Hunting and Fishing in Tarquinia, from the end of the sixth century B.C. The rich garments of the guests, the earrings of the woman, the number of servants, and the quality of the vases illustrate the affluence of the married couple buried in the tomb.

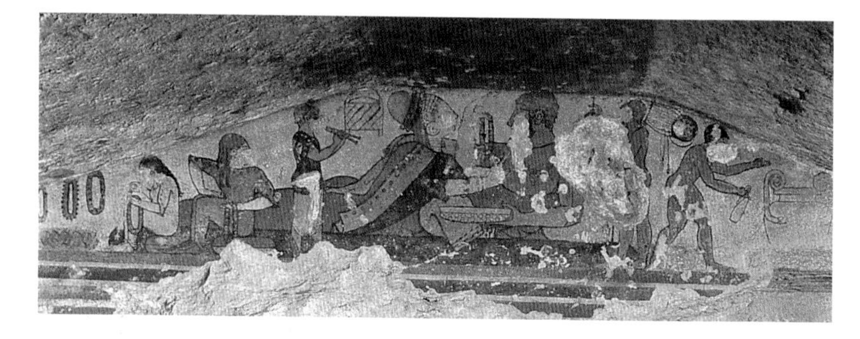

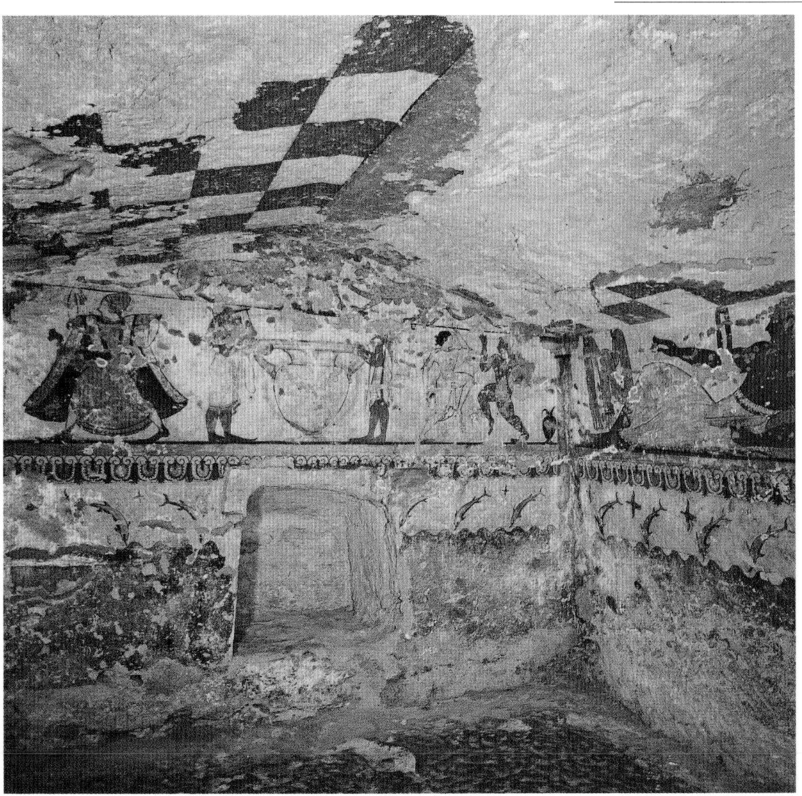

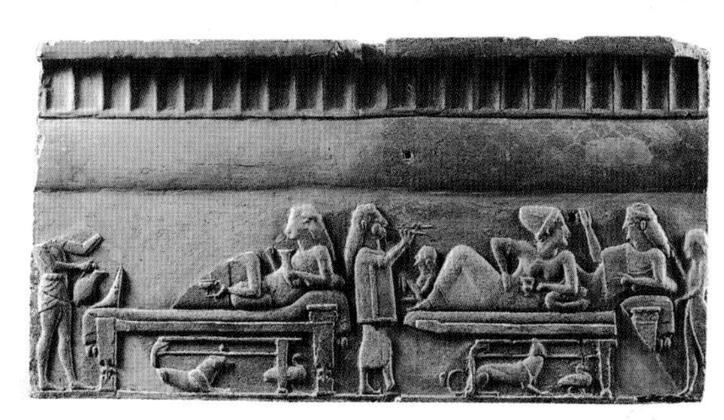

▲ The Tomb of the Lionesses in Tarquinia, datable to the last decades of the sixth century B.C. The two lateral walls show banquet guests, while the back wall shows dancing figures on each side of a huge krater.

▲ Terra-cotta plaque from Velletri. Naples, Museo Nazionale. Male and female figures attend the banquet—whose representation stylistically recalls the Ionic figurative tradition—and lie upon *klinai*.

▶ Small cinerary urn from Chiusi, from the end of the sixth century B.C. Florence, Museo Archeologico. Pairs of male figures, probably relatives of the deceased, repose on *klinai*.

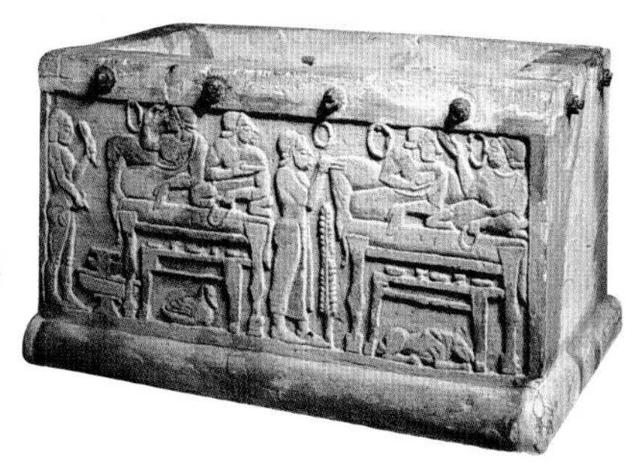

Attic Pottery in Etruria

At the beginning of the sixth century B.C., figurative vases from Attica began to be imported alongside the amphorae of oil from that region. They arrived via the Tyrrhenian Sea thanks to commercial ties established in the previous centuries. The tombs of Cerveteri, which received the largest number of these vases during this first stage of importation, held the works of the first Attic potters, such as the Gorgon Painter. The Etruscan aristocracy's keen demand for vases decorated in the black-figure technique can be demonstrated by the presence of Tyrrhenian and Nikosthenic amphorae that were expressly made by Attic workshops to suit Etruscan tastes. Vases in the red-figure technique also apparently pleased Etruscan clients in Tarquinia, Cerveteri, and Vulci, who brought to their symposia functional vases, such as *kylikes* (drinking bowls) by Oltos and the Penthesilea Painter. However, the defeat of the Etruscan fleet at Cumae in 474 by the Syracusans caused trade routes to shift, and the massive imports of the end of the sixth century experienced a sharp downturn.

▼ Black-figure *kylix*. Tarquinia, Museo Archeologico. The struggle between Hercules and Triton is shown at the center. Greek myths were transmitted not only orally but also through the iconography of figurative vases that were imported from Attica at the behest of Etruscan buyers.

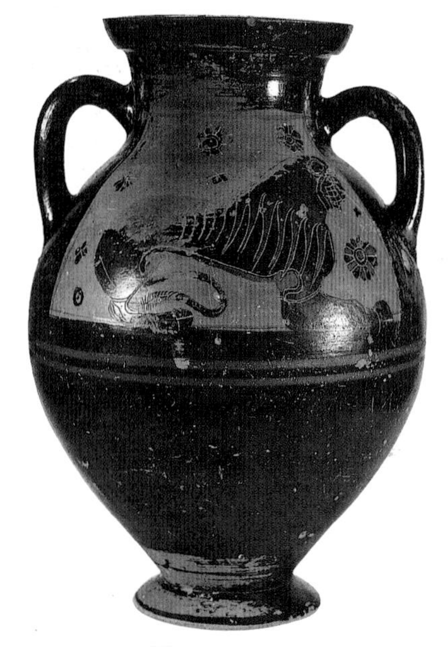

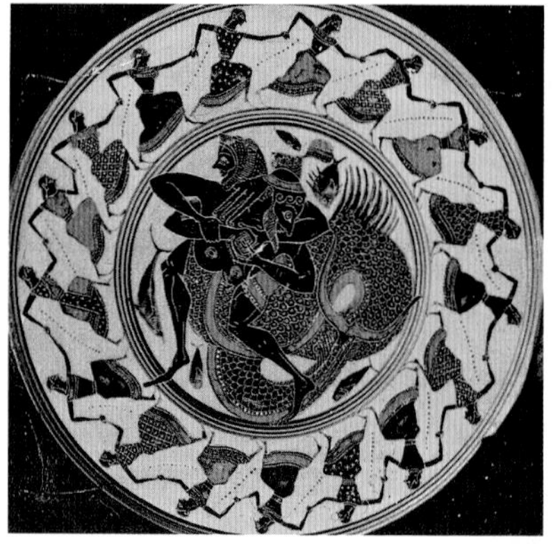

◀ Attic black-figure amphora from a Cerveteran tomb, from the first quarter of the sixth century B.C. Its shape and the decoration of a crouching lion with a huge mane allow it to be attributed to the Gorgon Painter, whose works were much in demand by the Etruscans.

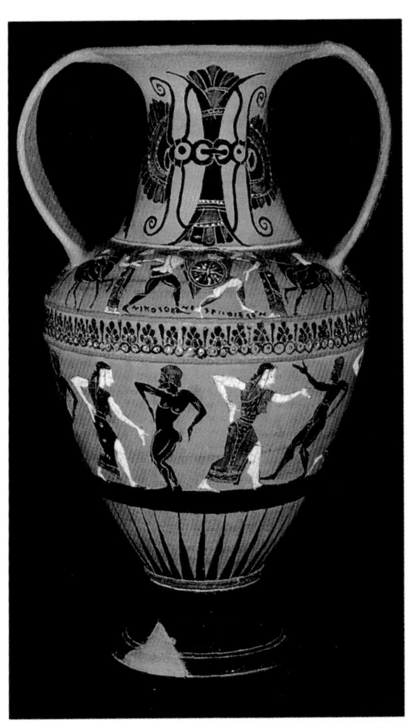

◀ Nikosthenic amphora. Rome, Museo di Villa Giulia. This amphora is one of a number of vases that were executed for Etruscan customers in workshops that specialized in creating, in the Attic black-figure technique, vase-shapes that were foreign to the Athenian repertory but taken directly from bucchero vessels. This was the case with the workshop of Nikosthenes, after whom these "Nikosthenic" amphorae are named.

▶ Amphora richly decorated with superimposed friezes. Rome, Museo di Villa Giulia. It belongs to a class of Tyrrhenian amphorae that were produced in Attica during the second quarter of the sixth century B.C. and found almost exclusively in Etruria. These amphorae seem to have been intended for the Etruscans, who took its iconographic models from Greek mythology and imitated them locally.

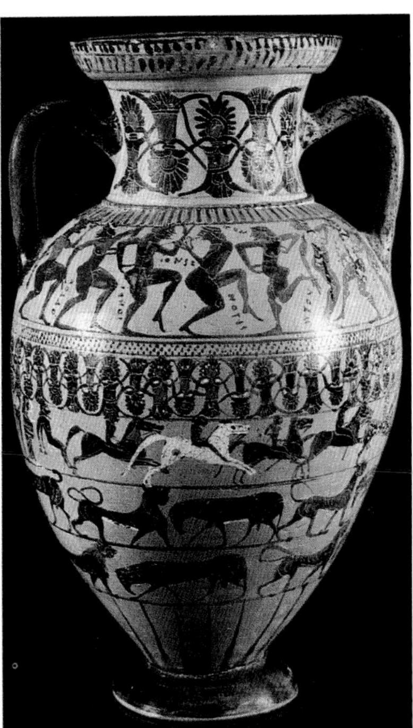

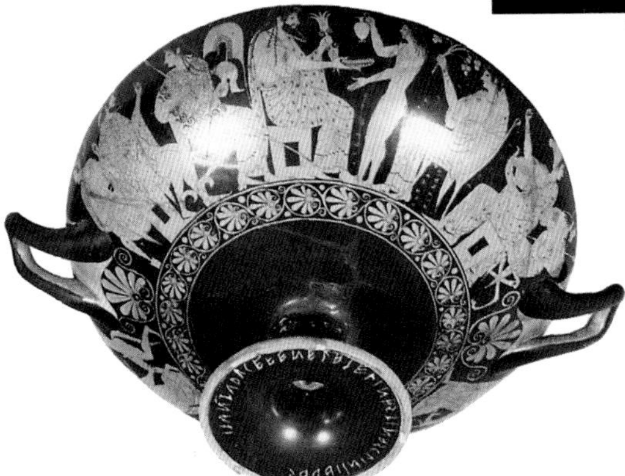

◀ Red-figured *kylix* from Attica, sixth century B.C. Tarquinia, Museo Archeologico. This bowl's exterior has been decorated with figures of divinities gathered at an assembly. An inscription written in the Etruscan alphabet under its base is dedicated to the Dioscuri.

Etruscan Figurative Pottery

Parallel to the continuous importation of vases from Attica, artisans from eastern Greece emigrated to Etruria and adapted their experience to the needs of the local markets. Painters from northern Ionia specialized in producing *hydria* in Cerveteri and *dinoi* in Vulci; the former were decorated with mythological or hunting scenes, the latter with scenes connected to the myth of Dionysus. Also in Vulci and Cerveteri, ceramic workshops sprang up that produced vases that mixed eastern Greek elements with the contemporary iconography of Attic pottery. For example, in Vulci a workshop headed by the Paris Painter (active 550–525) produced Pontic vases. During this same period, the vase painters of the La Tolfa group were working in Cerveteri, creating Ionic-style amphorae that were decorated with figures of animals or mythological scenes. Also in Vulci, the workshop of the Micali Painter, influenced by Attic black-figure pottery, decorated vases of different shapes during the last quarter of the sixth century. At the beginning of the fifth century, black-figure production began to diminish. It was supplanted by red-figure works, which offered greater opportunities for expression.

▼ Black-figure *hydria* in the Ionic style, 520–510 B.C. Toledo, Museum of Art. A scene from the myth of Dionysus can be seen on the vase's body: After pirates abducted the god, they threw themselves into the sea out of fear and were transformed into dolphins.

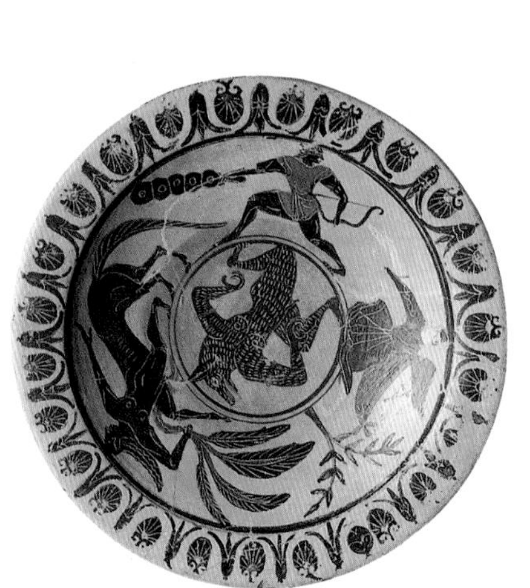

◀ The Tityos Painter, Pontic plate. Rome, Museo di Villa Giulia. This piece is interesting, both for the myth of Hercules and Deianira and for the figure in the central tondo, which may be an Etruscan demon.

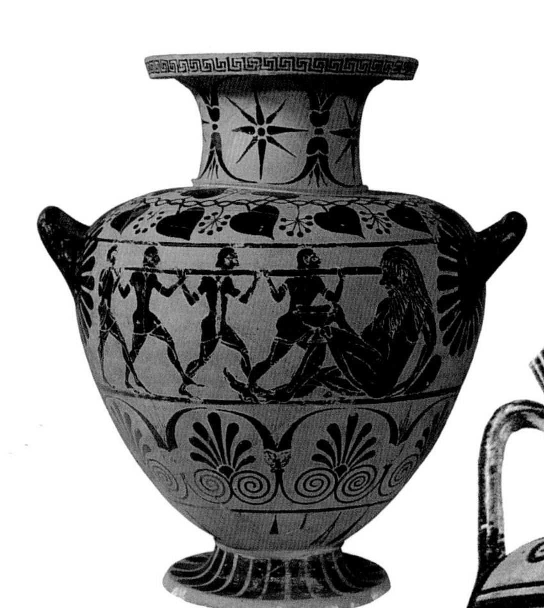

◀ Cerveteran *hydria,* 520–480 B.C. Rome, Museo di Villa Giulia. This is the sole example of a Greek-inspired work that features the myth of Polyphemus.

▼ The Eagle Painter, Cerveteran black-figure *hydria* from Cerveteri, about 525 B.C. Los Angeles, The J. Paul Getty Museum. Helped by Iolaus, Hercules battles the Lernean Hydra. The lively vegetal motifs were typical of Etruscan tastes.

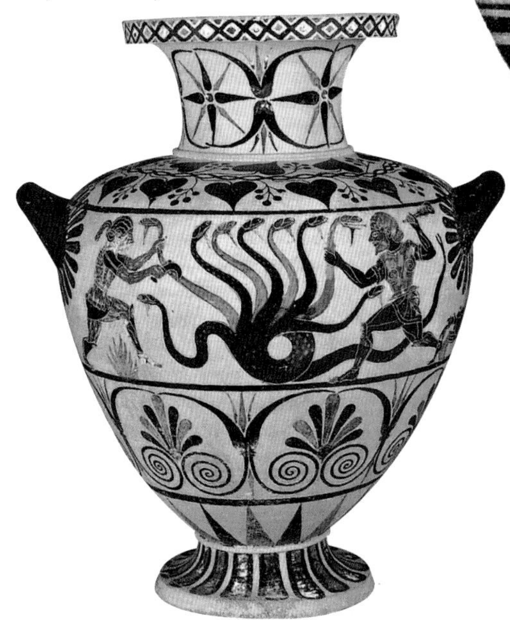

▲ The Workshop of the Micali Painter, an amphora decorated with figures of running athletes. Tarquinia, Museo Archeologico. This painter, to whom about two hundred known vases are attributed, can be placed in Vulci between 525 and 500 B.C. They constitute an important example of the passage from the late Archaic to the early Classical periods.

The Sarcophagus of the Married Couple

Preserved in Rome at the Museo di Villa Giulia, the extraordinary Sarcophagus of the Married Couple fashioned in terra-cotta is one of the most famous works of Etruscan art, together with the nearly identical example at the Louvre in Paris. Created by an Etruscan artist influenced by the Ionic tradition, the sarcophagus functioned both as a burial urn and a celebratory monument for the aristocratic couple. The deceased are portrayed as real people elegantly dressed and taking part in an eternal banquet in an attitude of profound union.

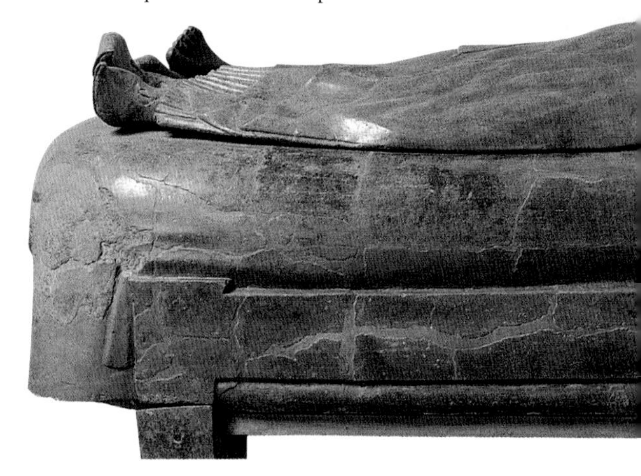

▼ Cinerary urn in the shape of a *kline* from a tomb in the Banditaccia necropolis at Cerveteri, from the second half of the sixth century B.C. Cerveteri, Museo Cerite. The use of terra-cotta urns in the shape of *klinai,* upon which married couples appear reclining during symposia, is typical of terra-cotta works from Cervetari. These were distinguished by a number of peculiarities, including polychromy.

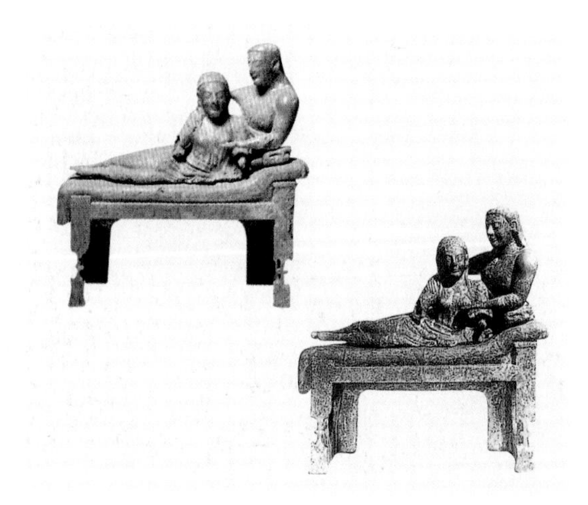

◀ Lid of a cinerary urn from the Banditaccia necropolis at Cerveteri, from the first quarter of the fifth century B.C. Cerveteri, Museo Cerite. The woman turns toward the viewer while the man watches her lovingly and offers her his left hand, which may once have held a cup. This was a typical position for figures on these urns: The man is shown with a naked torso while the woman is always clothed.

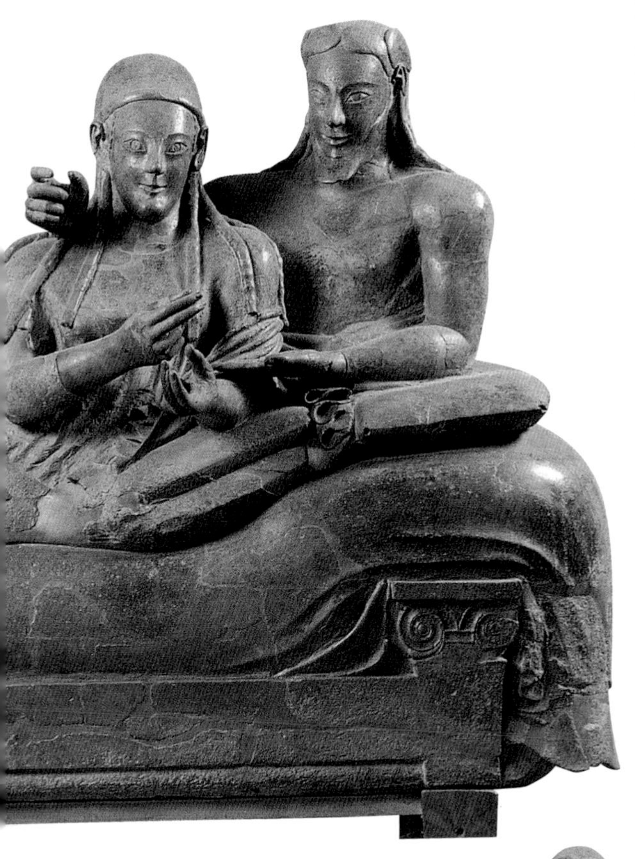

▼ The Paris example was found during the excavations at Cerveteri in the mid-1800s. It became part of the Campana Collection under the name "Lydian sarcophagus" and was considered one of the most outstanding pieces at the Museo Napoleone III. Traces of polychromy have survived on this masterpiece, characteristic of high-quality Cerveteran terra-cotta work made in the sixth century B.C. Technically, these sarcophagi were created in various sections using molds, as can be seen in the faces, which echo eastern Greek models. The upper parts of the bodies are disproportionately large in respect to the lower ones, and are rendered with decidedly more liveliness.

Stone Sculpture

The influence of the Ionic style, typical of artworks from the sixth century B.C., can be observed in the sculpture from cities such as Vulci, Chiusi, Fiesole, and Volterra, whose workshops specialized in common forms of funerary crafts. In the southern region, statues made in Vulci, which, from the Orientalizing period had had an apotropaic function, designed to protect against evil spirits, acquired Ionic elements in the sixth century B.C. One studio in Chiusi was active in producing statues of weeping figures and sphinxes, although a more consistent production of bas-reliefs would begin during the city's Archaic stage. These included *cippi* (commemorative pillars) with scenes of dances, banquets, and games in an Ionic style, which continued to appear through the first decades of the fifth century, when the workshops of southern Etruria were creating lively counterparts in terra-cotta. The Ionic language of products from Chiusi could also be found in stelae from Volterra and Fiesole, which in turn influenced the sculpture workshops of Etruria in the Po region.

▼ Stone lion from Blera, first half of the sixth century B.C. Viterbo, Museo Archeologico. This model is part of Blera's sculpture production. The figure of a seated lion guarding the sepulchre was quite common in monumental funerary sculpture, which also included panthers, sphinxes, and other imaginary animals, all with apotropaic functions.

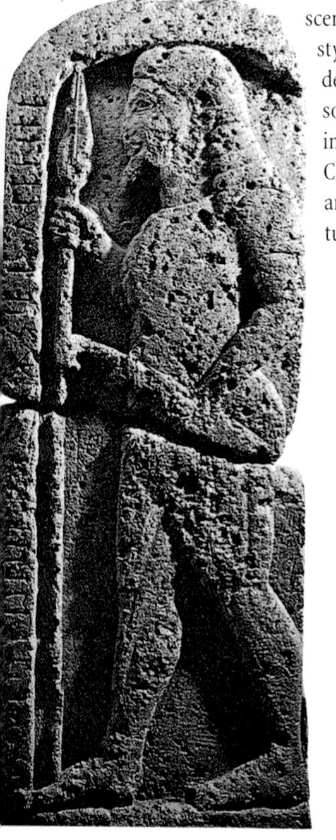

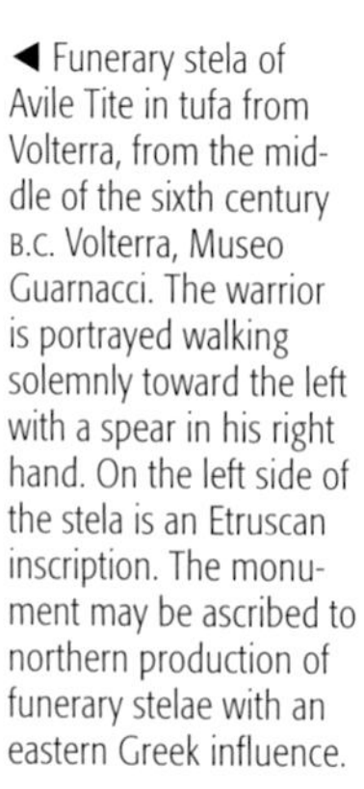

◀ Funerary stela of Avile Tite in tufa from Volterra, from the middle of the sixth century B.C. Volterra, Museo Guarnacci. The warrior is portrayed walking solemnly toward the left with a spear in his right hand. On the left side of the stela is an Etruscan inscription. The monument may be ascribed to northern production of funerary stelae with an eastern Greek influence.

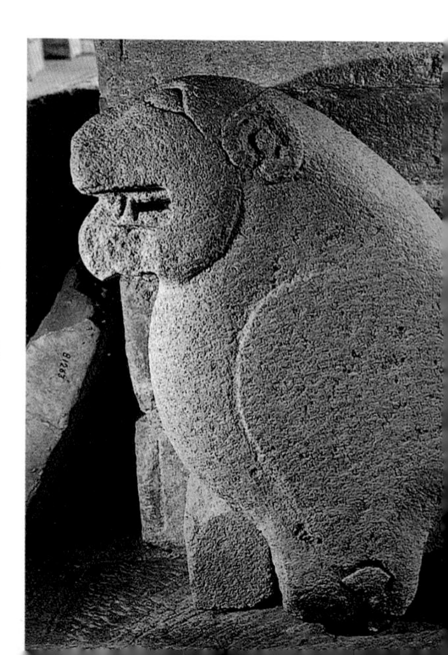

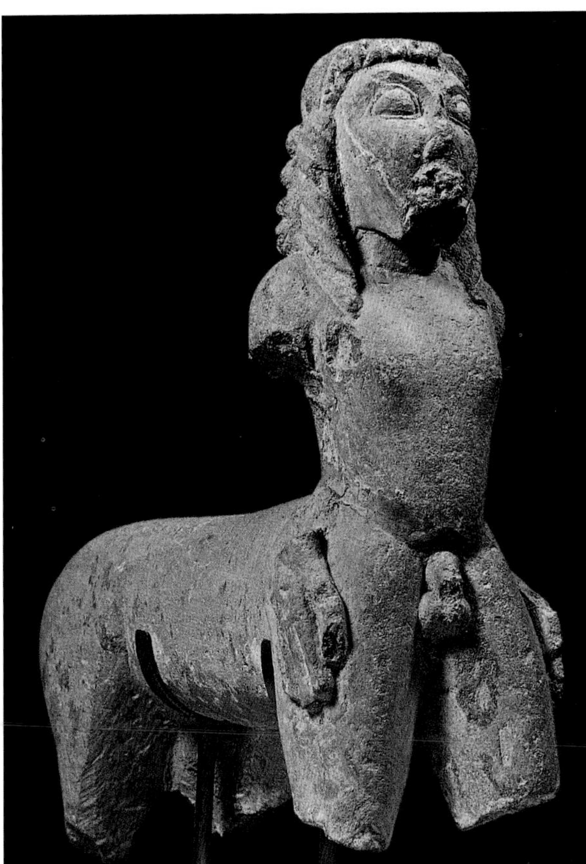

◀ Nenfro centaur from 590–580 B.C. Rome, Museo di Villa Giulia. During the first thirty years of the sixth century, Vulcian workshops created statues of imaginary beings that were derived from Greek mythology and had the function of protecting tombs. This centaur in the Villa Giulia seems to be the earliest example of this production, which stylistically recalls Daedalic art in its typically layered hairstyle and its treatment of volumes.

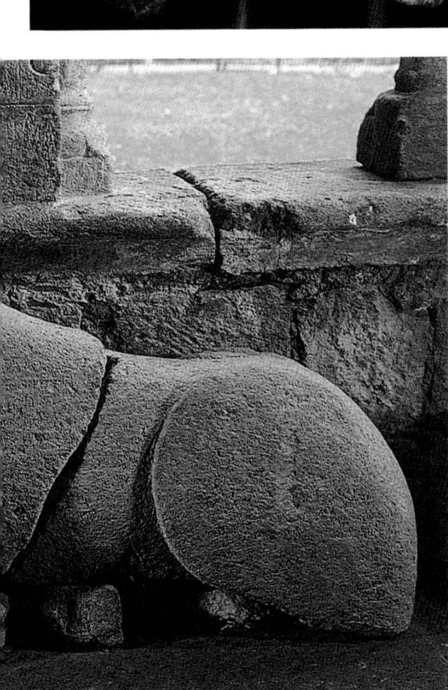

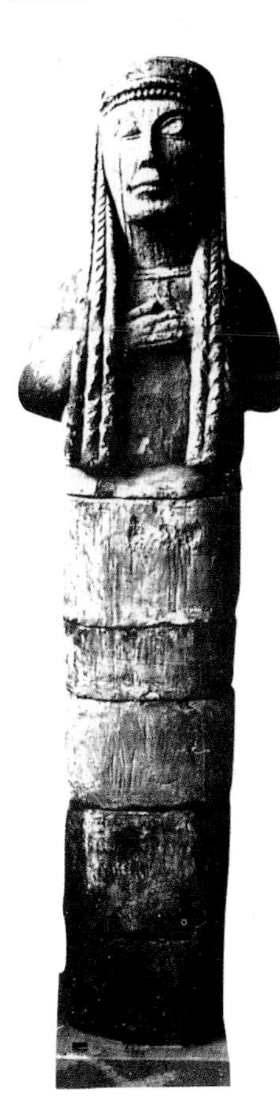

▶ Statue of a mourning figure in local stone, the product of a Chiusi workshop, dating between 580 and 560 B.C. Florence, Museo Archeologico. Besides these weeping figures, the workshop created statues of sphinxes with the same apotropaic function and with the same stylistic traits, which were quite similar to contemporary Vulcian production.

Etruscan Expansion

Rich epigraphic evidence, ancient literary sources, and archaeological discoveries have provided a precise picture of the Etruscans' presence outside of Etruria proper. The best-recorded sites are those of Lazio, Campania, and the Po Valley, where archaeological evidence has confirmed a close relationship between the inhabitants of these regions and the Etruscans. The rich Orientalizing tombs of Palestrina and discoveries relating to the era of the Etruscan monarchy in Rome enrich already abundant historiographic evidence concerning this period of Lazio's history. Archaeological discoveries in recent years in the cities of Capua and Pontecagnano, documenting their cultural and material similarities, have confirmed that the Etruscans were in Campania from the Villanovan era onward. In the Po plain, Villanovan culture left important traces in the region of Bologna beginning in the ninth century B.C. Relations between the Etruscans and the inhabitants of Campania and the Po plain developed differently in the following centuries because of diverse geographic, political, and social conditions.

▶ Between the end of the sixth and the beginning of the fifth centuries B.C., the Po plain was the main focus for a colonizing movement by the population of northern Etruria. Spina and Marzabotto were settled, and the great city of Felsina, present-day Bologna, was built. Archaeological evidence and epigraphic records indicate similarities between the settlement of the Po plain and that of Etruria, with a pre-urban phase of well-organized villages and an urban stage based on a trade economy.

▶ The coastal settlements of Campania functioned as commercial ports for inland cities with agricultural economies. The discovery of inscriptions proves a consistent Etruscan presence in the Campanian area until the end of the sixth century B.C.

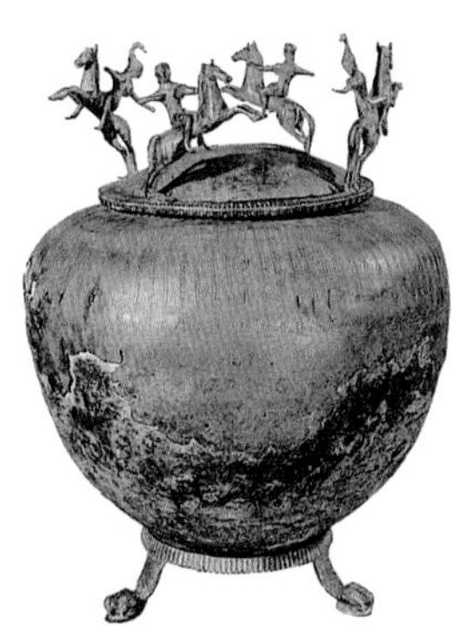

▲ Bronze *lebes* from the Campanian area, from the beginning of the fifth century B.C. London, The British Museum. This is part of a Campanian production of large vases that were used during funerary *ludi,* or games in honor of the deceased.

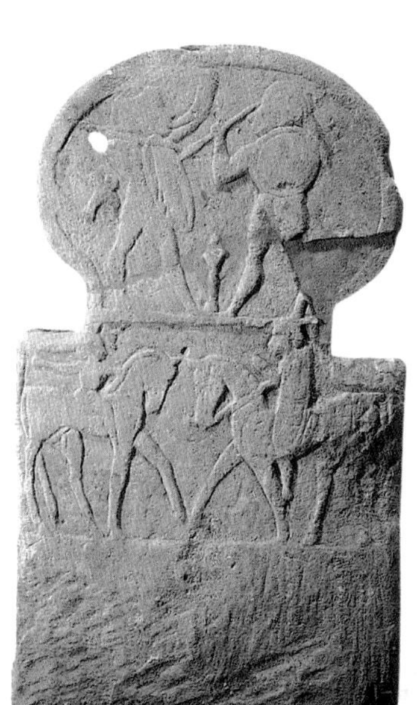

◀ Stela from Felsina, 530–520 B.C. Bologna, Museo Civico Archeologico. As was typical for the Bologna region, the stelae produced there recall the sculptural tradition of northern Etruria.

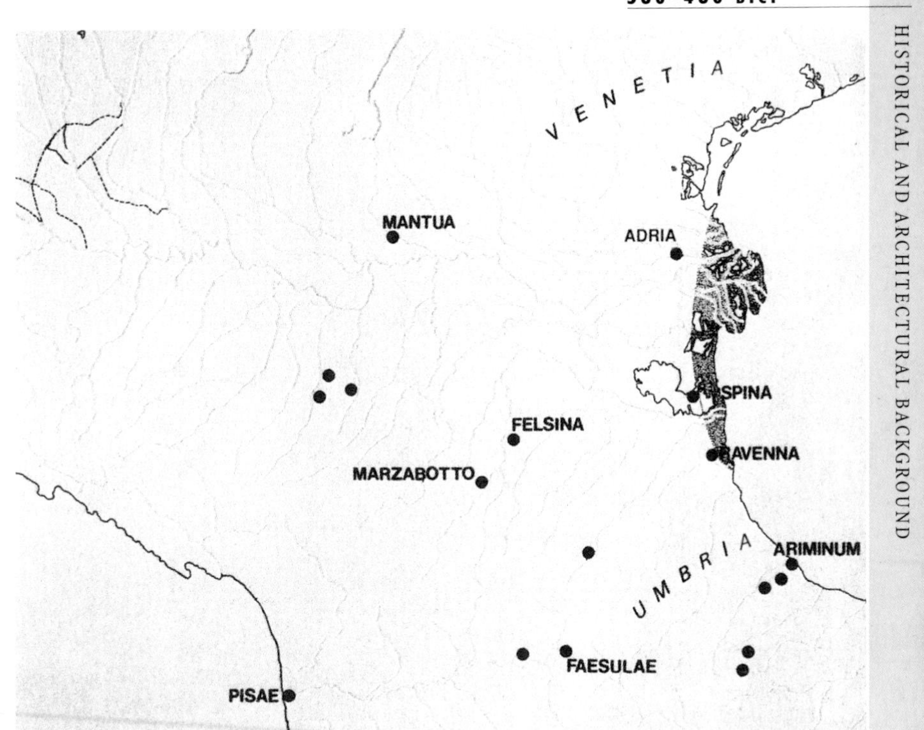
VENETIA
MANTUA
ADRIA
SPINA
FELSINA
RAVENNA
MARZABOTTO
ARIMINUM
UMBRIA
FAESULAE
PISAE

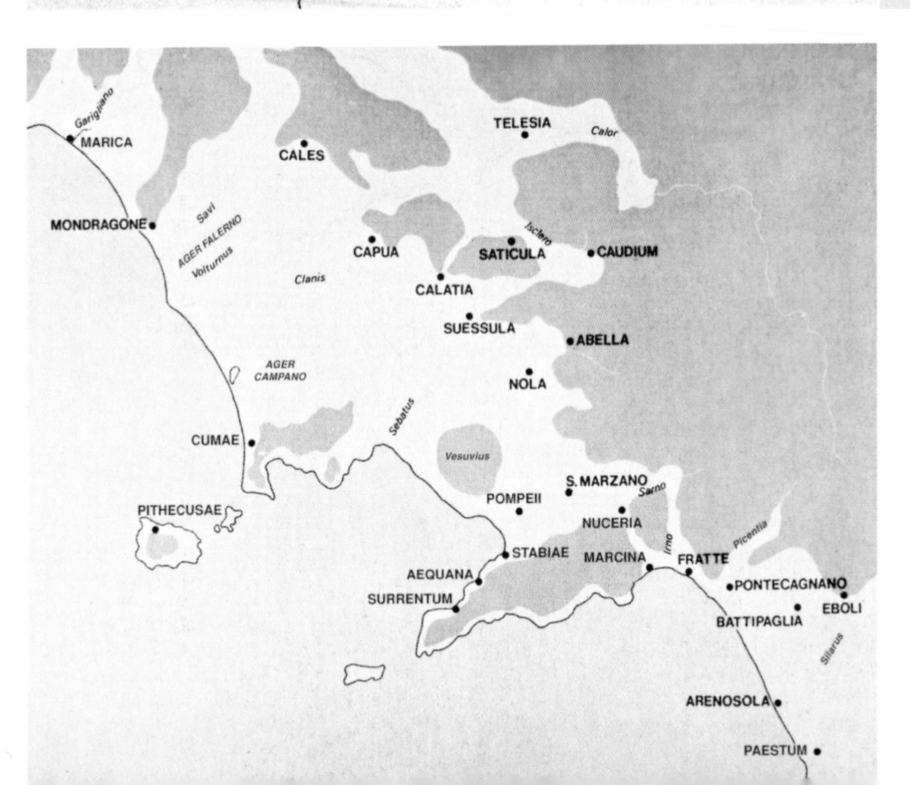
Garigliano
MARICA
CALES
TELESIA
Calor
MONDRAGONE
Savi
AGER FALERNO
Volturnus
CAPUA
Isclero
SATICULA
CAUDIUM
Clanis
CALATIA
SUESSULA
ABELLA
AGER
CAMPANO
NOLA
Sebatus
CUMAE
Vesuvius
S. MARZANO
Sarno
POMPEII
PITHECUSAE
NUCERIA
Picentia
Irno
STABIAE
MARCINA
FRATTE
AEQUANA
PONTECAGNANO
SURRENTUM
EBOLI
BATTIPAGLIA
Silarus
ARENOSOLA
PAESTUM

Cippi from Chiusi

In the final years of the sixth century B.C., artistic activity in Chiusi made a name for itself with the production of sculpted urns and *cippi* with scenes from the usual iconographic repertory of the aristocratic ideology, enriched with funerary significance.

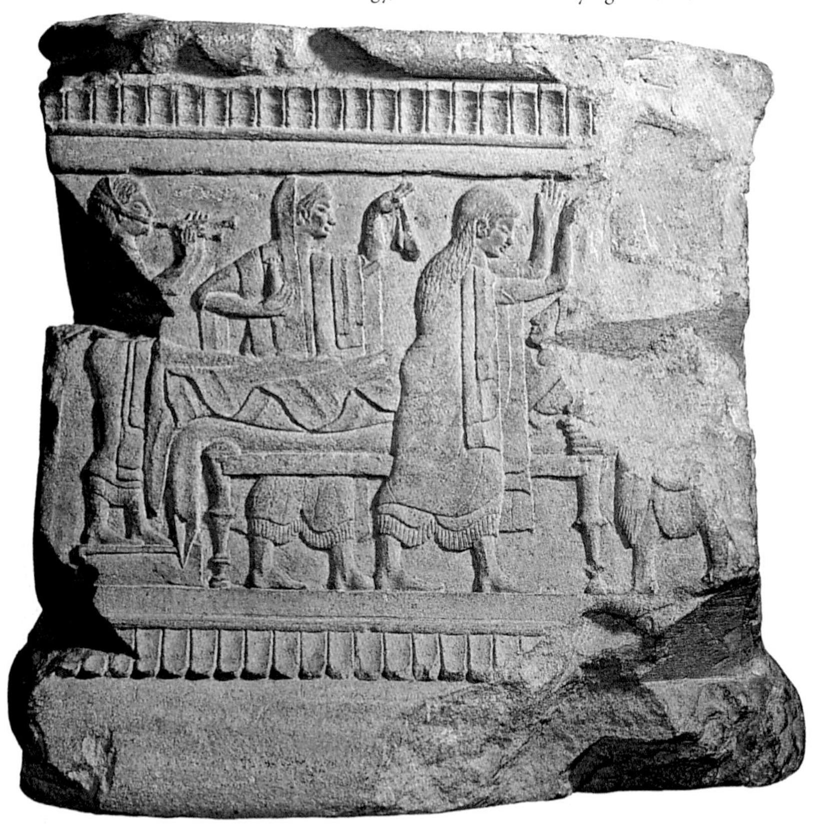

▲ *Cippus* base from the Scalabrini collection in Chiusi. Rome, Museo Barracco. One of the base's four sides depicts the *prothesis,* the ritual display of the dead. This ritual, during which the body was prepared for burial, took place inside the house. A solemn procession then accompanied the deceased to its definitive resting place, where a funeral ceremony was performed. These rites were illustrated in the tomb frescoes themselves and in a number of *cippi* from Chiusi.

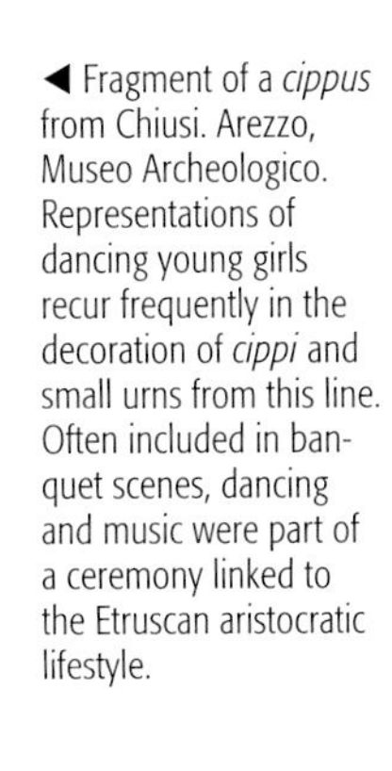

◀ Fragment of a *cippus* from Chiusi. Arezzo, Museo Archeologico. Representations of dancing young girls recur frequently in the decoration of *cippi* and small urns from this line. Often included in banquet scenes, dancing and music were part of a ceremony linked to the Etruscan aristocratic lifestyle.

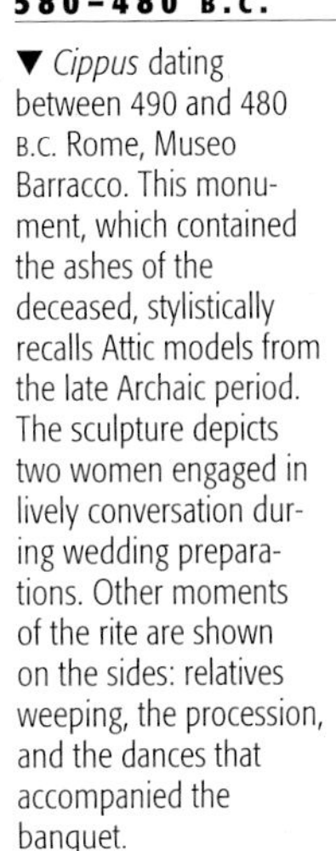

▼ *Cippus* dating between 490 and 480 B.C. Rome, Museo Barracco. This monument, which contained the ashes of the deceased, stylistically recalls Attic models from the late Archaic period. The sculpture depicts two women engaged in lively conversation during wedding preparations. Other moments of the rite are shown on the sides: relatives weeping, the procession, and the dances that accompanied the banquet.

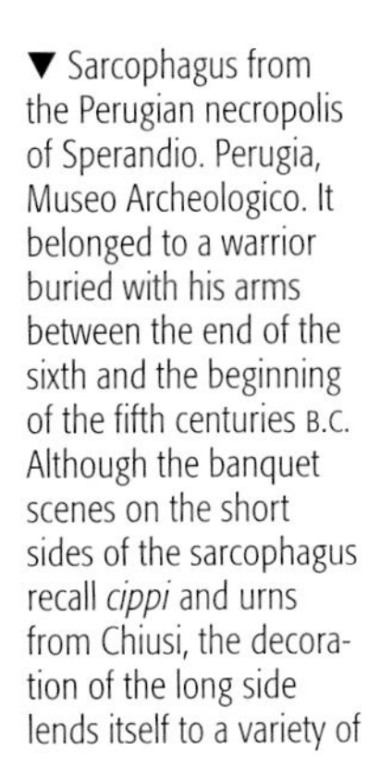

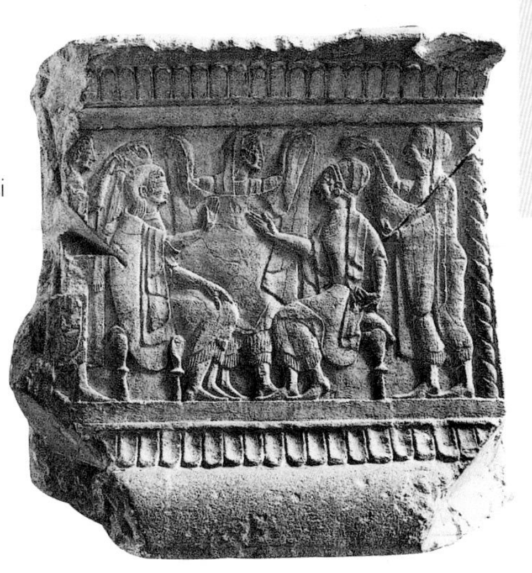

▼ Sarcophagus from the Perugian necropolis of Sperandio. Perugia, Museo Archeologico. It belonged to a warrior buried with his arms between the end of the sixth and the beginning of the fifth centuries B.C. Although the banquet scenes on the short sides of the sarcophagus recall *cippi* and urns from Chiusi, the decoration of the long side lends itself to a variety of interpretations. It shows a cortege of people and animals that could refer to the emigration of a family group from Chiusi to Perugia in the era of King Porsenna, or to a triumphal ceremony by which a leader celebrates his feats and parades his wealth and status. In any case, the image would be unique among *cippi,* which the sarcophagus recalls in style and type.

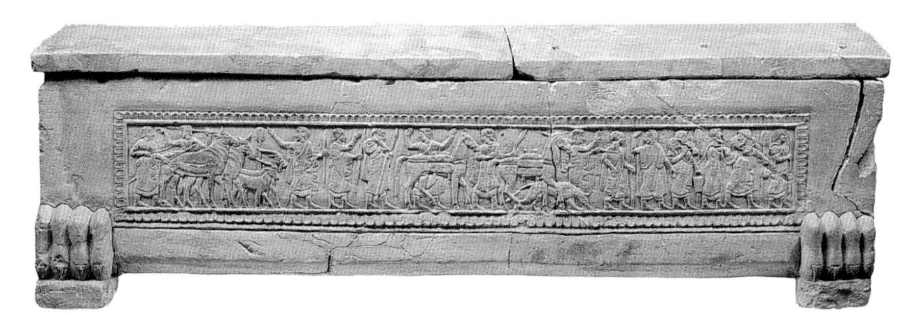

Bucchero Artisans

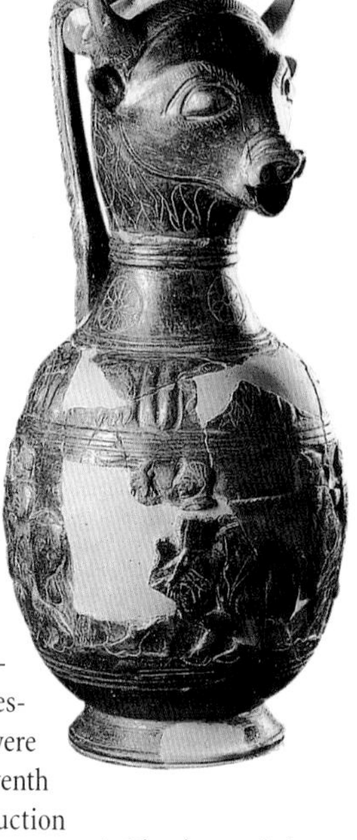

The production of bucchero began in the first half of the seventh century B.C. in Cerveteri, where artisans specialized in creating vases for the symposia and for personal use. From the second half of the seventh century, other workshops in southern Etruscan cities and Campania began to assert themselves, and their work shows a close relationship to Cerveteran production. Bucchero from this period, a valued ceramic because of its many uses, is mostly thin and adorned with incised or stamped motifs such as fans, spirals, and animal decorations. The shapes, which recall those of impasto, metal, or ivory vessels, recur in vases used for drawing, pouring, and drinking that were found throughout the Mediterranean between the end of the seventh and first half of the sixth centuries. Due to high demand, production intensified over the course of the sixth century and expanded to various cities in Etruria. Among these, Chiusi emerged as the northern Etrurian city most active in the production of vases in *bucchero pesante* decorated with narrative scenes, made by rotating a carved roller with a negative image over fresh clay. The popularity of this ware even forced Attic craftsmen who worked for the Etruscan market to imitate some of its shapes.

▲ *Oinochoe* made in Chiusi in the first half of the sixth century B.C. Florence, Museo Archeologico. This work features a bull's head for its upper part, while the body of the vase is decorated all over with motifs that are incised or modeled in relief.

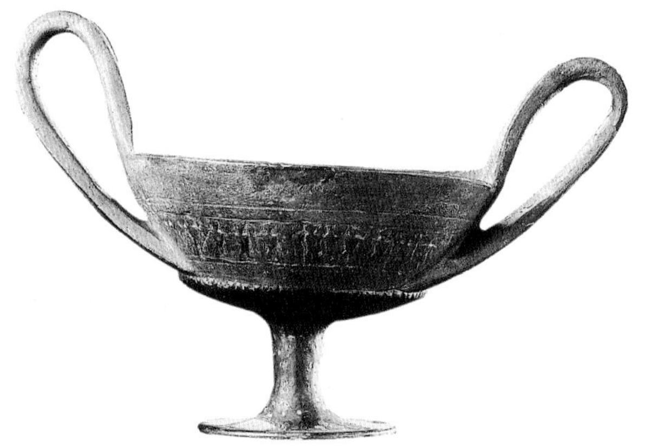

◀ The *kantharos* was produced in its most common form during the last quarter of the seventh century B.C. and was exported throughout the Mediterranean. This specimen from Florence shows a rolled decoration with a frontal arrangement of figures.

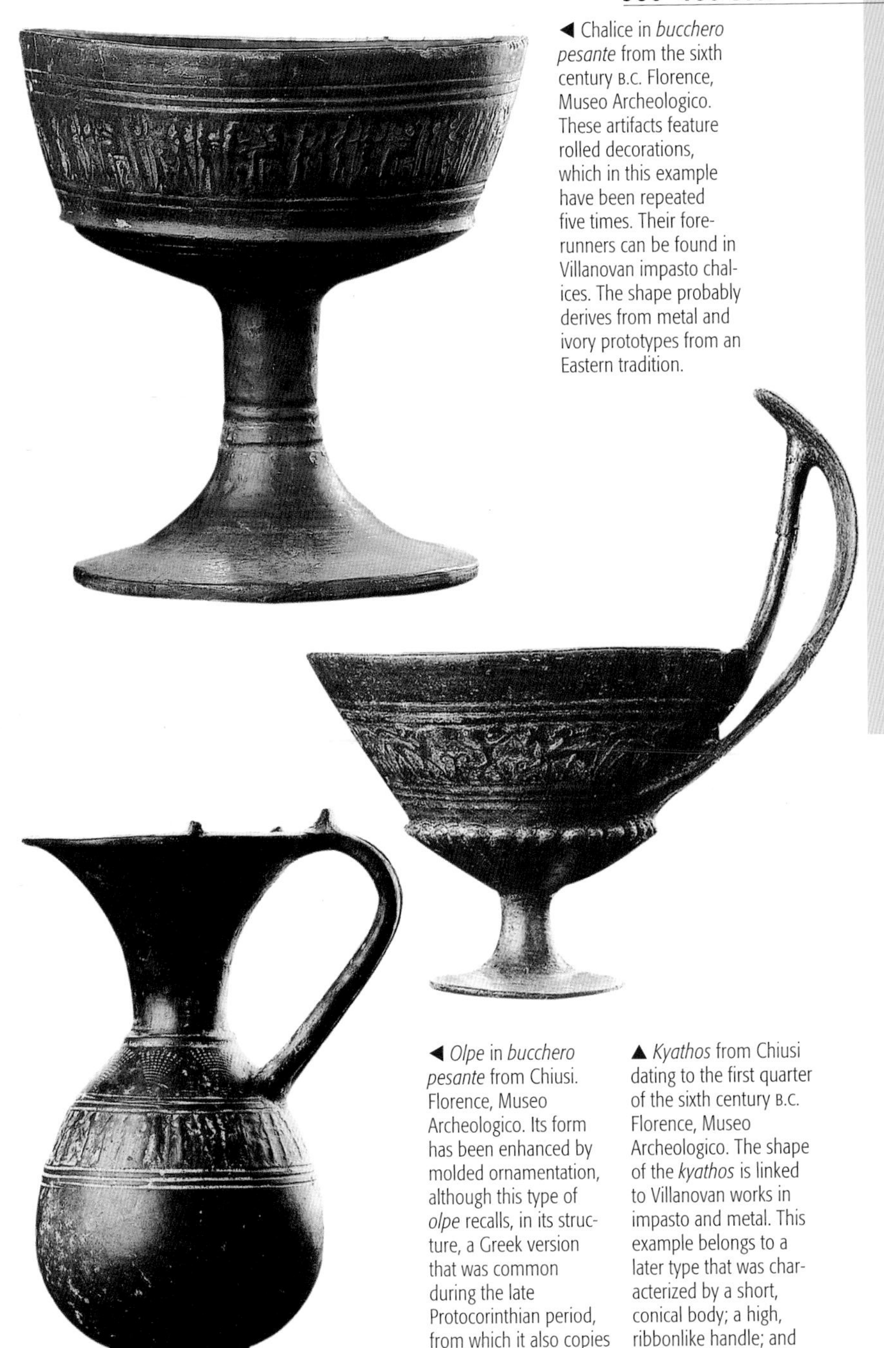

◀ Chalice in *bucchero pesante* from the sixth century B.C. Florence, Museo Archeologico. These artifacts feature rolled decorations, which in this example have been repeated five times. Their forerunners can be found in Villanovan impasto chalices. The shape probably derives from metal and ivory prototypes from an Eastern tradition.

◀ *Olpe* in *bucchero pesante* from Chiusi. Florence, Museo Archeologico. Its form has been enhanced by molded ornamentation, although this type of *olpe* recalls, in its structure, a Greek version that was common during the late Protocorinthian period, from which it also copies decorative motifs.

▲ *Kyathos* from Chiusi dating to the first quarter of the sixth century B.C. Florence, Museo Archeologico. The shape of the *kyathos* is linked to Villanovan works in impasto and metal. This example belongs to a later type that was characterized by a short, conical body; a high, ribbonlike handle; and rolled decorations.

Cerveteri

The necropolises of southern Etruria furnish important evidence about the cult of the dead. They also provide information about town planning, types of houses, and aspects of everyday life. The development of funerary architecture can easily be followed within the necropolises of Cerveteri, where tombs carved out of local tufa stone have been well preserved.

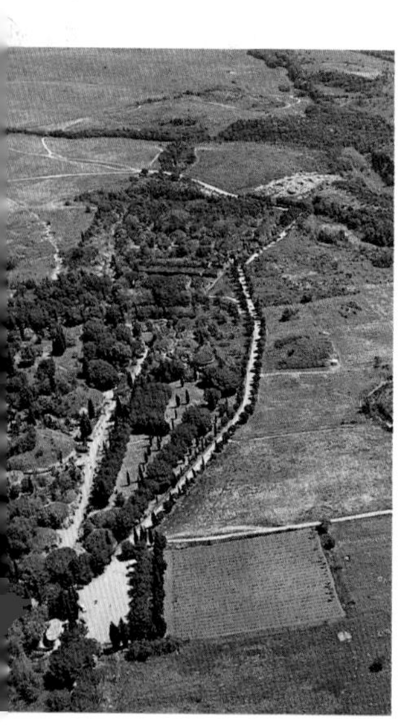

▲ Various types of tombs can be seen at the necropolis of Banditaccia, from a simple *fossa* or trench burial to a tumulus, or round tomb, with a retaining wall, a cube tomb, and a great hypogeum.

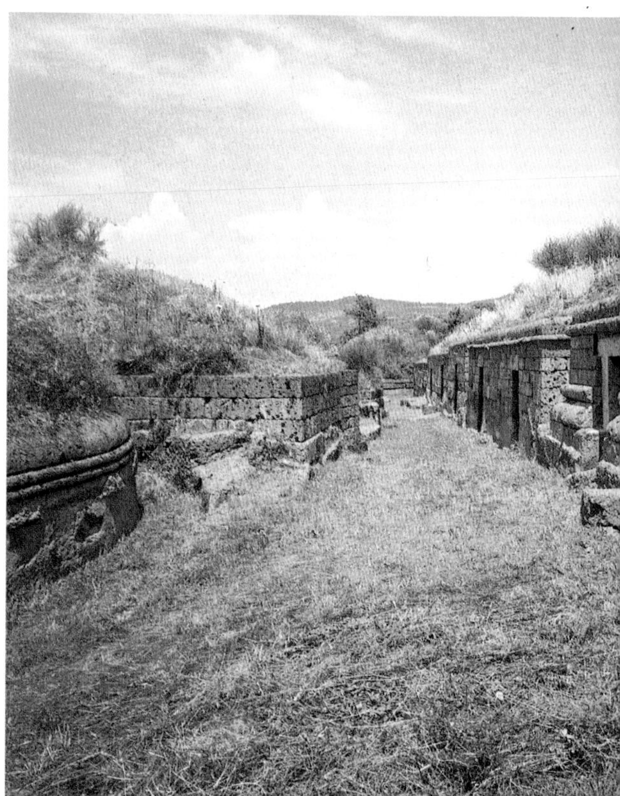

▲ Roads and squares characterize the necropolis, resembling the cities of the living. The urban organization of the necropolis featured a grid layout. Cube tombs, built with blocks of tufa that were perfectly cubed, were aligned along the sides of the roads, as were the oldest monumental tumuli.

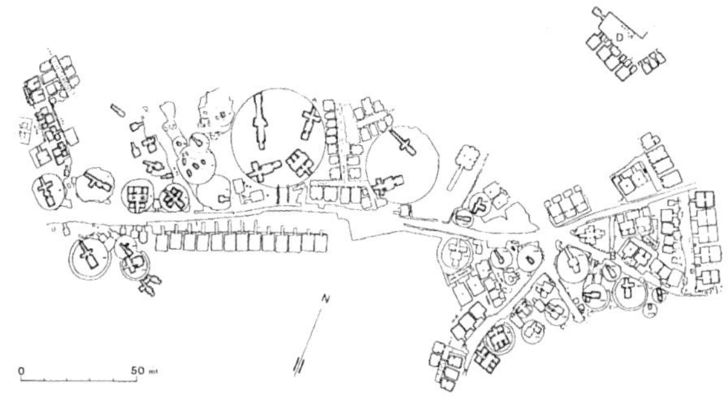

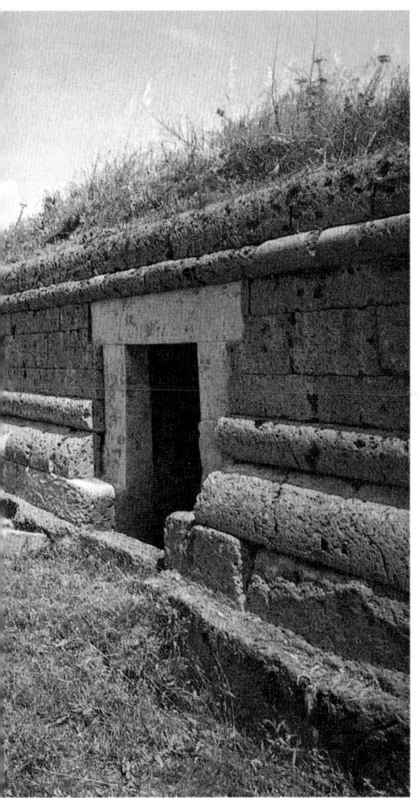

▲ In the plan of the necropolis of Banditaccia, which was used between the seventh and third centuries B.C., the urban structure of this "city of the dead" is evident. The tombs overlook an actual road. The great tumuli of the seventh and sixth centuries can be seen, with their burial chambers carved into the tufa, as can the cube tombs of the sixth century, and, to the south of the road, a line of more recent tombs.

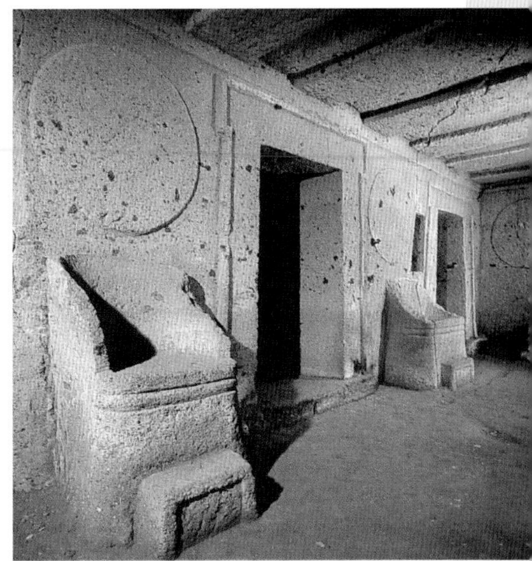

▲ The Tomb of the Shields and Seats. To the sides of the central entrance are two stone thrones, above which are two round, sculpted shields. The tomb features, in a central nucleus that recalls houses from the first half of the sixth century B.C., a vestibule with three doors that lead to the burial chambers.

The Painted Tombs of Tarquinia

The strong link between the art of pottery decoration and that of painting has been accepted for some time, as are the stages of development in the funerary painting tradition of Tarquinia during the second half of the sixth century B.C. During this period, there is documentation of a large influx of potters, ceramic decorators, and painters of eastern Greek origin lending their services to local workshops catering to wealthy Etruscan buyers. The earliest examples of painting in Tarquinia can be found in the Tomb of the Lionesses and the Tomb of the Hut. In the former the ornamentation is limited to a back wall, where two feline figures face each other. In the latter, again on the back wall, a false door has been depicted. In the second half of the sixth century, the decorations grew richer with the addition of a figurative frieze along the tomb's other walls. This led to the creation of figurative scenes in the Tomb of the Bulls, which show a close affinity with Pontic ceramics; the delicate landscapes and lively narrative taken from the style of Samnite wall painters in the Tomb of Hunting and Fishing; and the funerary games and dances in the Tomb of the Augurs, which are similar to works by artists from northern Ionia. Thus the tombs of Tarquinia record how the nobility acquired new styles and iconography that mirrored aristocratic principles.

▼ Games in honor of the deceased, portrayed along the lateral walls of the Tomb of the Augurs, 530–520 B.C. Two vigorous, naked athletes wrestle before a judge, who holds a staff of command used by referees. Three *lebetes* stacked on top of each other, the prize for the competition, are shown between the two contenders. At the right is the masked player called a Phersu, engaged in a cruel game that was a forerunner of gladiatorial contests.

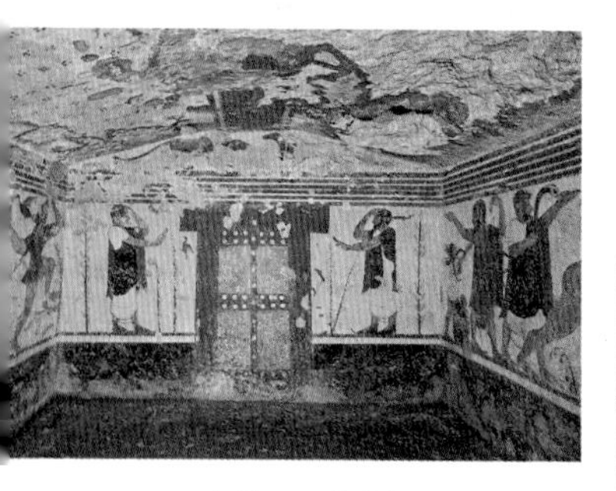

▲ The motif of the closed door on the back wall of the Tomb of the Augurs can be found in other tombs and has a clear symbolic meaning, alluding to the passage from life to death.

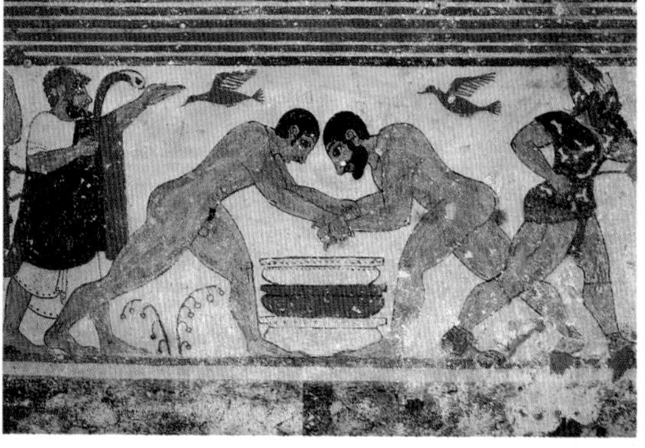

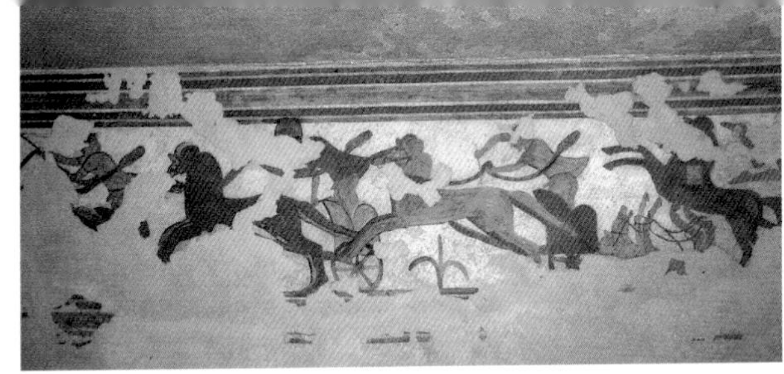

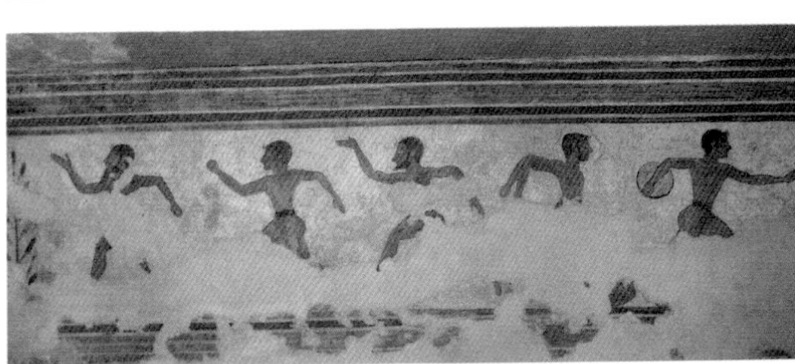

◀ Games of sport dominate the center of the decoration of the Tomb of the Olympic Games. Young athletes of noble rank took part in chariot races, boxing and running contests, the high jump, and discus throwing, which were all part of funeral rites.

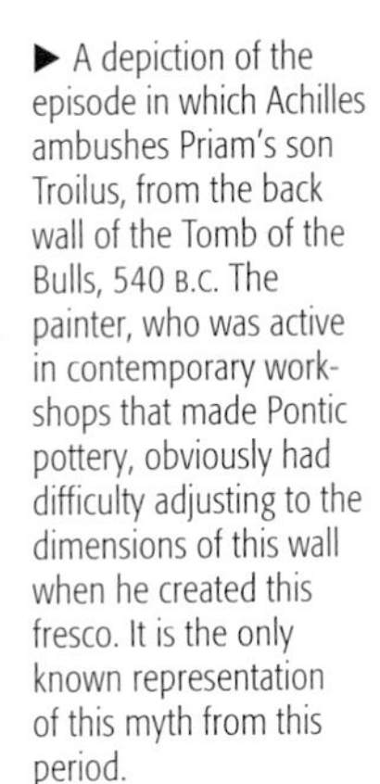

▶ A depiction of the episode in which Achilles ambushes Priam's son Troilus, from the back wall of the Tomb of the Bulls, 540 B.C. The painter, who was active in contemporary workshops that made Pontic pottery, obviously had difficulty adjusting to the dimensions of this wall when he created this fresco. It is the only known representation of this myth from this period.

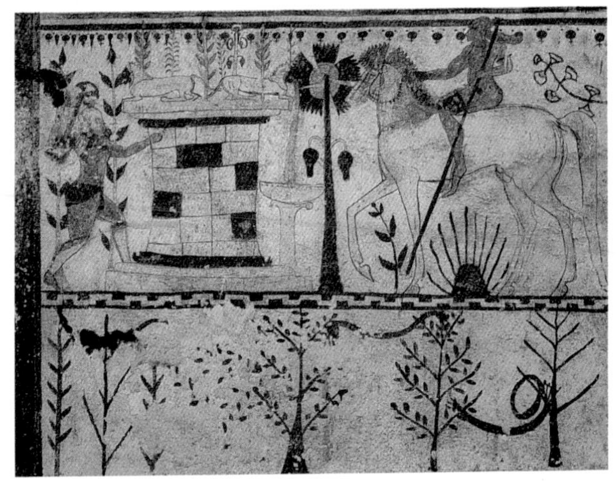

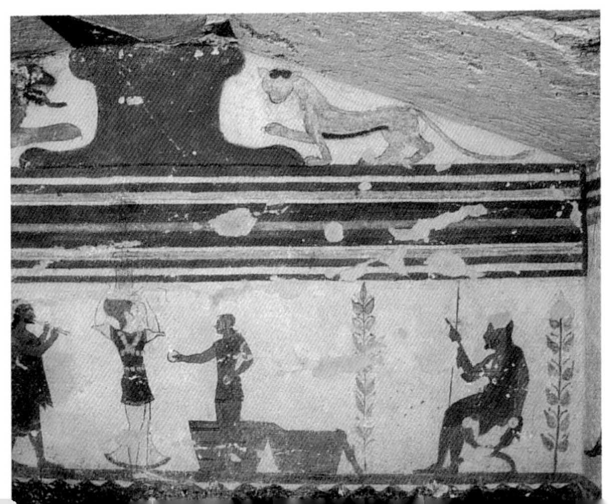

◀ The Tomb of the Jugglers, 520 B.C. Stylistically akin to the Tomb of the Augurs in its Ionic tastes, the tomb ornamentation, which proves the close relations between vase painting and wall painting, is marked by elegant figures dancing to the sound of the pipes.

The Benvenuti *Situla*

The most highly valued examples of *situlae,* which were widespread in a large part of northern Italy and in east-central Europe from the end of the seventh century on, were produced in Bologna and Este.

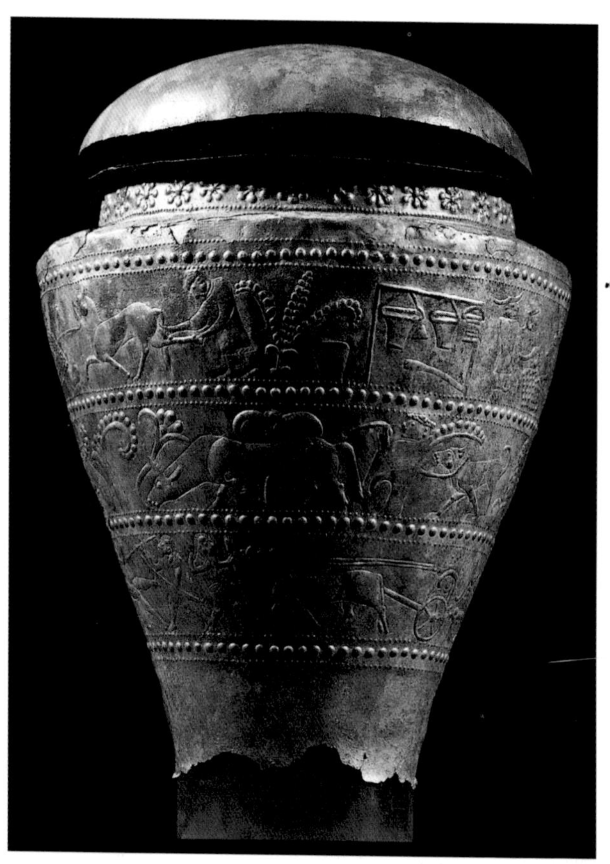

▼ Details from the "Providence" *situla,* dating to the end of the sixth century B.C., of unknown provenance. Providence (R.I.), Rhode Island School of Design Museum. Some of the decorative details, such as the rendering of the figures, their headwear, and the shields of the warriors, allow it to be placed alongside the Certosa *situla* for its value and significance. The inscription, in a northern Etruscan alphabet, underscores its function as a prestigious gift and an object for trading among members of the aristocratic class.

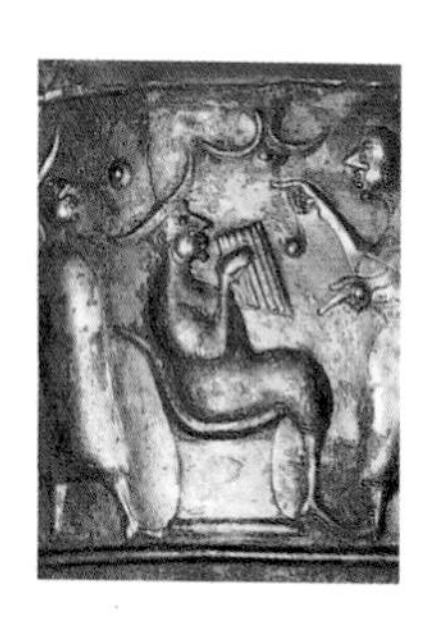

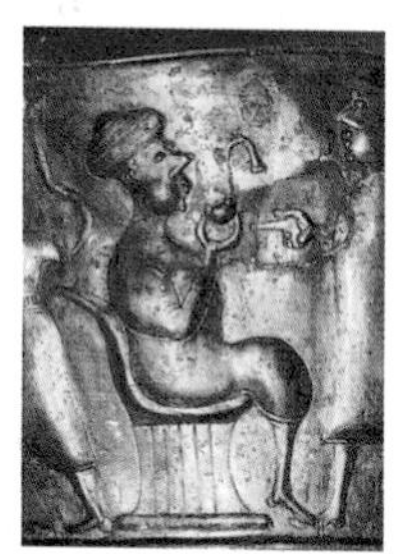

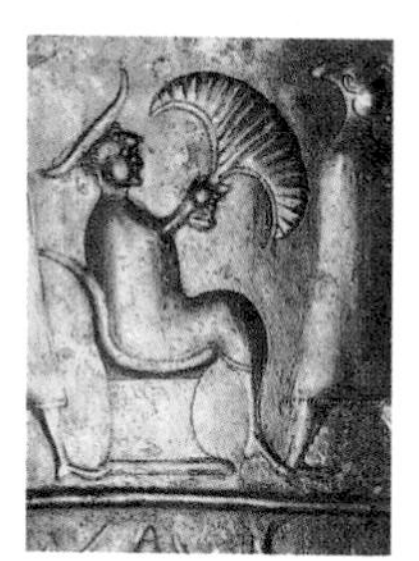

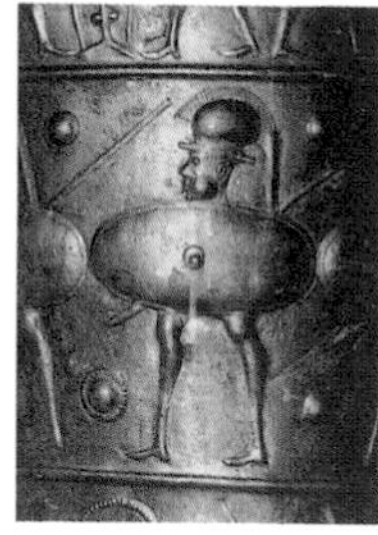

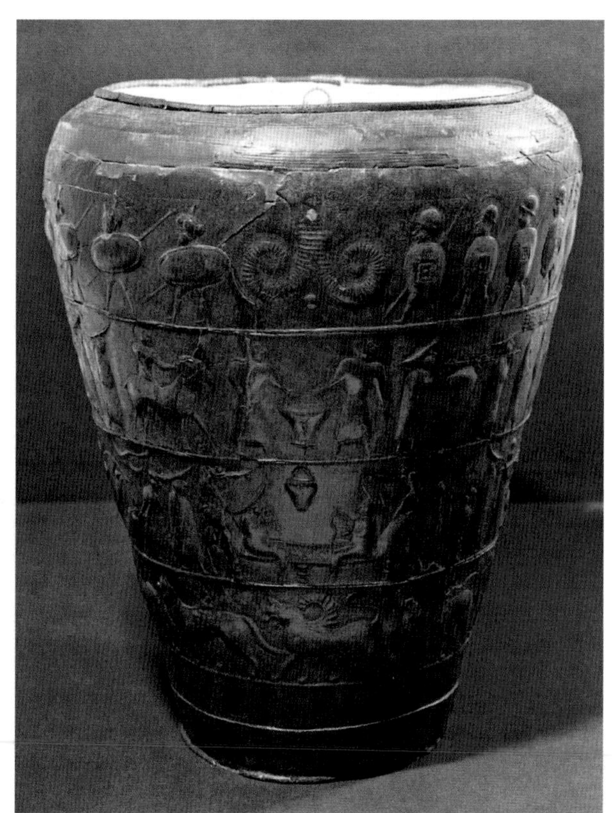

◀ The Certosa *situla*. Bologna, Museo Civico Archeologico. This object was found among the modest grave-goods of a woman's cremation tomb from the beginning of the fifth century B.C., although its age, based on comparisons with other works from northern Etruria, can be moved back to the first half of the sixth century. This object had been kept for a long while before being used as a cinerary urn. The decoration is arranged on four levels: from top to bottom, a military parade, a sacred procession, scenes from life in the palace and the field, and a line of imaginary animals. The significance of the depictions has been variously interpreted, although the intention of celebrating the exploits of an aristocratic figure seems obvious.

◀ The Benvenuti *situla* from Este, dating to the end of the seventh century B.C. Este, Museo Nazionale Atestino. This masterpiece of *situla* production from Este belonged to the rich grave goods from a woman's tomb dating to the end of the seventh century. The iconographic repertory of imaginary animals and vegetal motifs is from the recent Etruscan Orientalizing phase, while the scenes of real life reveal the local elite's fondness for celebrating itself.

▶ Ivory figurine of a helmeted warrior from a *tholos* tomb in Comeana. Florence, Museo Archeologico. The warriors on the first level of the Certosa *situla* from Bologna come from the same artistic environment as works in ivory from this tomb. In fact, specialized ivory workers are recorded among the Orientalizing artists of northern Etruria.

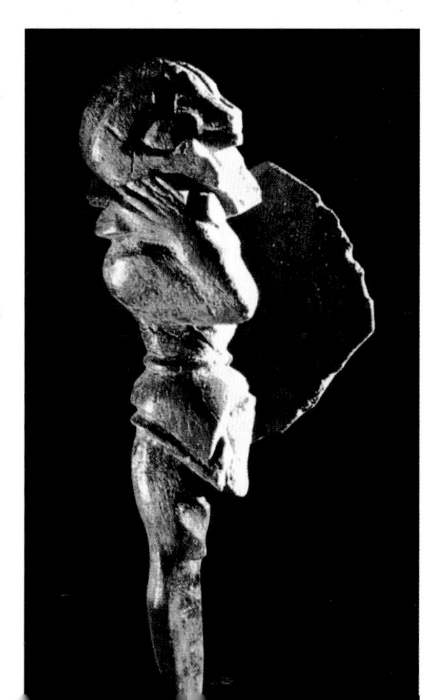

Bronzeworking

The fame of Etrurian bronzes reached as far as Greece, where sources from the fifth century B.C. attest that cultured Athenians appreciated the quality of Etruscan works. Besides the valued but less common toreutics (embossed metalwork) from Chiusi and Perugia during the sixth century, the activity of bronze workers was mainly focused on producing furnishings and votive objects on an industrial scale. Vulcian artisans were quite active. They created wares for symposia, tripods, incense burners, and candelabras in an Ionic style; these spread beyond Etruria and were highly prized. Still, this production falls within the Peloponnesian tradition, and more typically Etruscan incense burners and candelabras have been discovered predominantly in the cities of the Po Valley. The small bronzes preserved in burial deposits are a reflection of large bronze statues that unfortunately have been completely lost. It is not always possible, however, to distinguish precisely where these Greek-styled figurines of warriors and girls were made, even if they can be attributed to artisans who were influenced by Ionic art.

▼ *Oinochoe* with a Rhodian-type trilobed mouth from Campovalano. Chieti, Museo Archeologico. It belongs to a group of Etruscan vases discovered in the tombs of Picena-area leaders from the sixth century B.C. These were vases for symposia, a ritual that the Etruscans introduced to the area.

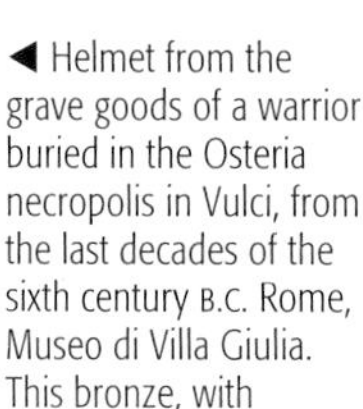

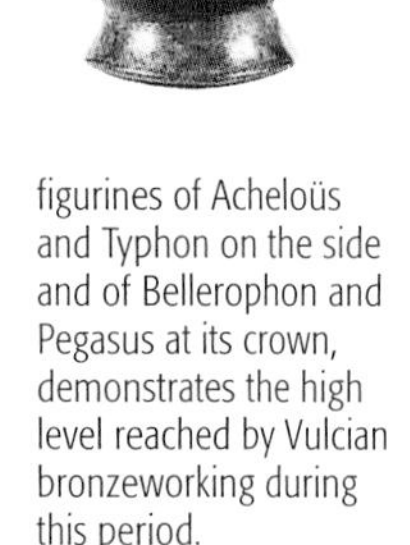

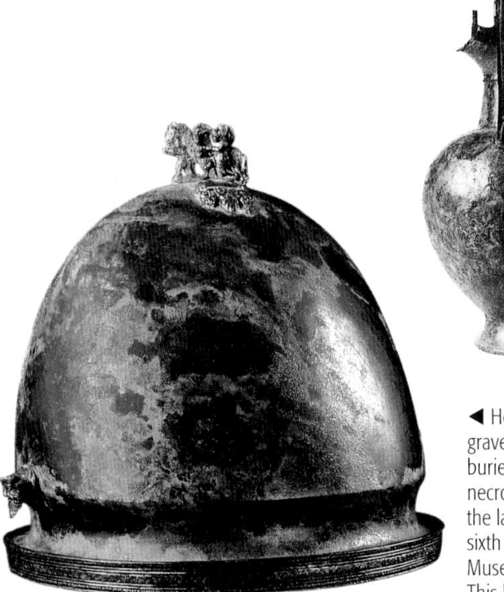

◄ Helmet from the grave goods of a warrior buried in the Osteria necropolis in Vulci, from the last decades of the sixth century B.C. Rome, Museo di Villa Giulia. This bronze, with figurines of Acheloüs and Typhon on the side and of Bellerophon and Pegasus at its crown, demonstrates the high level reached by Vulcian bronzeworking during this period.

▼ A small bronze of a warrior from the votive deposit of Brolio, Val di Chiana, 560–550 B.C. Florence, Museo Archeologico. This statue, together with two similar figures and a female figure, must have been used to decorate a larger object, as demonstrated by the presence of similar pins in all of the pieces. They were made in Chiusi.

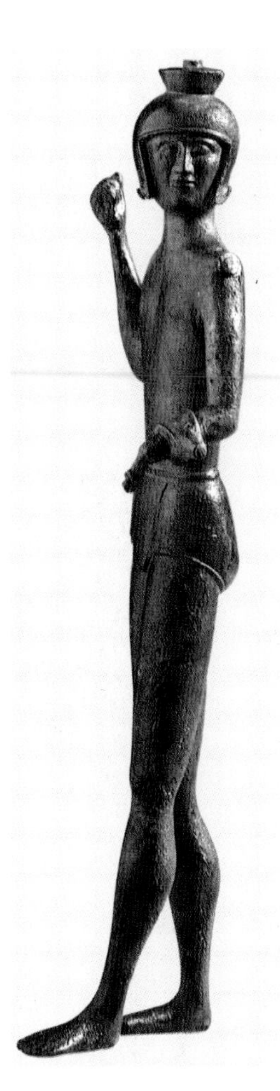

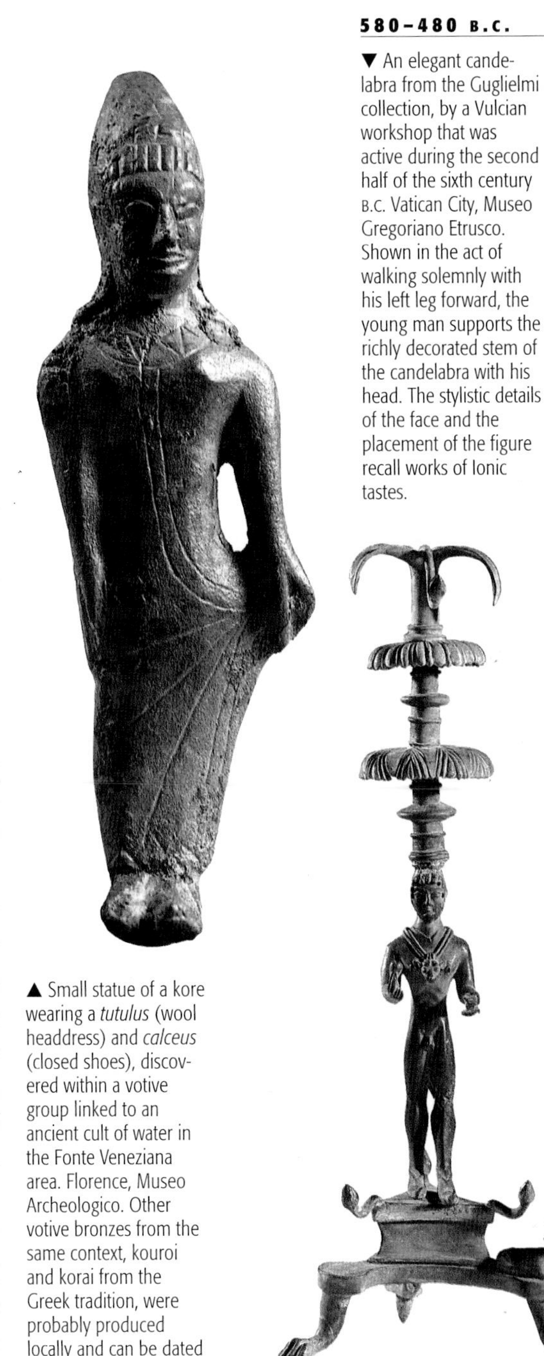

▲ Small statue of a kore wearing a *tutulus* (wool headdress) and *calceus* (closed shoes), discovered within a votive group linked to an ancient cult of water in the Fonte Veneziana area. Florence, Museo Archeologico. Other votive bronzes from the same context, kouroi and korai from the Greek tradition, were probably produced locally and can be dated to the middle of the sixth century B.C.

▼ An elegant candelabra from the Guglielmi collection, by a Vulcian workshop that was active during the second half of the sixth century B.C. Vatican City, Museo Gregoriano Etrusco. Shown in the act of walking solemnly with his left leg forward, the young man supports the richly decorated stem of the candelabra with his head. The stylistic details of the face and the placement of the figure recall works of Ionic tastes.

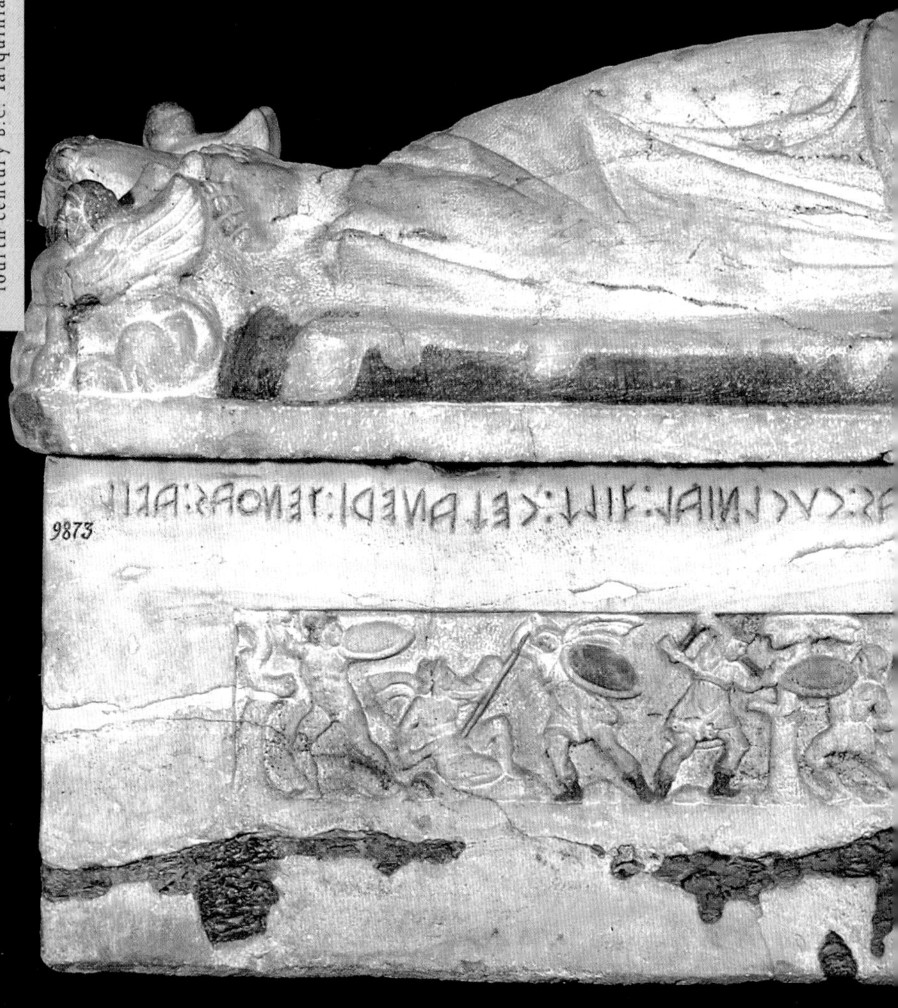

The Sarcophagus of Velthur Partunus, from the third quarter of the fourth century B.C. Tarquinia, Museo Archeologico

The Classical Period

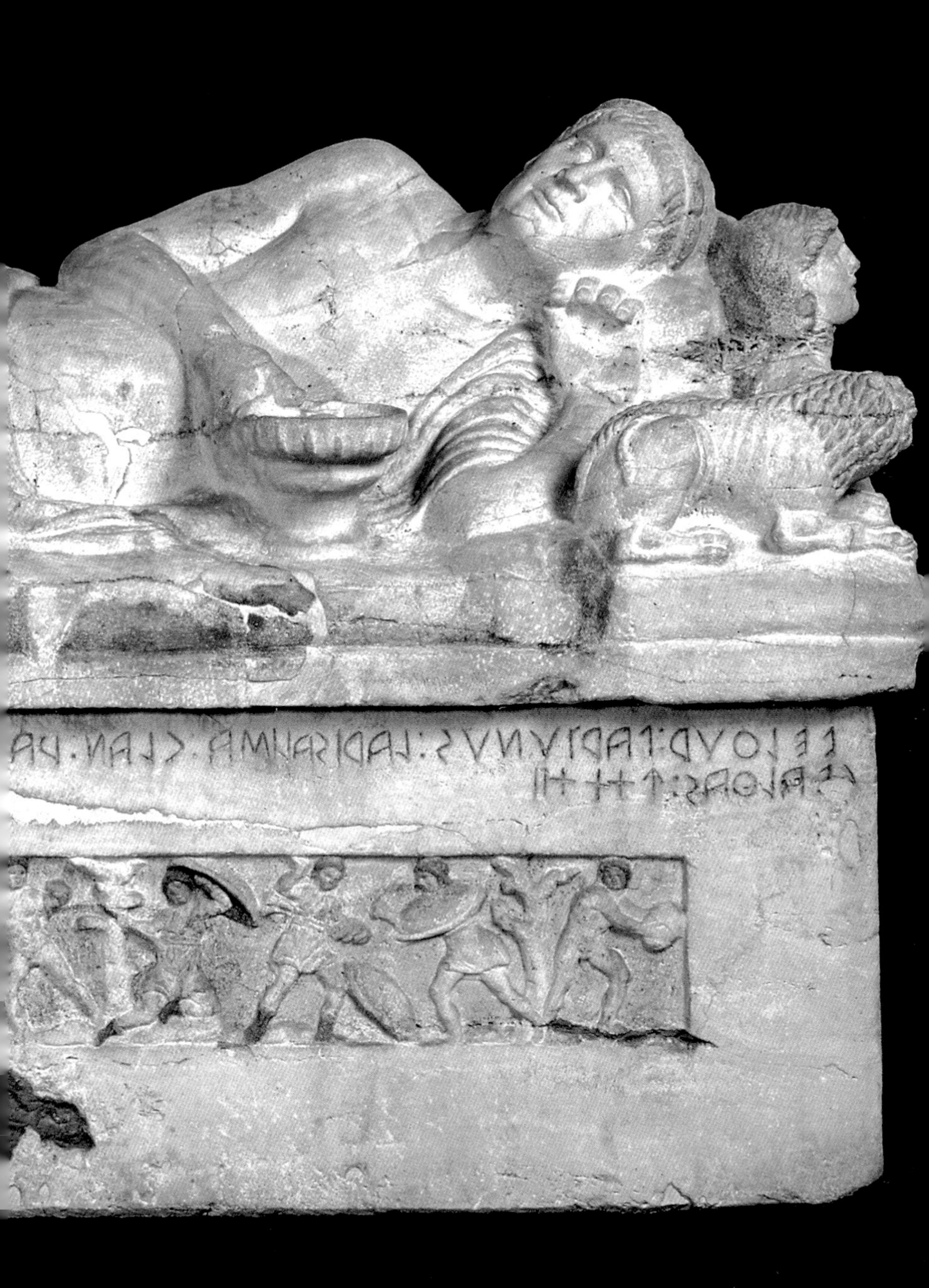

The War between Rome and Veii

Veii enjoyed an advantageous geographic position, being surrounded by fortified sites in the low valley of the Tiber, and had been appointed to manage the saltworks at the river's mouth for the entirety of the fifth century B.C. It became the target of Roman hostilities, especially from the *gens* Fabia. Resistance from Veii must have been tenacious, since Marcus Furius Camillus was only able to force its surrender in 416. The city asked for help from the Etruscan League a number of times, but, other than aid in 480, it was left to its own fate. The *populi etruriae* decided to deny it solidarity, as Livy writes, as long as it remained a monarchy. These events illustrate sociopolitical changes in action. The so-called crisis of the fifth century in reality showed that ancient forms of aristocratic government were evolving in the direction of a republican oligarchy. The new governments, preferring collective hoarding and less transparency, favored the concentration of imports and products in the votive deposits of the great federal sanctuaries, rather than in private residences. Many preexisting socioeconomic conditions, which differed from city to city, intersected with this change. As a result each city became a separate capital, in which social tensions, local culture, and unequal levels of development determined its own particular situation.

▲ Female head in bronze from Chiusi, 450 B.C. Paris, Musée du Louvre. The hair parted in the center; the large forehead; the long, straight nose; and the large eyes show early Classical influence.

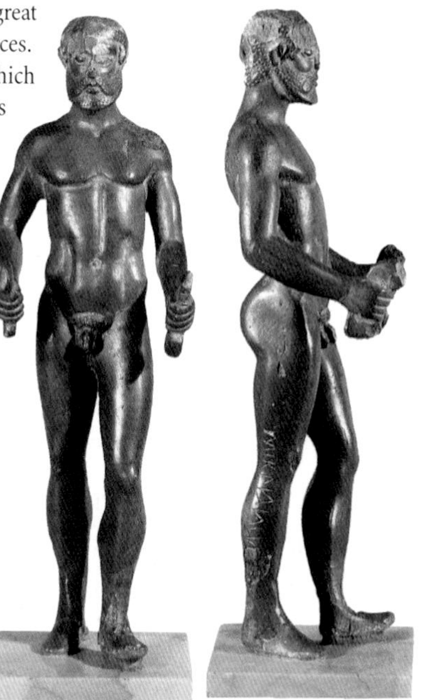

▶ Bronze statue of an athlete from Quarata, 460–440 B.C. Paris, Bibliothèque Nationale. A production from either Chiusi or Arezzo, this bronze represents a jumper. The short hair, almond-shaped eyes, and a fan-shaped beard are all features from the iconography of a group of athlete statues from late Archaism. He holds two weights in his hands, and his chest and abdomen have been rendered dynamically in three dimensions, making this votive offering conform to the aristocratic ideal.

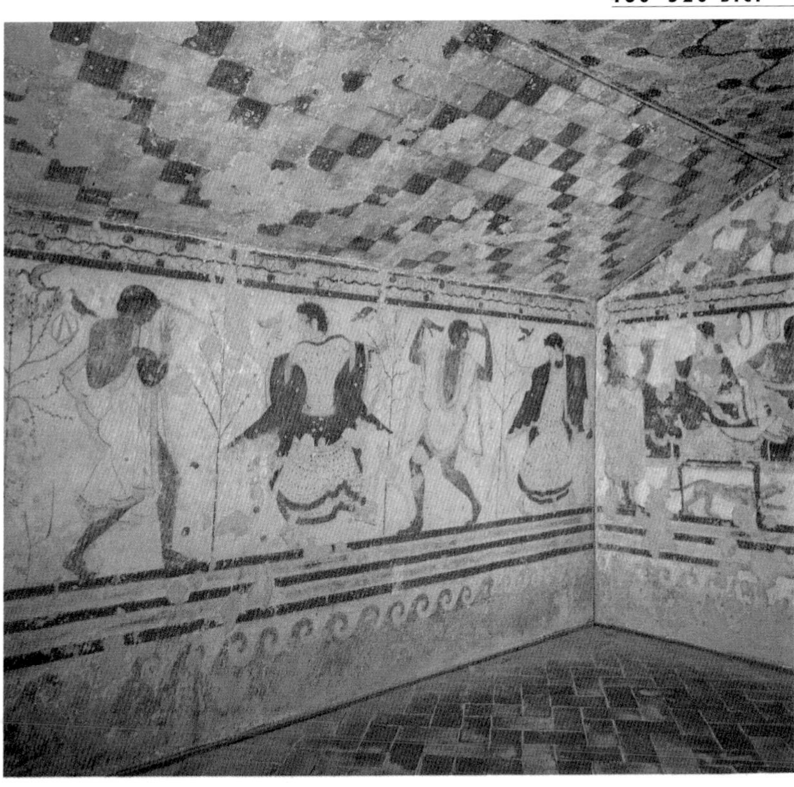

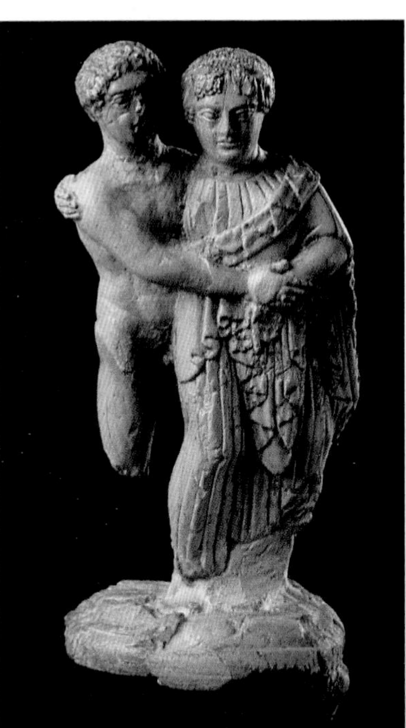

◀ Bronze and ivory candelabra from Spina, fifth century B.C. Ferrara, Museo Archeologico. The ivory group portrays a youth who embraces a young girl wearing a chiton and himation (a loose-fitting robe). The couple stands over a three-legged support with lion's paws on spherical elements. The foundation of Spina was part of a reorganization plan for Etruria in the Po Valley, aimed at revitalizing markets that had dwindled due to Carthaginian and Greek competition. The necropolises there give proof of vibrant markets and trade.

▲ The Tomb of the Triclinium, 480–470 B.C. Tarquinia, Museo Archeologico. On the left lateral walls, between trees and birds, a musician wearing a blue cloak with a red border plays a lyre and dances. A female dancer, wearing a chiton with red flowers similar to her cloak, faces left. Next to her are a male dancer with a blue cape and a female dancer in a flowered chiton. These paintings evolve from an Archaic tone toward a balance that is comparable to the greater Attic potters.

Monumental Terra-Cottas in the Fifth and Fourth Centuries B.C.

The monumentalizing of the sacred urban or rural areas provides evidence of the strong growth of the polis during the Classical period. If in the previous centuries holy places had been architecturally incorporated into aristocratic residences, the new urban structure demanded an exclusive area near a public space, a true dwelling dedicated to the gods. The Etruscans absorbed the mythological sagas of the Greek world and transferred them to the local environment, identifying the gods of the Greek pantheon with indigenous divinities. These became the decorative themes for their houses of worship. The flourishing craftsmanship of Etruscan terra-cotta techniques, enriched by the presence of Greek artisans in the local studios, softened the Ionic tones of the previous generation. New compositional schemes emerged, with the superimposition of multiple levels and figures that were articulated from modeled work and followed stylistic methods and iconography popular in the Hellenic tradition. Such schemes had once been used in aristocratic residences, due to their strong propagandistic endorsement of the power of the elite. Now, they became exemplars for an entire political community of citizens. The temple pediments were animated and colored by struggles and allusions to mythical tensions in which the collective society reconstructed its origins and dominance, justifying and ennobling them. During that fortunate moment for the Etruscan League, antefixes, antepagmenta, moldings, and statues emphasized the wisdom of the divine plan from the buildings on high. It was the zenith of the entrepreneurial economy of an entire nation, not just that of a narrow aristocratic elite.

▼ High-reliefs in terra-cotta from the Belvedere temple in Orvieto, from the fifth and fourth centuries B.C. Orvieto, Museo Claudio Faina. These figures, fully articulated above and connected to slabs below, were uncovered at the rear of the temple. The slanted edge of the slabs shows that they were positioned along the slope of the roof. From left to right, the figures are those of a youth in armor, two seated females, and the head of a bald older man. These and other figures from the temple are enlivened by twists of the body and Phidian gazes that look toward the center of the tympanum, but they struggle to free themselves of the solemn Archaic rhythm.

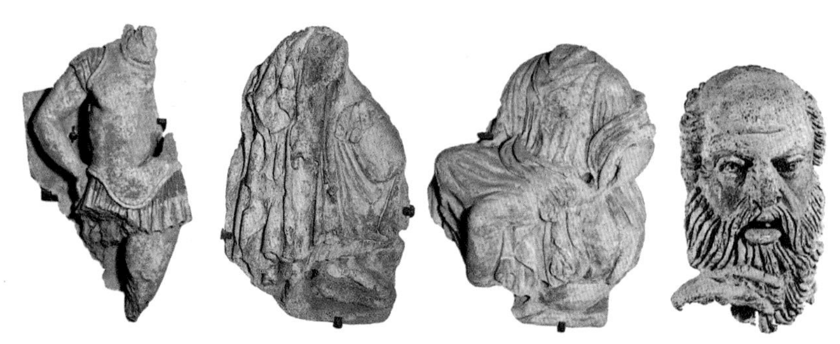

◀ Antefix with the head of Silenus from Pyrgi, 460 B.C. Rome, Museo di Villa Giulia. The snail-like hairstyle and the bulbous eyes, framed by arched eyebrows in relief, evoke the Archaic. The nimbus, a large halo encircling the head, is decorated with palm and lotus leaves in a bronzeworking-style relief that can be compared to works from Cervetari.

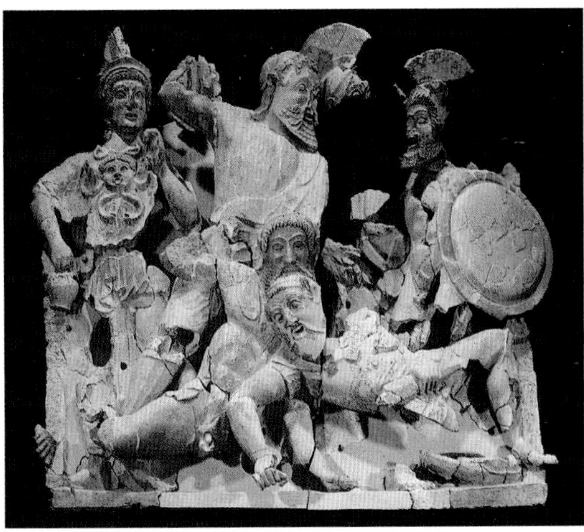

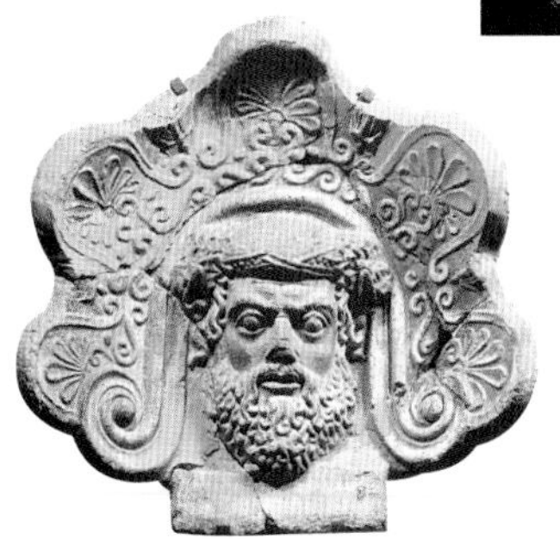

◀ Antefix of the head of Silenus with a nimbus, from the Belvedere temple, fifth and fourth centuries B.C. Orvieto, Museo Claudio Faina. Echoes of early Classical art emerge from the face of Silenus, both in the dignified facial features and the modeling.

▲ Terra-cotta high relief from the rear pediment of Temple A in Pyrgi, from the beginning of the fifth century B.C. Rome, Museo di Villa Giulia. The subject, taken from the saga of *Seven against Thebes,* has been rendered in a multilevel composition.

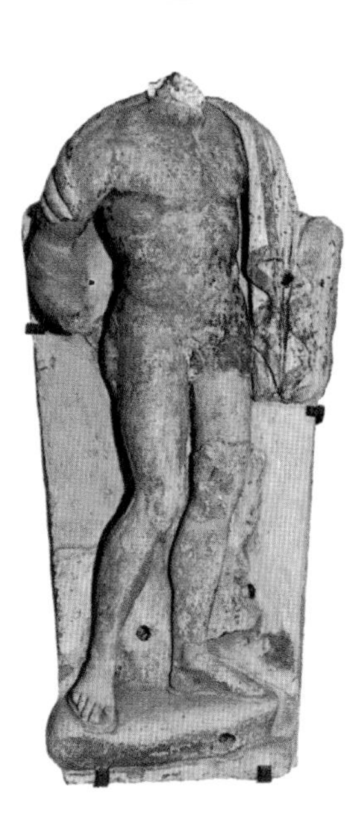

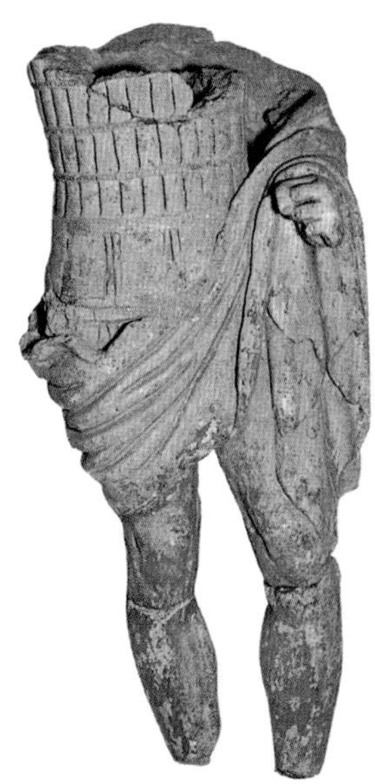

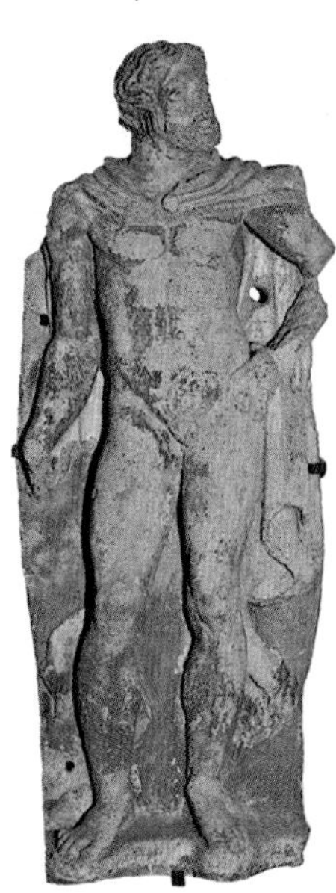

The Winged Horses of Tarquinia

At the head of a line of *columen* in Tarquinia's Ara della Regina temple is one of the finest examples of Classical sculpture: a pair of winged horses pulling a *biga* on which, most likely, sat a figure of a female deity, although only a fragment of drapery belonging to the right section has survived. The figurative language, influenced by post-Phidian teachings, is directly reminiscent of Attic pottery, mediated by the Magna Graecia and Italic environments.

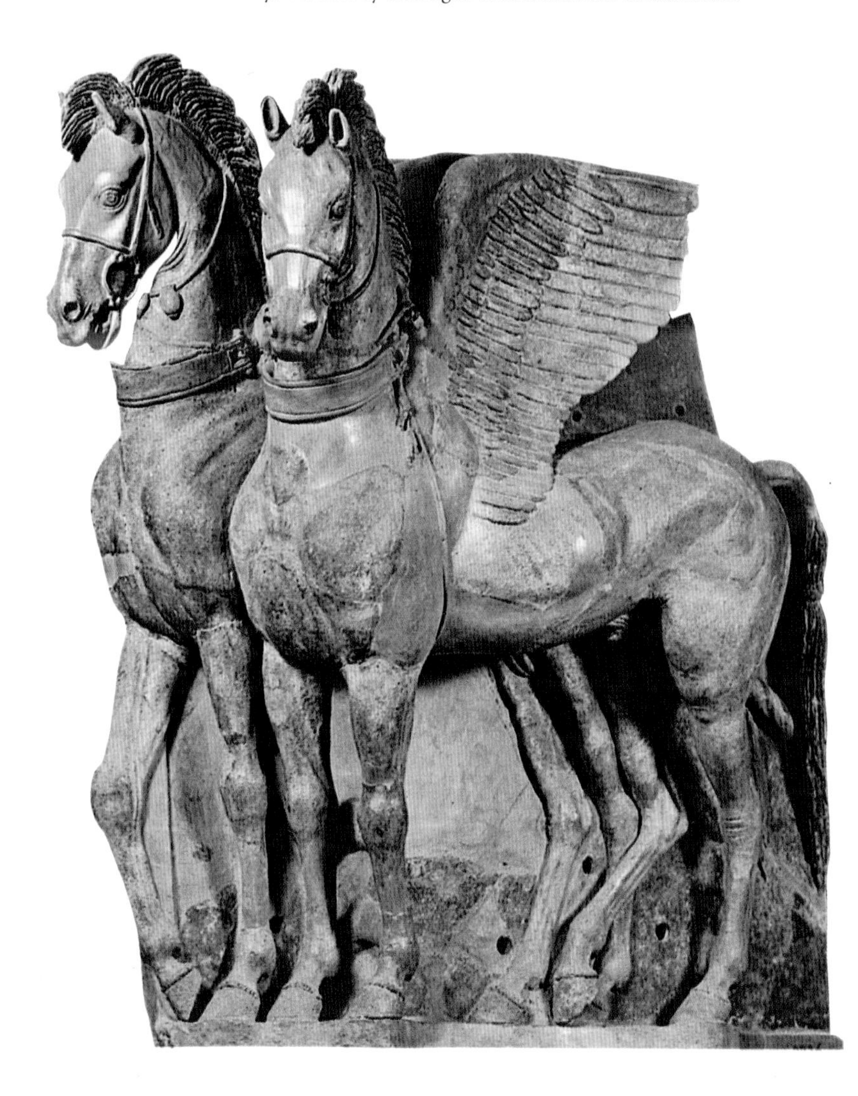

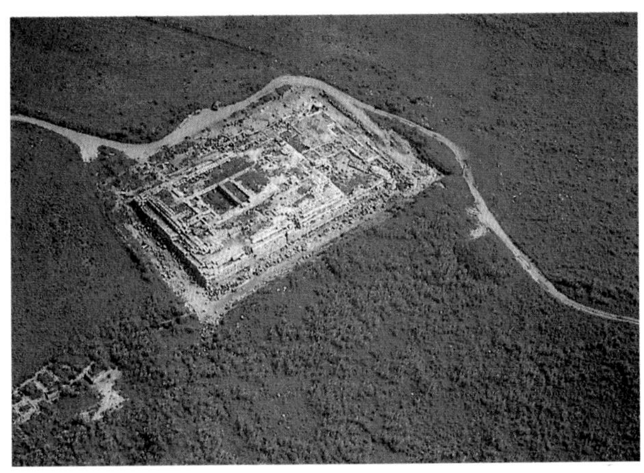

◀ Aerial view of the Ara della Regina temple, fourth century B.C. Tarquinia. This temple plan has eliminated the *posticum,* lengthened the alae, and subdivided the *cella* into three rooms. It is surrounded by a peristyle of columns that rose from a monumental podium of stairs. The crest of the hill was augmented with landfill to form the foundation.

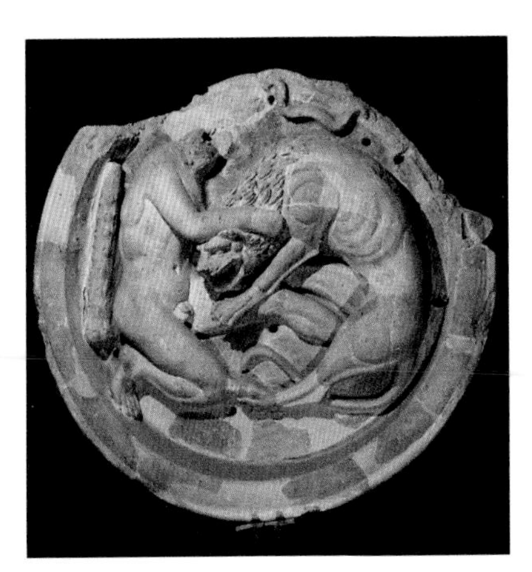

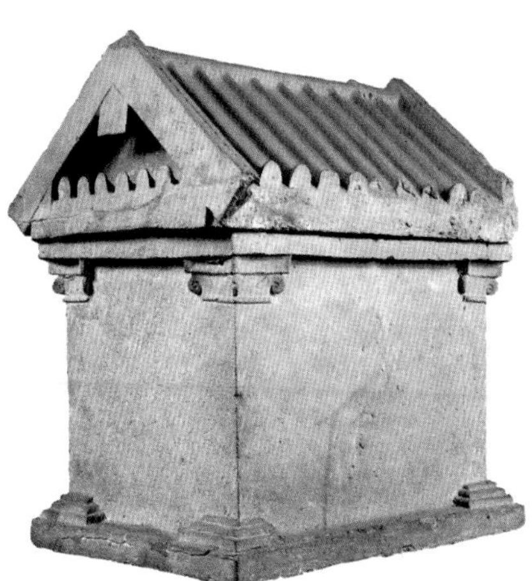

▲ Disk acroterion showing Hercules strangling the Nemean lion, fourth century B.C. Salerno, Museo Provinciale. It is comparable to Etruscan examples that were applied to the heads of the *columen* (ridgeboards) and to *mutules* (decorative soffit blocks).

▶ Lateral acroterion from Cerveteri, from the middle of the fourth century B.C. Vatican City, Museo Gregoriano Etrusco. This Pegasus is an ancestor of the Tarquinian horses in its expressive protome and open mouth.

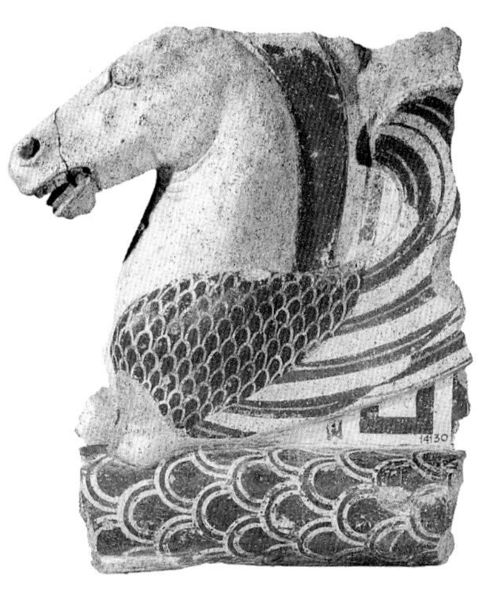

▲ Clay cinerary urn in the shape of a small temple, from Volterra, fourth and third centuries B.C. Florence, Museo Archeologico. The characteristics of Etruscan temples have been faithfully reproduced here. It lacks decorative pediments, but it is rich in antefixes of maenad or sileni heads, pediment molding, perforated cornices, and pedimental antepagmenta. These characteristics have been documented through both archaeological discoveries and Vitruvius's *De Architectura*.

Greek Influence

Etruscan craftsmanship in the fifth and fourth centuries B.C. was animated by lively Classical vibrations, thanks to an industrious acceptance of Greek teachings that was not frozen in slavish imitation. Variations on Classical models occurred not because the craftsmen lacked ability or understanding, as has been thought in the past, but rather because Classical stylistic techniques were used in various combinations, at times incoherently and with local contributions, leading to a Tyrrhenian union with reference typologies. The evolution of a formal language proceeded in tandem with the articulation and eventual decay of the Archaic aristocratic ideology, which had determined the accepted iconography. The stylistic delays that appear in votive bronzes and antefixae and in works of a higher artistic level should be interpreted in this light. The defeat of Cumae, the consequent Syracusan presence in the Etruscan region, and the shrinking of the oligarchy laid the foundations for the chronic Archaic lateness of southern Etruria's main crafts. Devotional sculptures, however, show a passage from the more composed and severe shapes of the Classical style to the shaded softness of the school of Polyclitus.

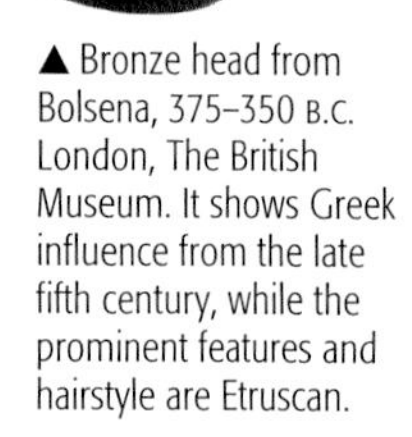

▲ Bronze head from Bolsena, 375–350 B.C. London, The British Museum. It shows Greek influence from the late fifth century, while the prominent features and hairstyle are Etruscan.

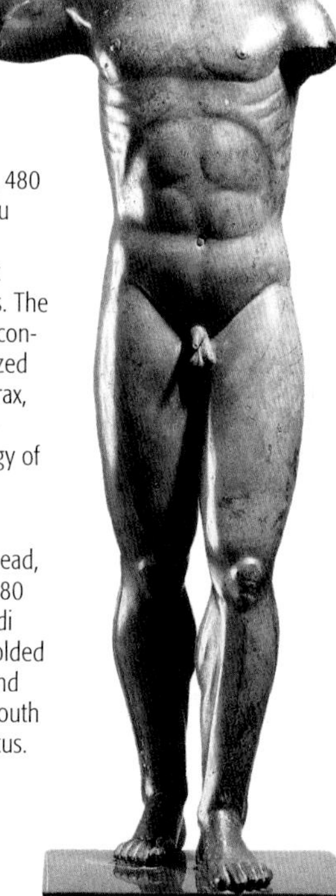

► Javelin thrower, 480 B.C. Paris, Musée du Louvre. This piece evokes late Archaic kouroi from Samos. The rigidity of the arm contrasts with the stylized delicacy of the thorax, whose narrowness dampens the energy of the legs.

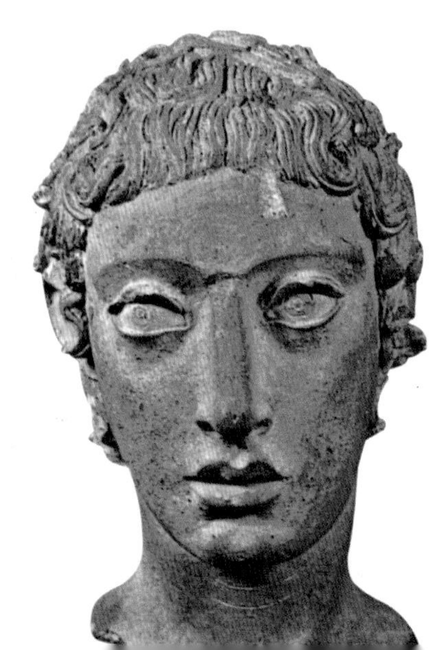

◄ The Malavolta head, in clay, from Veii, 480 B.C. Rome, Museo di Villa Giulia. The molded locks, large eyes, and the pronounced mouth derive from Polyclitus.

▶ Bronze head of a male wearing a diadem, from Cagli. Ancona, Museo Archeologico. Made in Orvieto, its eyes are of vitreous paste. The late Phidian influence of the hairstyle with ringlets over the temples and a number of recurring details from terra-cottas of Falerii lead it to be dated toward the second quarter of the fourth century B.C.

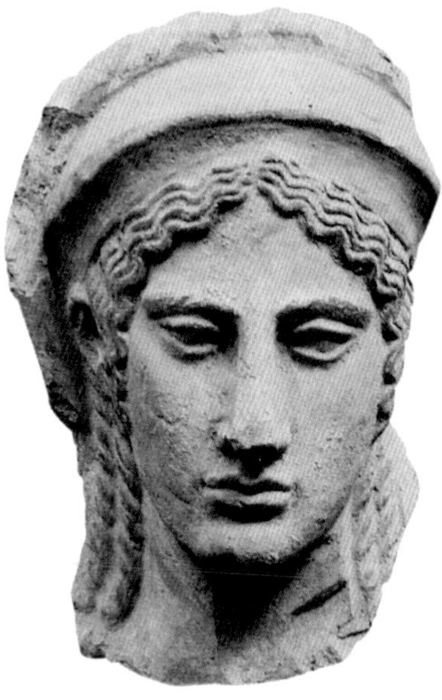

▲ Antefix of a female head, from the Paolozzi collection, second half of the fifth century B.C. Chiusi, Museo Archeologico. Greek influence can be seen in the rendering of the hair, which features a center part, waves on the head, and cascading vertical curls. The soft planes and severe expression of the face's structure denote an inner composure imbued with Classical teachings, which overcome the neutral ideal of its type.

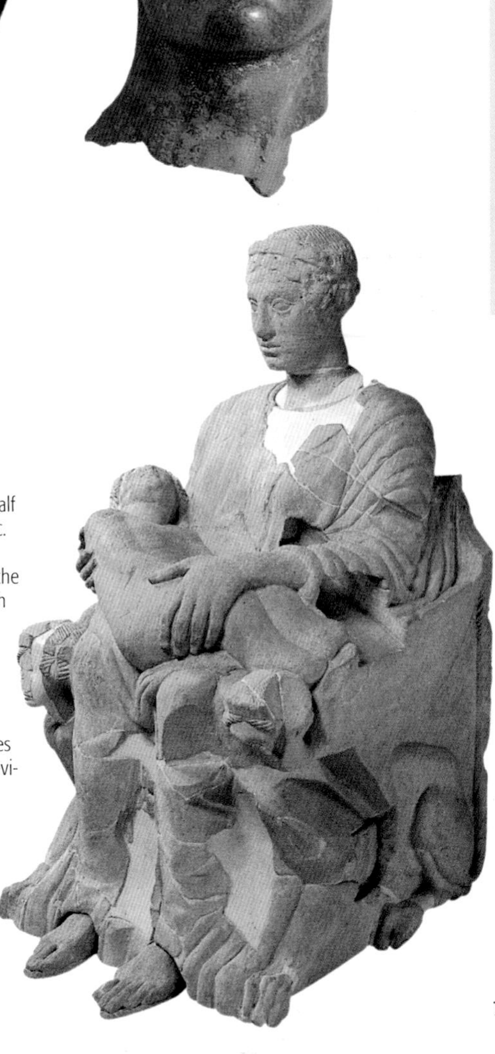

▶ Cinerary statue of Mater Matuta, from Chianciano, second half of the fifth century B.C. Florence, Museo Archeologico. This is the only example in which the woman, seated on an oriental-type throne, holds a child in her arms. A full acceptance of Attic Classicism via the cities of Magna Graecia is evident in its pose and expressiveness.

Language and Written Text

From the moment Etruscan was identified as a language isolate, it became clear that using an "etymological method"—based on genealogical connections between different languages—would be of no help in determining the morphology and syntax of the Etruscan language. Scholars have applied various complementary methods to try to decode it. First, they have used the "combining method," which identifies, compares, and catalogues the words and forms present in the texts. Due to the highly formal nature of this type of analysis, however, it cannot by itself yield meaning from the texts. It needs to be augmented with other information, such as the context of the inscription, the medium, the type of object on which it was found, and any proper names used. This last type of analysis naturally combines with a third method, called "bilingual" or "parallel text," which uses a known language to help interpret an unknown one. It is based on cultural similarities between peoples of the same region, pointing out parallels between forms in analogous texts. Finally, a typological analysis of a language's morphology and syntax reveals the presence of certain linguistic characteristics that yield clues to others: for instance, a language that places the subject before the verb tends also to place the genitive before the noun.

▼ A lead sheet in lenticular form from Heba, Magliano. Florence, Museo Archeologico. The text, which has been engraved in a spiral toward the center on both sides, mentions completed rituals and others to be carried out in honor of various divinities. Since the majority of the long texts that have survived are of a ritual nature, the repertory of words we have is limited.

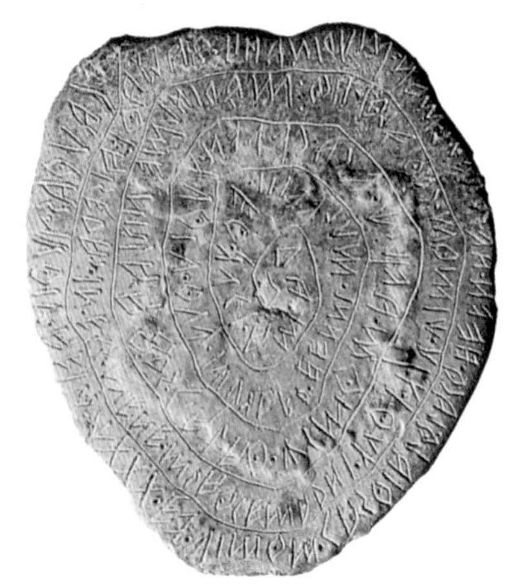

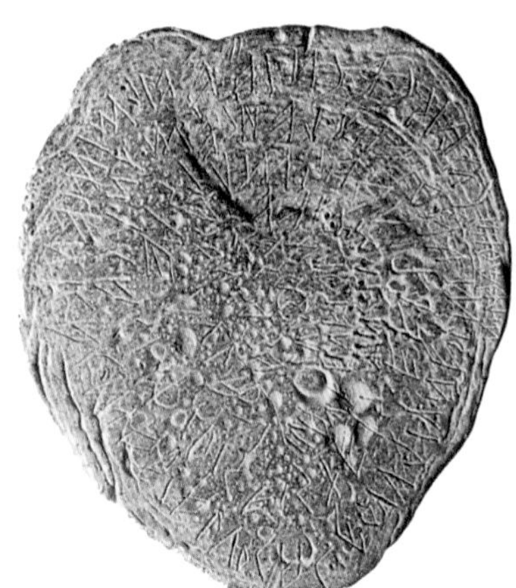

▼ Border *cippus* from the Perugia area. Perugia, Museo Archeologico. The lower, unfinished section was buried in the ground. The inscription transcribes a deed regarding an agreement between the Velthina and the Afuna families of Perugia on the definition and transfer of landholdings. The text is rich with juridical terms.

► Egg-shaped bronze and lead weight from Cerveteri, third century B.C. Rome, Museo di Villa Giulia. The dedicatory engraving of ten lines gives evidence of names and political and military careers: Larth Penthe and Vel Lape dedicated the object, which belongs to Turms (although it previously belonged to Vel di Archmsi), in the sanctuary of Hercules during the magistracy of Zilc.

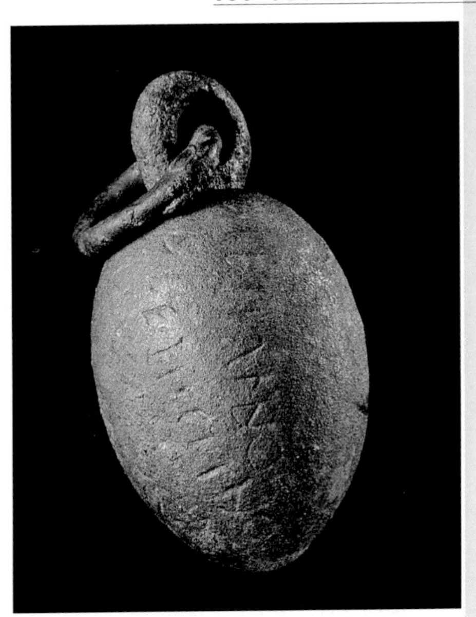

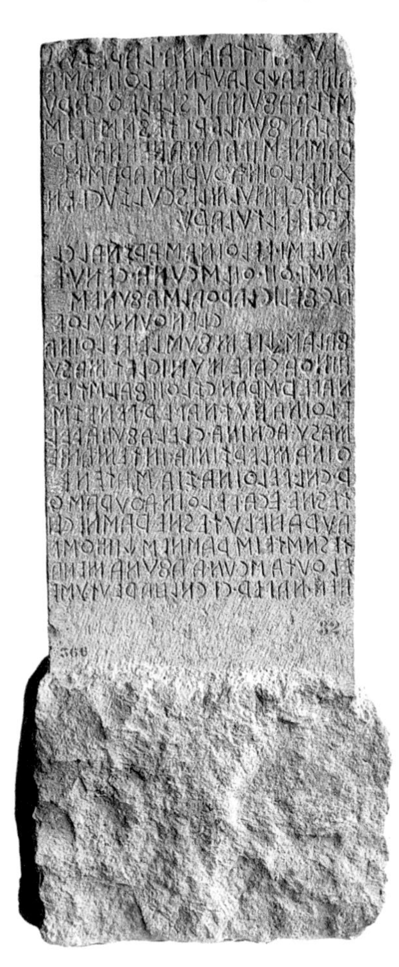

▲ Terra-cotta roof tile from Capua, fifth century B.C. Berlin, Staatliche Museen. A ritualistic text is written on its surface, the longest of which concerns the gods of the Underworld, with prescriptions for ritual acts to propitiate various divinities. The lines of writing alternate in their direction.

The Inscribed Gold Sheets of Pyrgi

Two engraved gold sheets were unearthed in the sanctuary at Pyrgi, together with a third in Phoenician. Dating to the beginning of the fifth century B.C., they are the oldest historical epigraphic sources from Etruria. The Phoenician text and the Etruscan text of Lamina A, which loosely correspond in content, tell how the local Etruscan ruler, Thefarie Velianas, "ruler over Cerveteri for three years," dedicated a "sacred place," Temple B, and a statue to the goddess Uni (the Phoenician Astarte), with whom the sovereign had a privileged relationship. The goddess herself, it is explained, requested a gift from him. Lamina B, which has no Phoenician parallel, lists Thefarie's successive gifts to the sanctuary.

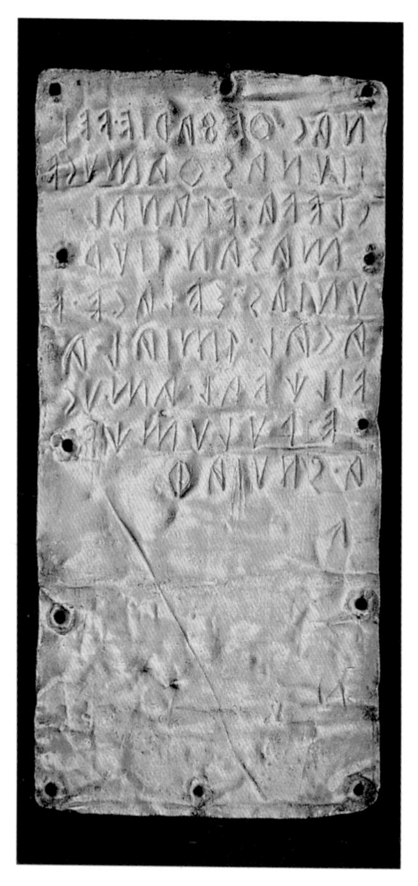

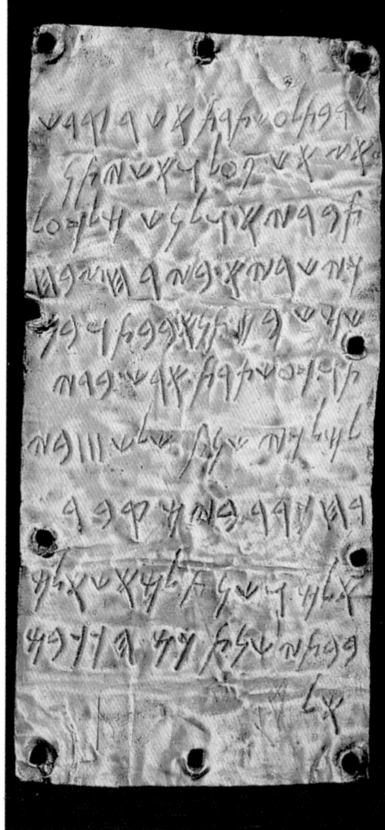

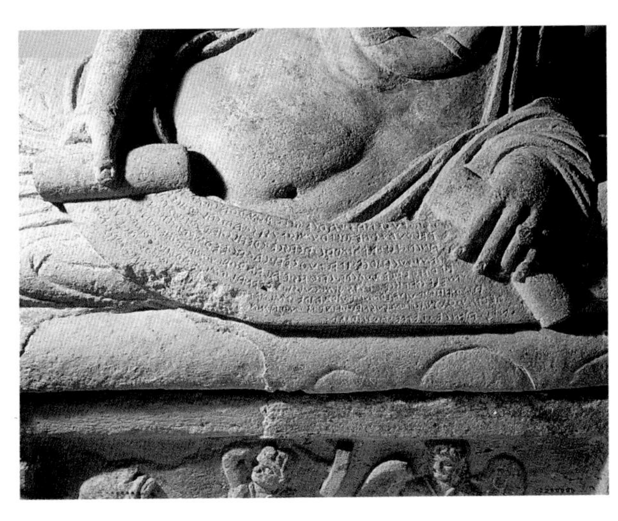

◀ The sarcophagus of Laris Pulena, Tarquinia, from the middle of the third century B.C. Tarquinia, Museo Archeologico. A scroll unrolls from the hands of the deceased containing his genealogy and biographic information. Scrolls were made of strips of animal skin, linen, or papyrus and the text was written in columns. Unrolled from right to left, they must have been used for texts that had wide circulation.

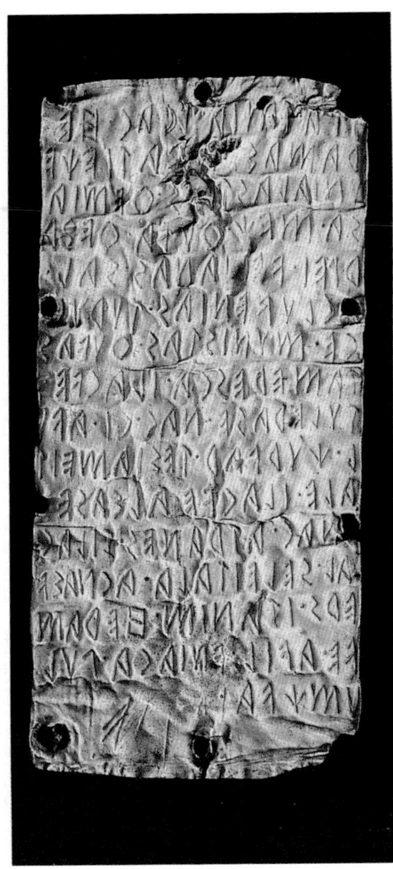

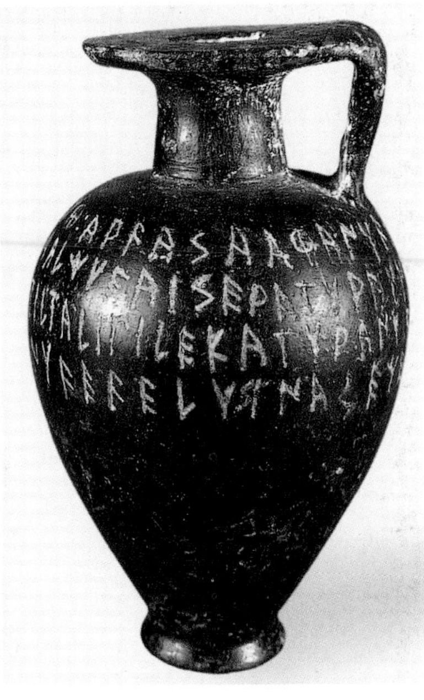

▲ Bucchero *aryballos* from Cerveteri, from the end of the seventh century B.C. Rome, Museo di Villa Giulia. It features a continuous inscription of 174 letters filled with white paste. Among the words that can be isolated are three groups of letters that include the Etruscan name Turan and the Greek Aphrodite, which lead some to believe that this could have been an amorous inscription.

An Urban Apogee

The defeats suffered by the Etruscan navy at the hands of the Syracusans in 474 B.C. at Cumae and, in 453, in the waters off the island of Elba caused them to lose control over the Tyrrhenian Sea. Thus began the decline of the flourishing commercial ports of the Archaic period. Economic interests turned northward, and new commercial centers opened in the Rhine Valley toward the regions beyond the Alps. A new vigor animated the two trading centers of the Upper Adriatic, Adria and Spina, where the Greeks came to exchange oil and wine for grain. The political and economic restructuring produced a second colonization of Etruria in the Po Valley. Existing cities were rejuvenated, including Bologna, which grew from an agricultural district into an urbanized city, and new ones were founded, such as Marzabotto and Spina, which had long stood along the routes to northern Europe. The rules that determined the foundation and planning of cities were moving away from religious ideology, according to which an earthly microcosm mirrored a celestial and geometric macrocosm. Nevertheless, the orientation of city streets—the weave of the urban fabric—was determined by sacred augurs, who followed the Hippodamian principle of orthogonal planning.

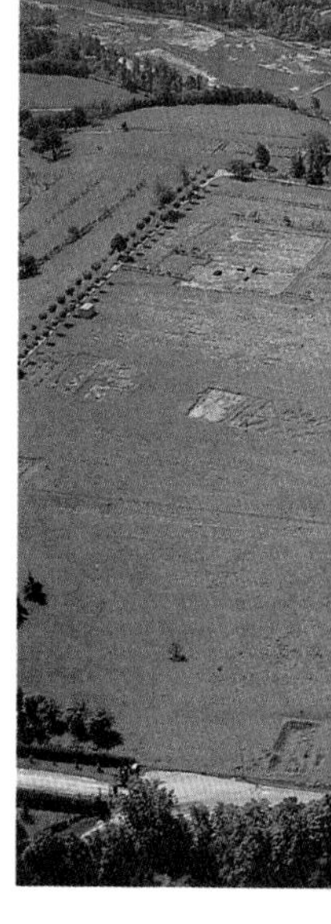

▲ Aerial view of the Etruscan settlement of Marzabotto, fifth century B.C. The orthogonal plan, in which streets cross each other at right angles and form rectangular insulae (blocks) of houses, was Hellenic and inherited via Magna Graecia. It was adopted and adapted to the rules of the *disciplina etrusca*.

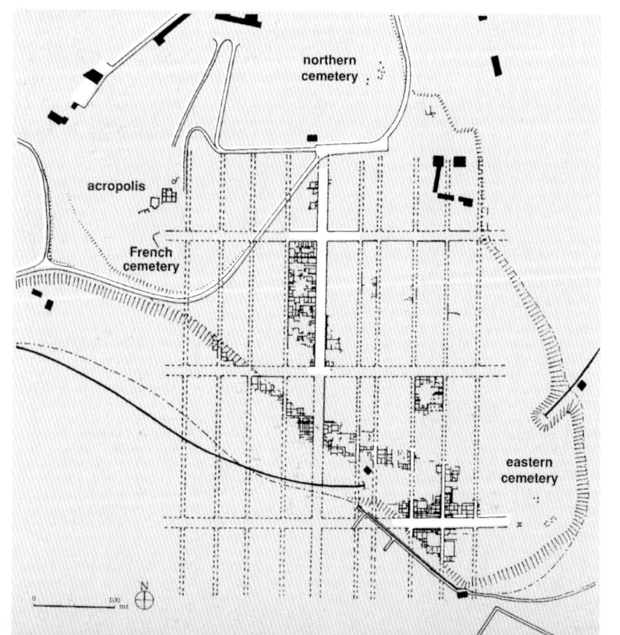

◀ Plan of the city of Marzabotto. There are three large, equidistant arteries, more than 15 meters (49 feet) wide and oriented in an east–west direction. They cross another street of equal width, at the sides of which narrow parallel lanes are laid out at less rigidly equal intervals. They combine to form elongated rectangular blocks.

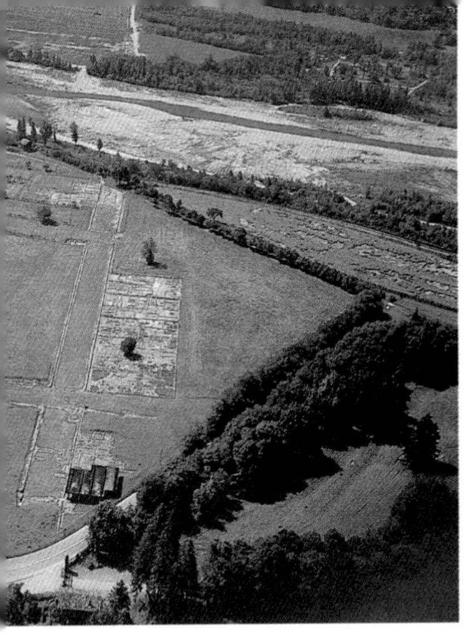

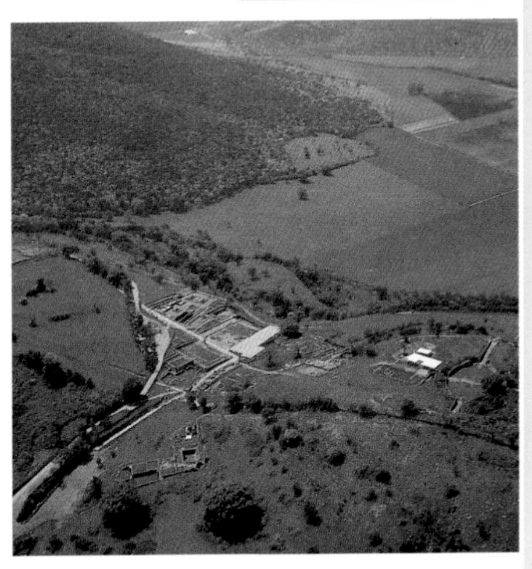

▲ Aerial view from the northeast of the built-up area of Roselle. *At center* is the Valley of the Forum, with a roof to cover the buildings; *at left,* the south hill.

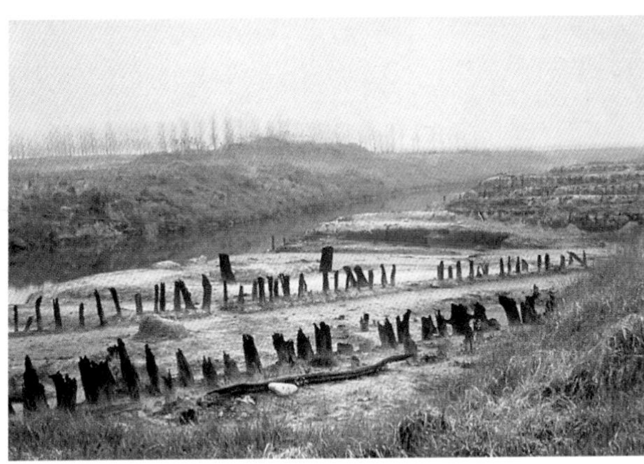

◀ View of the pilings in the *agger* that surrounded the built-up area of Spina, Mezzano Valley, fifth and fourth centuries B.C. The regular roads, laid out in an orthogonal pattern, were sometimes replaced by navigable canals, a striking anticipation of what was to develop centuries later in Venice.

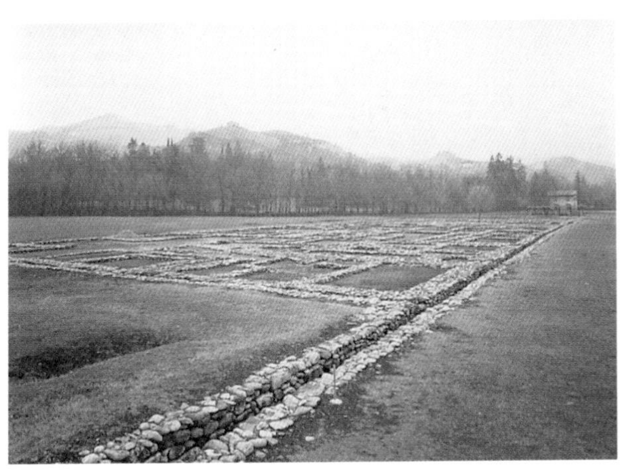

◀ Marzabotto, fifth century B.C. The first block of Region IV adjoined the north–south *platea,* which was bordered by an uncovered canal. Besides functioning as a sewer system for the adjacent houses, it marked the end of the public area.

Marzabotto and Domestic Architecture

The orthogonal urban framework of the fifth and fourth centuries B.C. corresponded to an evolution in private dwellings. These lost the solemnity of the palatial residences of Murlo or Acquarossa in favor of a general planimetric standardization, which points to the emergence of a middle class. The blocks at Marzabotto housed up to seven or eight units of up to 800 square meters (8600 sq. ft.), which shared certain general features: road access; a long hallway flanked by rooms used as shops or workshops; a large, central, cross-shaped courtyard with a well; and three other rooms in back that echoed the three-part division of the houses at Acquarossa. Vitruvius defined the "Tuscan" atrium as that of a house with a central, open-air courtyard. It was covered by a roof that sloped toward the interior opening (*compluvium*) and gathered rainwater into a storage tank (*impluvium*), which in the house at Marzabotto corresponded to the well. The pitched roof was supported by wooden trusses and ran horizontally along the perimeter walls.

▼ A gabled roof and a roof with a *compluvium* and an *opaion* to allow smoke to exit. Marzabotto, Museo Nazionale Etrusco. The first includes ridge tiles that are aligned with the roof tiles, which were fired in a kiln. In some cases the openings along the facade were found to be the work of potters or foundries.

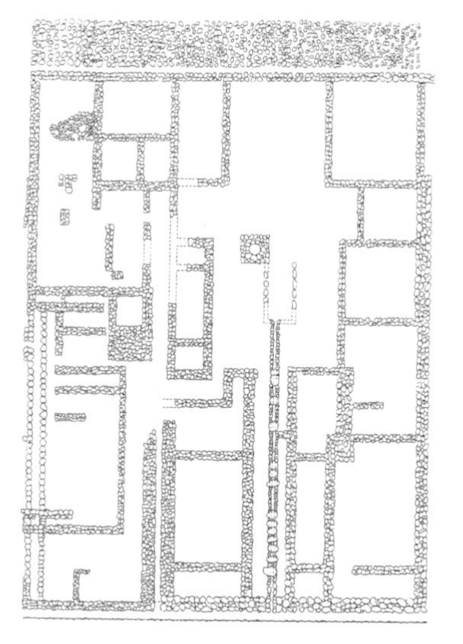

◀ Plan of a Marzabotto residence from the beginning of the fifth century B.C. The roof was tiled and the walls built with a lattice framework or with unfired bricks. The courtyard pavement was of river stones while the interior floor was clay, and a drainage channel ran under the corridor floor.

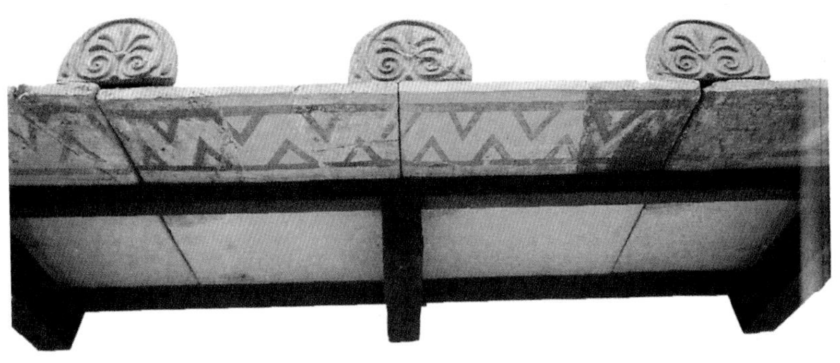

▲ Roofing tiles from residences. Marzabotto, Museo Nazionale Etrusco. These tiles were painted on their interior side and had palmette antefixes above them that were found in the well at *platea* D.

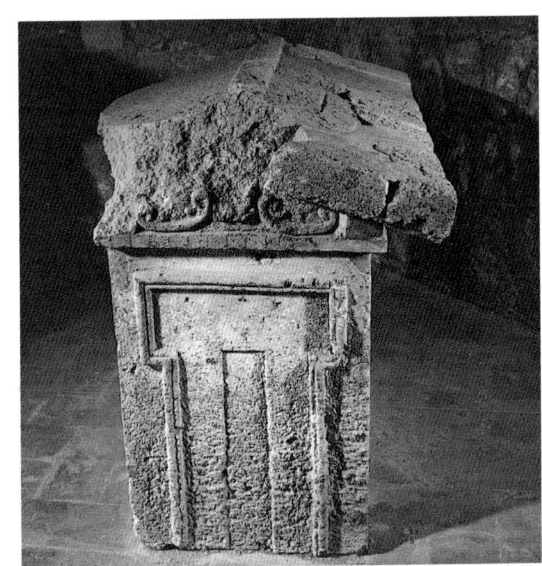

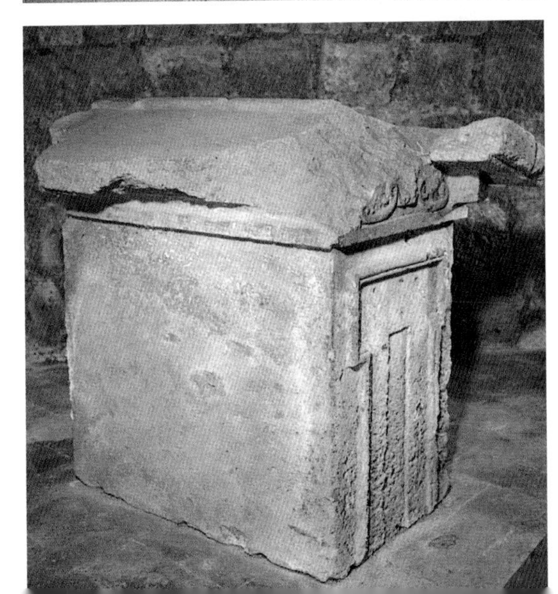

▶ A funerary *cippus* in nenfro, shaped like a house with a projecting gable roof, from Casale Signorelli, fifth century B.C. Viterbo, Museo Archeologico. At the top of the walls runs a cornice decorated with small squares sparingly painted red or black. The model matches Vitruvius's descriptions of Etruscan buildings. The open plan of the courtyard, with an atrium and *tablinum,* was to become canonical for upper-middle-class homes. It would be carried into the Roman world, where the houses in Pompeii are the most well-known examples.

The Gods

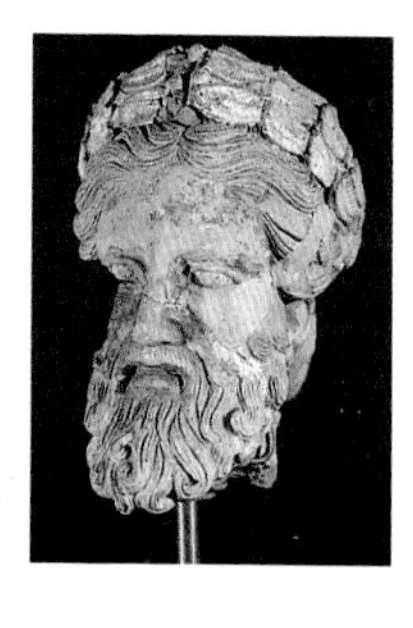

▲ Votive terra-cotta of Tin, identified through analogous iconography as the Greek Zeus, from the Belvedere temple in Orvieto. Orvieto, Museo Claudio Faina. The Phidian stylistic characteristics date this to the beginning of the fourth century B.C.

Originally the Etruscan concept of religion did not include anthropomorphic divinities, but instead was ruled by a teratomorphic vision of the forces of nature. Elemental beings resided in the heavens and within the bowels of the earth; they had terrifying features and various sexual connotations. A primitive group of "monstrous" gods was joined by others that originated in the surrounding Italic environment, especially the Latin, Faliscan, and Umbrian worlds. The distant roots of this religion can be found in domestic rituals and the exaltation of heroized ancestors. In the middle of the seventh century B.C. the religion shifted its center from noble families to the collective society, paralleling the passage from a village to an urban civilization. The adoption of the Greek gods and myths was the most obvious result of the evolving ideology of the nobility. Comprehending the motives behind and changing assumptions of myths helps to illuminate the process by which anthropomorphic divinities were accepted. The process was clearly more complex than simple religious syncretism and a passive acculturation in form but not substance. By the fourth century, the identification of native with Greek divinities was complete, and the Olympic pantheon was fully represented.

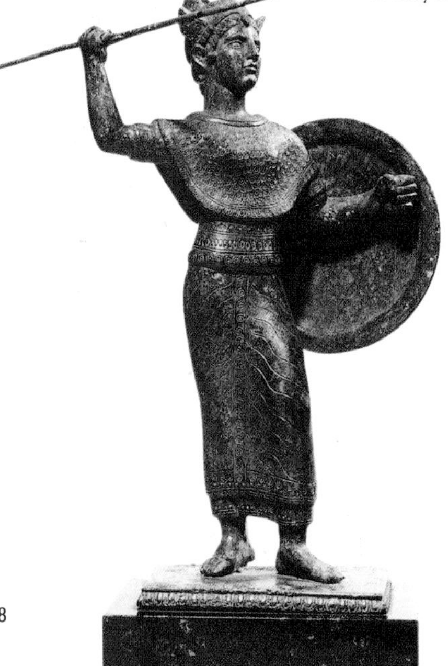

◀ Minerva Promachos, from Apiro, middle of the fifth century B.C. Berlin, Staatliche Museen. This deity is comparable to the Greek goddess Athena.

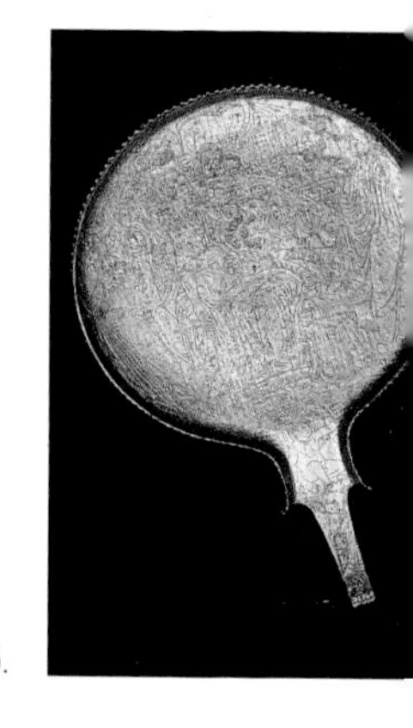

▶ Mirror from Volterra, middle of the fourth century B.C. Florence, Museo Archeologico. It portrays a myth that was originally Greek: the nursing of Hercle (Hercules) by Uni (Hera).

▶ Statue of Fufluns, Greek Dionysus, 480 B.C. Modena, Galleria Estense. The Hellenization of the divinities was complex, woven together with "native variations" from the Archaic phase that could change in function and appearance, and with "dialectical variations" on a divinity that, beyond the variables of Hellenization, remained univocal.

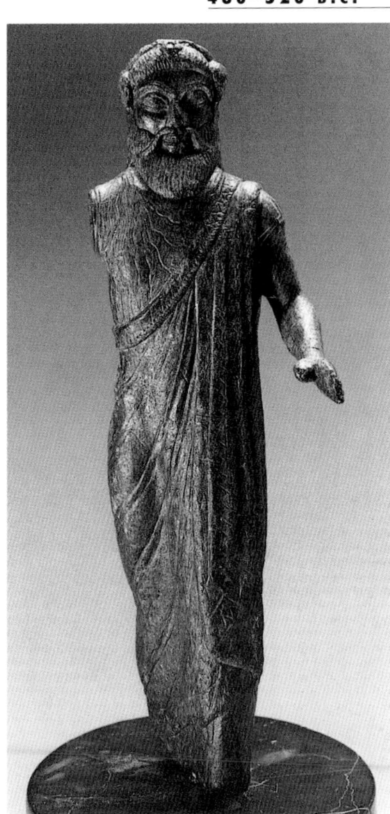

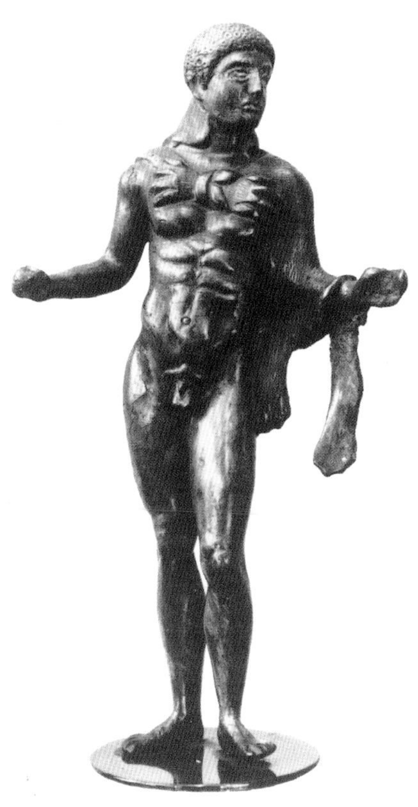

▲ Statue of Hercules from Mount Falterona, 450 B.C. London, The British Museum. The god is wearing only the skin of the Nemean lion, tied across the chest, which descends from his head down his back like a cape. This piece is firmly linked to Greek models in its iconography and style, which recalls Polyclitus.

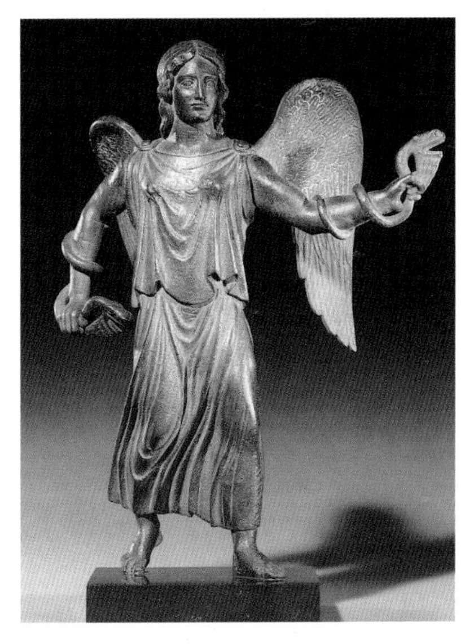

▶ Statue of Vanth from the end of the fifth century B.C. London, The British Museum. The winged Fury wears a chiton, and her loosened hair is parted twice. Her arms are wrapped in snakes. The iconography of this divine regulator of destiny and goddess of the Underworld assumed connotations of the Greek Erinyes.

Tages and the Mirror of Tuscania

In his *De Divinatione,* Cicero tells one of the few myths that is entirely Etruscan: One day in Tarquinia, a farmer was plowing his field. All at once a boy named Tages, possessed of the wisdom of an old man, bounded out of a furrow in the ground. He told the farmer of the *disciplina etrusca,* the collection of rules that regulated the relationship between god and man.

▼ Scarab in carnelian from the fourth or third centuries B.C. Rome, Museo di Villa Giulia. On its base, within a frame fashioned like a thin cord, the farmer kneels over Tages, who is depicted as he emerges from the earth. The Tagetic revelation of the haruspex discipline (augury from animal entrails) places the Etruscan religion among the revealed religions, the only one from the Mediterranean basin in the classical pagan world other than the Jewish religion. Since the earliest times, Etrurians boasted of their written revelation.

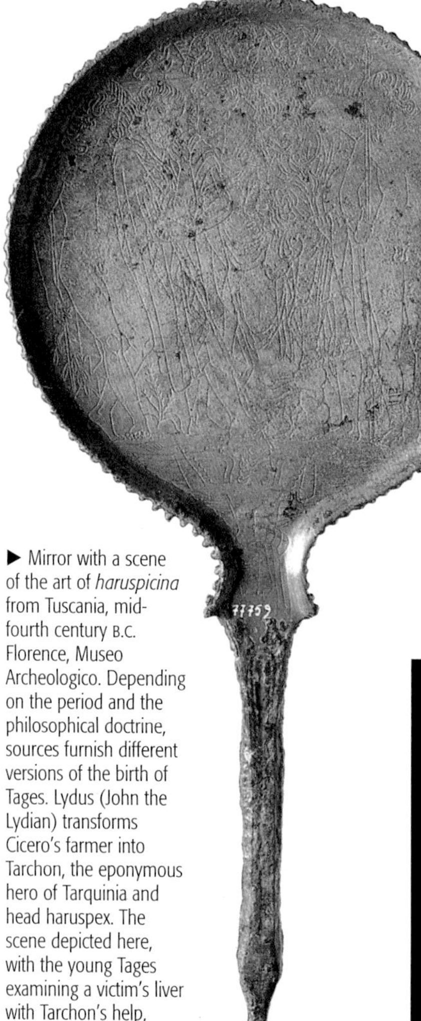

► Mirror with a scene of the art of *haruspicina* from Tuscania, mid-fourth century B.C. Florence, Museo Archeologico. Depending on the period and the philosophical doctrine, sources furnish different versions of the birth of Tages. Lydus (John the Lydian) transforms Cicero's farmer into Tarchon, the eponymous hero of Tarquinia and head haruspex. The scene depicted here, with the young Tages examining a victim's liver with Tarchon's help, seems to refer to Lydus's version.

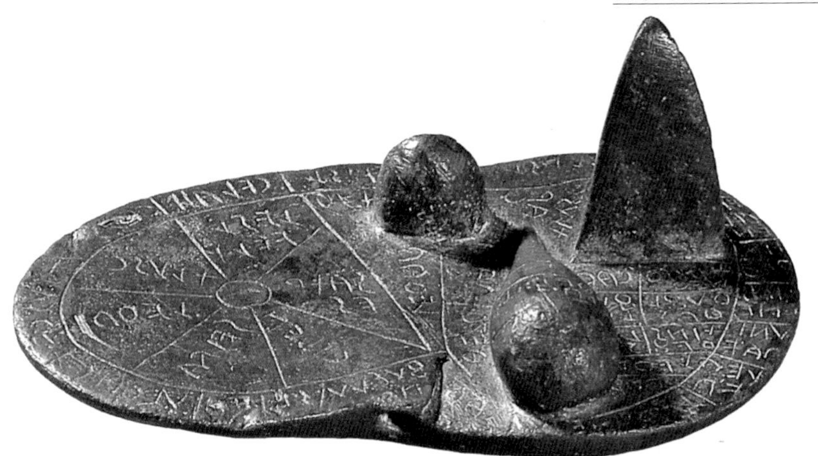

▲ Bronze model of a sheep liver from Settima, from the end of the second or beginning of the first centuries B.C. Piacenza, Museo Civico. In the Etruscan religion, the liver of sacrificial animals was a microcosm of the celestial macrocosm. The sixteen divisions engraved along the edge correspond to sixteen divisions of the heavens, each belonging to a specific deity. The parts of the liver that give "signs" to the haruspex reveal the divine location from which an omen emanated.

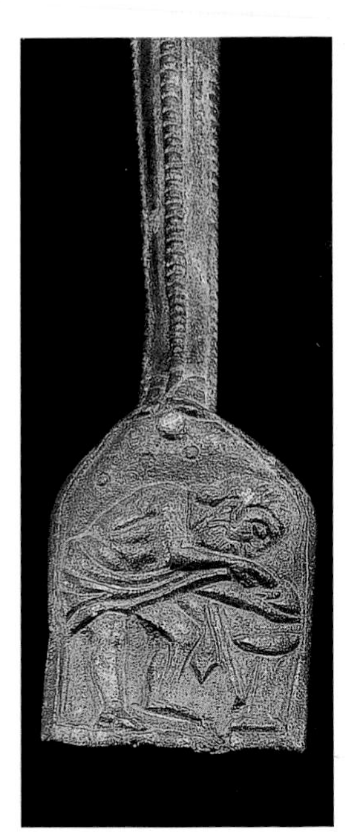

▼ Bronze plaque from a Schnabelkanne, 400–375 B.C. Amsterdam, Allard Pierson Museum. A bearded haruspex leans forward with a liver in his left hand. The reading of livers took place on an altar.

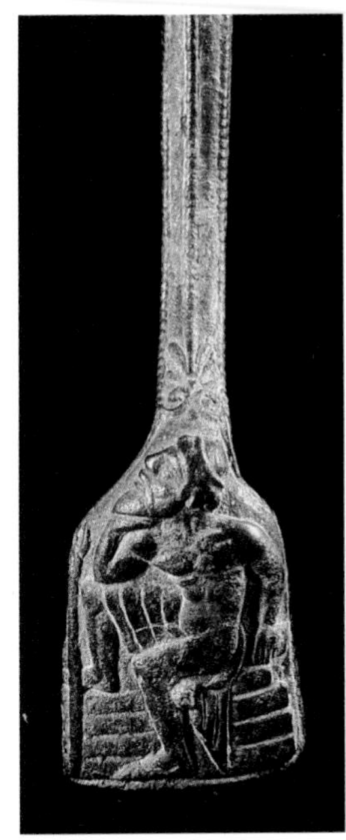

◀ Bronze Schnabelkanne handle, from the end of the fifth century B.C. Arezzo, Museo Archeologico. A naked and bearded man, wearing a cloak over his right leg and the pointed hat of the haruspices, sits on a block structure and gazes upward. The interpretation of lightning was also a part of the haruspices' art. The *disciplina etrusca* is part cosmogony, that is, reading the history of the world; part prophecy, or divining future history; and part intervention, a ritual act aimed at deferring divine punishment of cities or peoples by prayer or atoning for guilt.

Bronzeworking

The social shift toward oligarchy during the fifth century B.C. did not affect artistic work in bronze, which had one of its centers in Vulci. The transfer of the commercial axis toward Etruria in the Po Valley and the Upper Adriatic not only revitalized Vulcian production, which found new patrons and business in that new setting, but also the artisan class that supported itself through this work. Volsinii, the site of the federal sanctuary of Fanum Voltumnae, and Arezzo, which was located close to the mines, increased their local bronze production. Works were commissioned by the emerging middle class, which sought representative offerings that displayed their status, just as the Archaic aristocracy had. The Mars from Todi and the Chimaera of Arezzo are emblematic of the great bronzework of this period, although there are numerous lesser works that can be placed alongside those prime examples: candelabras with figured cymatia, vases, strigils, and, from the entire fourth century, toiletry objects, mirrors, and ex-voto statuettes. Along with the economic ascent of Etruria's interior, central, and northern regions during the fourth century came the easing of social tensions: The broadening of the political fabric to include the artisan class narrowed the gap between lords and servants. The coastal districts, meanwhile, had become less structured because of the loss of traffic on the Tyrrhenian. There, the social gap continued to widen.

▲ Bronze lamp, 400 B.C. Cortona, Museo dell'Accademia. Heads of Acheloüs jut out between apertures decorated with sileni playing panpipes and double-reed instruments, alternating with sirens sprouting birds' wings and tails. *Above,* the Gorgon's head at the center of a wave motif with leaping dolphins.

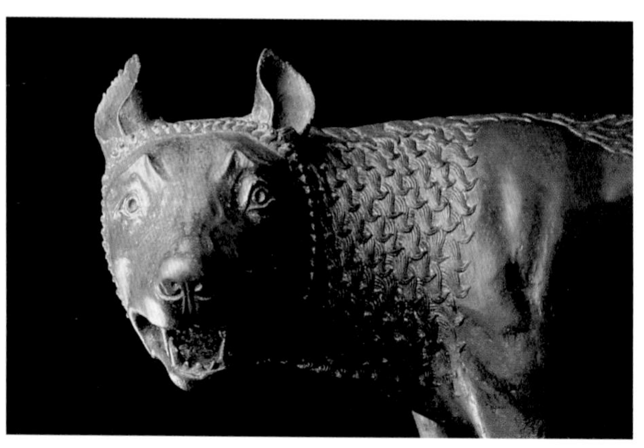

◀ Detail of the Capitoline She-Wolf, 450–430 B.C. Rome, Musei Capitolini. Despite the Archaic treatment of its coat, the rendering of the muzzle shows distinct naturalism. The beast faces left, with a guarded attitude emphasized by the stiff ears and the half-open mouth.

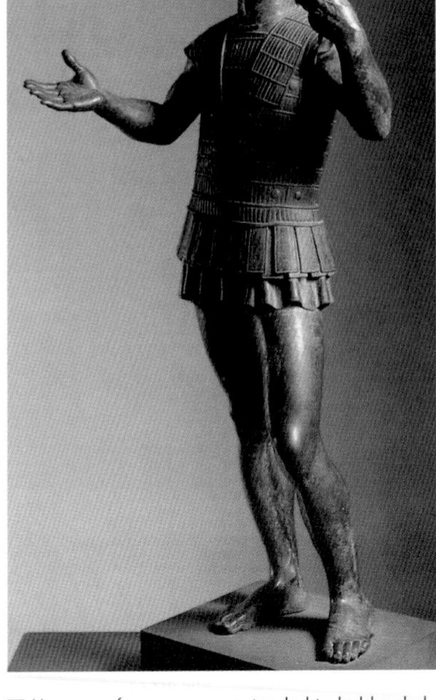

◀ Statue of a warrior, the so-called Mars from Todi, 400 B.C. Vatican City, Museo Gregoriano Etrusco. The cuirass, which has been represented realistically according to a clay prototype that draws on the statue in the Belvedere temple, emphasizes the figure's Italic-Etruscan character.

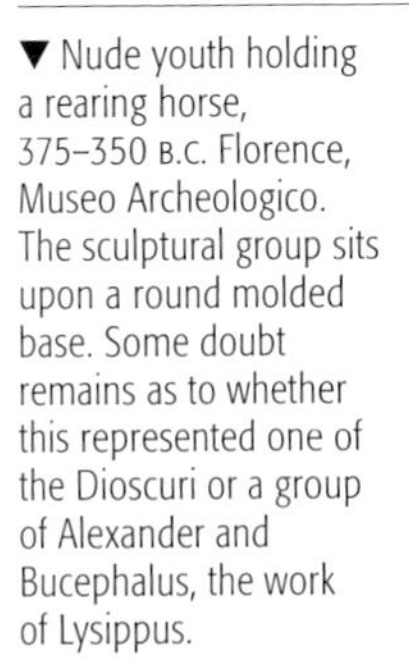

▼ Nude youth holding a rearing horse, 375–350 B.C. Florence, Museo Archeologico. The sculptural group sits upon a round molded base. Some doubt remains as to whether this represented one of the Dioscuri or a group of Alexander and Bucephalus, the work of Lysippus.

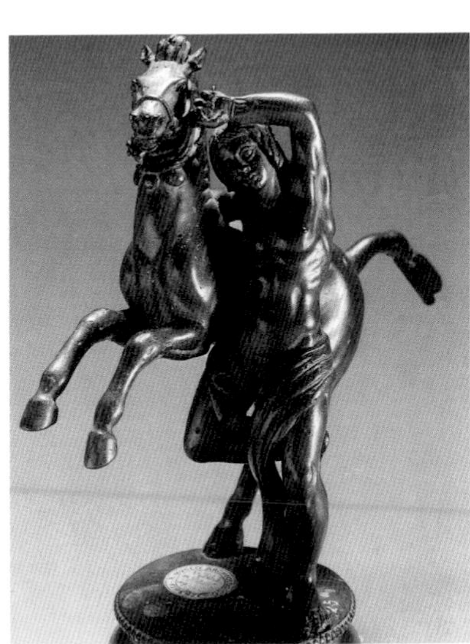

▼ Urn cover from Perugia, 400–375 B.C. St. Petersburg, Hermitage. The young bacchant is reclining with his left hand open and extended to hold a shallow bowl (*patera*). The Phidian influence is quite vivid in the structure of the face and in the young man's hair.

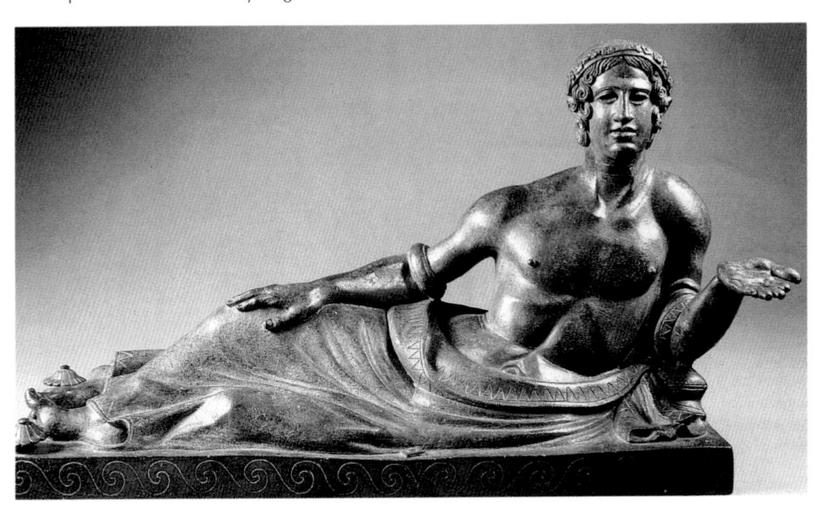

The Chimaera of Arezzo

Created through the technique of lost-wax casting, the beast is shown on the attack. It leans back on its hind legs with its lion head turned right and its goat head facing left. The Archaic aura and echoes of Greece and Magna Graecia emitted by the rigid and repetitive framework of the mane contrast with the lively naturalism of the wild animal's sleek body, which is completely Etruscan.

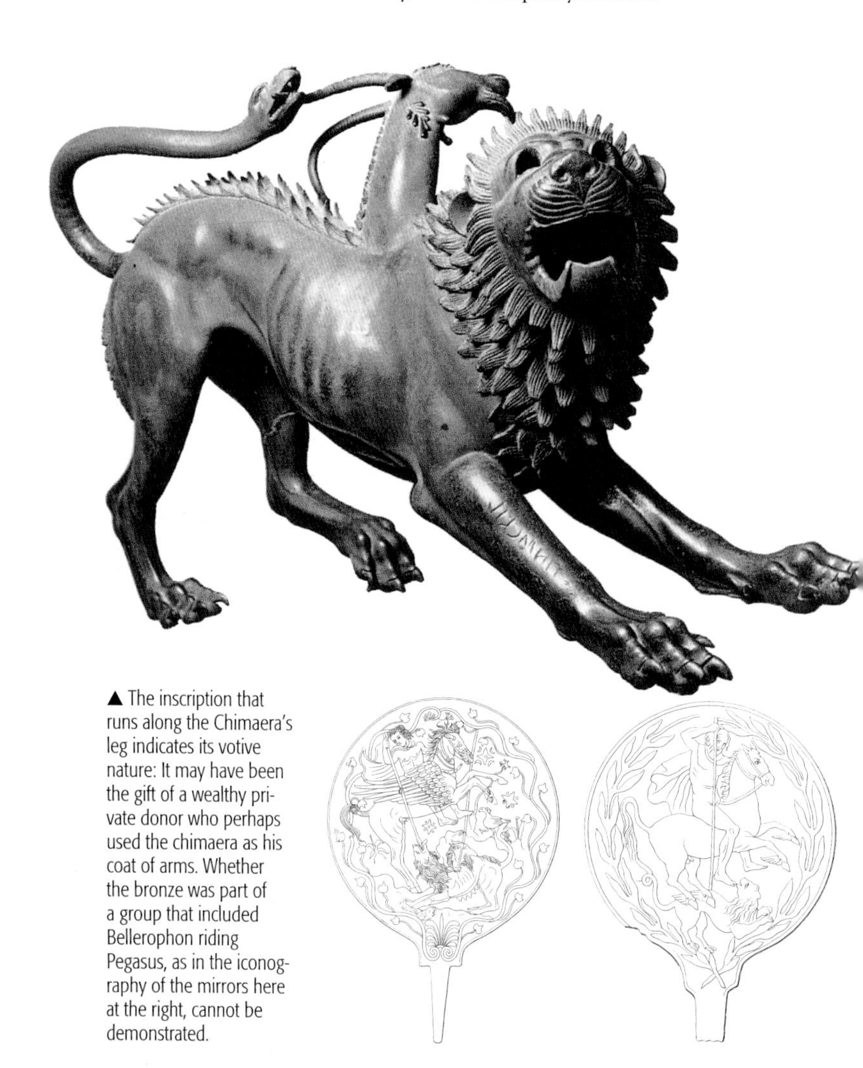

▲ The inscription that runs along the Chimaera's leg indicates its votive nature: It may have been the gift of a wealthy private donor who perhaps used the chimaera as his coat of arms. Whether the bronze was part of a group that included Bellerophon riding Pegasus, as in the iconography of the mirrors here at the right, cannot be demonstrated.

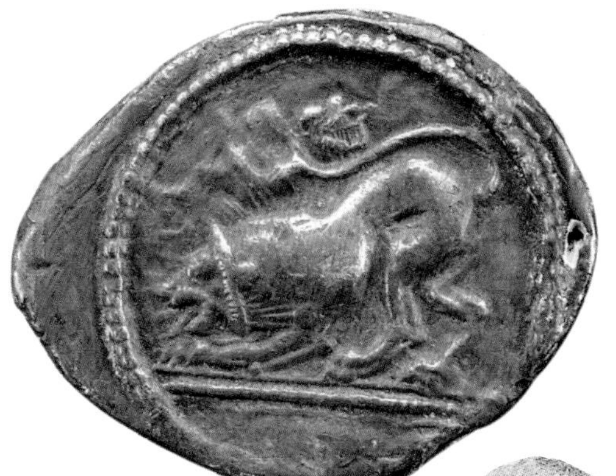

◀ Silver coin from the late fifth century B.C., from Populonia. Florence, Museo Archeologico. This depiction of a lion, which the coin displays on one side, is an ancestor of the Chimaera in its attitude and pose. The image evidently took on heraldic meaning.

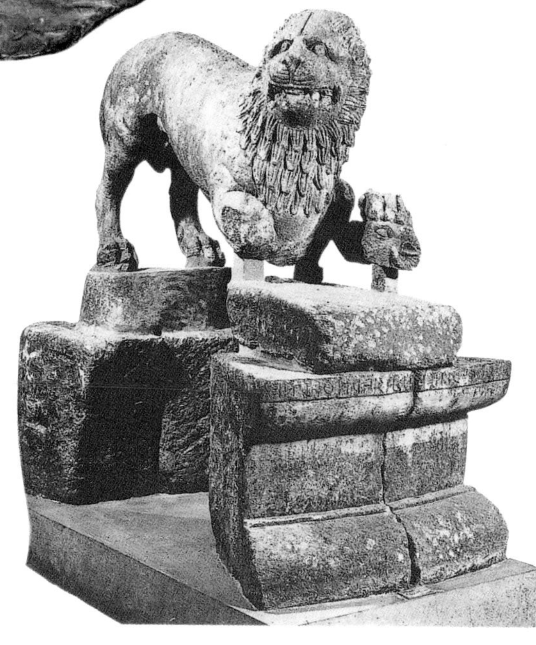

▶ Sepulchral statue of a lion from Tuscania, from the middle of the fourth century B.C. Florence, Museo Archeologico. Its anatomical details make this work the closest in iconography to the Chimaera. Its gnashing jaws, the mane formed of six concentric circles of flaming locks, its clawed paws, and its pose are the most obvious references to archaisms with roots in Magna Graecia, where this work was once mistakenly thought to have originated.

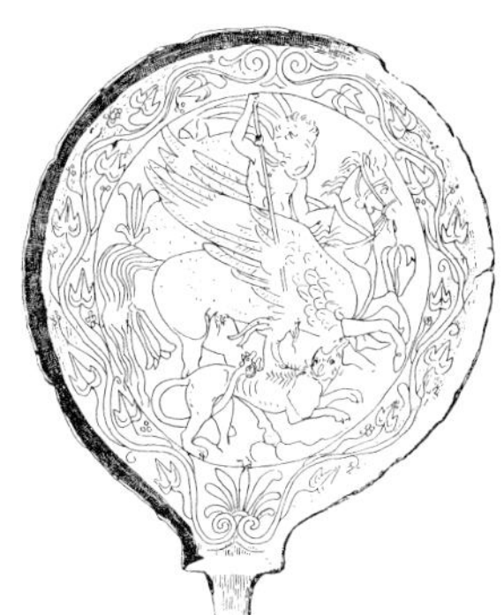

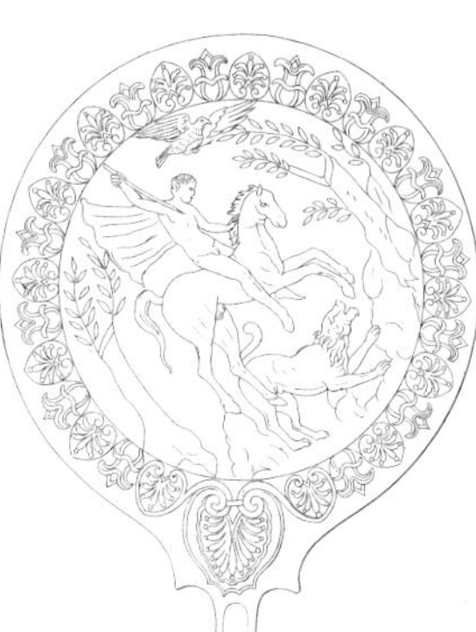

◀ The myth of Bellerophon and the Chimaera was quite popular with Faliscan and Vulcian vase painters of the fourth century B.C. and in depictions on mirrors from the same region, such as those reproduced at left. The leonine features of the Chimaera seem heightened in these visual records.

Aristocracy and the Middle Class at Tarquinia

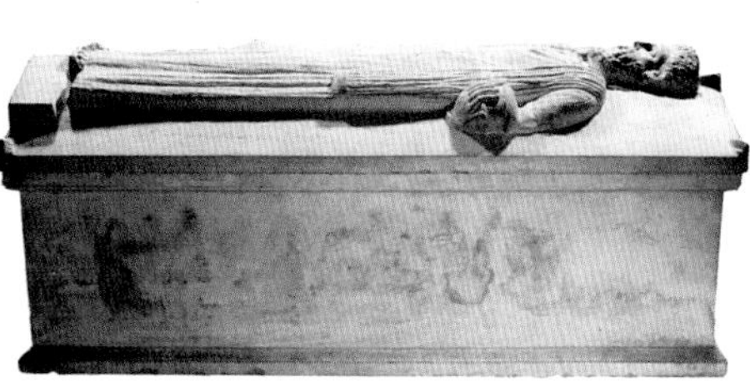

▲ The Sarcophagus of the Priest, Parian marble, 360–350 B.C. Tarquinia, Museo Archeologico. On the sloping lid, the deceased is portrayed carrying out a religious ritual. He wears a long-sleeved gown, hair styled in locks, and a curly beard. This high-quality work gives proof of the Tarquinian aristocracy's vitality.

The southern cities' loss of maritime supremacy set off a socioeconomic crisis. It caused the aged Tarquinian oligarchy to seek out, for its own survival, new resources in rural areas that had previously been deserted during demographic concentrations in urban areas. Thus, between the end of the fifth and beginning of the fourth centuries B.C., the repopulation of the countryside accelerated through the founding of new settlements or by the resettling of deserted areas. An arrangement of satellite cities around Tarquinia—Ferento, Tuscania, Norchia, and Castel d'Asso are the most well known—ensured both military security and food supplies, thanks to numerous farms. Members of the great aristocratic families attended the foundations of these colonies, and they depended upon the citizens of subordinate classes, either servants or *clientes,* the first nucleus of a middle class, to whom they distributed lands and conceded certain civil rights. The administration of public and religious power and land ownership, which had been the prerogatives of the oligarchic aristocracy, were increasingly shared with the intermediate classes through successive social reforms. The middle class, legitimized by a languishing aristocracy, expressed their new status through new figurative themes in the great underground burial chambers.

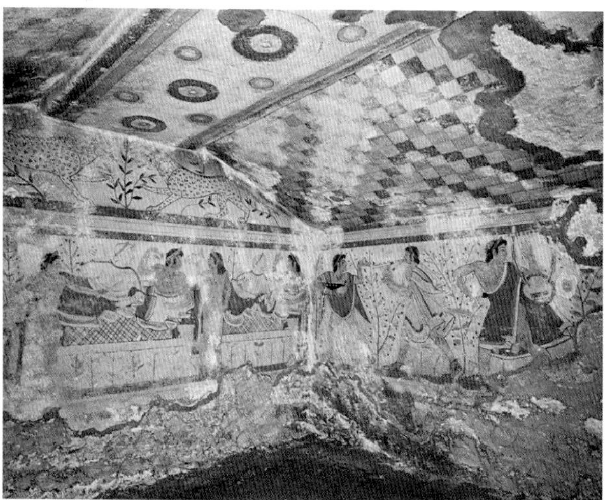

◄ The right wall of the Tomb of the Leopards, with a detail of the pediment for which the tomb is named, 480–470 B.C. Tarquinia. It is an example of late self-portraiture of the elites and their Greek aristocratic ideals, fixed within the canonial subjects of the symposium and the dance.

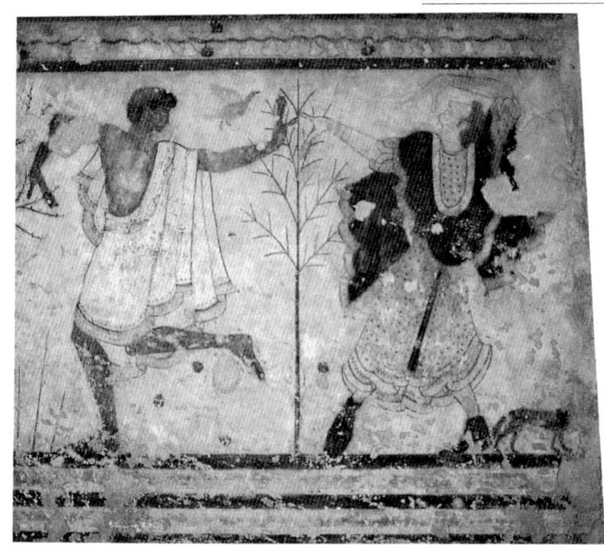

▶ Detail of the right wall of the Tomb of the Triclinium, 480–470 B.C., Tarquinia. In this tomb, alongside the Dionysian atmosphere of the dancers, the Archaic figurative repertory of felines—a symbol of the inevitability of death—is updated by the presence on the scene of two riders who have been identified as the Dioscuri. Their appearance introduces the representation of the afterlife.

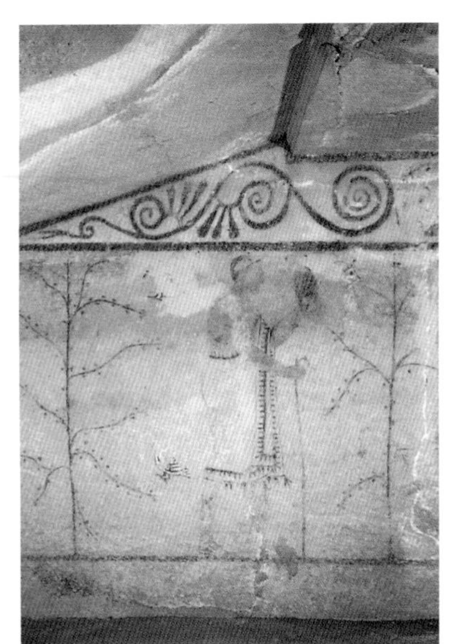

◀ Back wall of the Tomb of the Gorgoneion, 475 B.C., Tarquinia. Here the figurative language has been enhanced by a new measure, as evidenced by the rare garden scene, far removed from the festive Archaic atmosphere. The painted figures commingle with relatives under the tympanum of a *naiskos,* whose elegant Geometric volutes replace the already stereotypical felines.

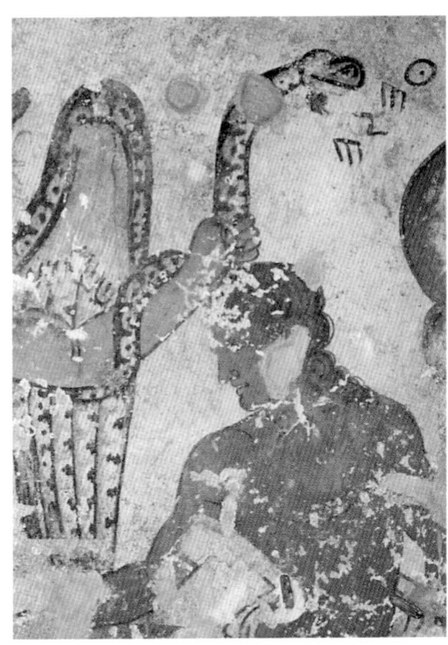

▶ The arm of Tuchulcha, a frightening Etruscan demon, wrapped by serpents. Detail from the right wall of the Tomb of the Underworld II, 425–400 B.C., Tarquinia. The changed sociopolitical context caused the nobility to take renewed pride in their status and to restore the great burial chambers to their royal sumptuousness, transforming them into the very kingdom of Hades and Persephone.

Classical Era Pottery

In Athenian red-figure pottery, figures were outlined with black slip (or paint). The year 480 B.C. marks the beginning of red-figure Etruscan pottery production. Oxidation during firing created the typical reddish color of the impasto. Etruscan red-figure, by contrast, was made by painting over the black surface with red paint for interior graffito details, or applying another color upon the painted surface. The reason for this choice of methods, which was more economical than the Attic method, was probably that Tuscan clay oxidized differently from the Greek variety and did not reach the desired red-orange color. It certainly was not due to a lack of skill, for during the initial phase of red-figure there were many Greek heads of workshops and many foreign potters who were children of Etruscanized Greeks through marriage: The signature "Arnth Praxias" evokes both origins. Vulci was the place of experimentation; a rich line of vase-painting is attributed to Chiusi during the course of the fifth century; and Falerii Veteres offered its own distinct history of this pottery's evolution.

▼ The cup of Aulus Vibenna, fourth century B.C. Paris, Musée Rodin. Inside on the medallion are two satyrs, with the one on the left carrying a wineskin on his back. The subjects are those of Attic pottery and are comparable to a cup from the school of Douris.

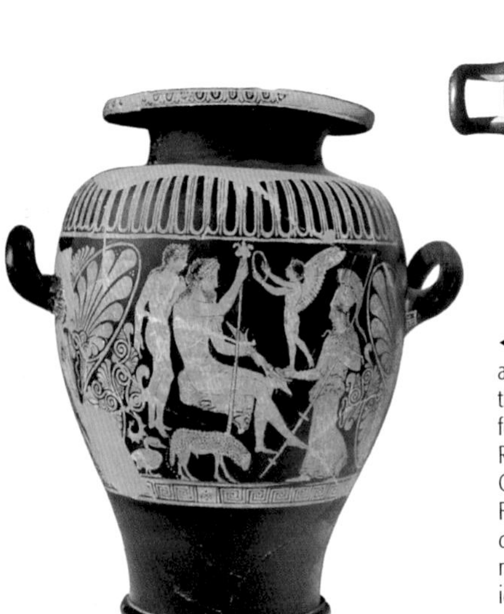

◀ The Diespater Painter, a Faliscan *stamnos* from the beginning of the fourth century B.C. Rome, Museo di Villa Giulia. This phase of Faliscan Attic production draws on a mythological repertory that is rich in ideological content.

▶ Black-figure amphora showing the Judgment of Paris from Vulci, 470 B.C. Berlin, Staatliche Museen. The subject integrates Attic red-figure innovations such as an interest in anatomy and space.

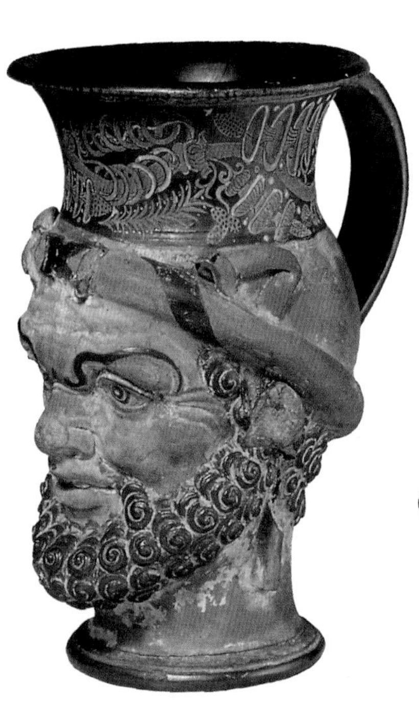

◀ Head-*kantharos,* a vase configured as a silenus, by the Montediano painter, 350 B.C. Paris, Musée du Petit Palais. Characteristic of Etruscan workshops was their specialization in particular vase shape.

▼ The Argonaut Painter, an Etruscan red-figure krater from Chiusi, from the second half of the fifth century B.C. Florence, Museo Archeologico. Italiot features are present in the nude masculine figures, which have been arranged in a cross pattern in the manner of the Protolucanian Amykos Painter.

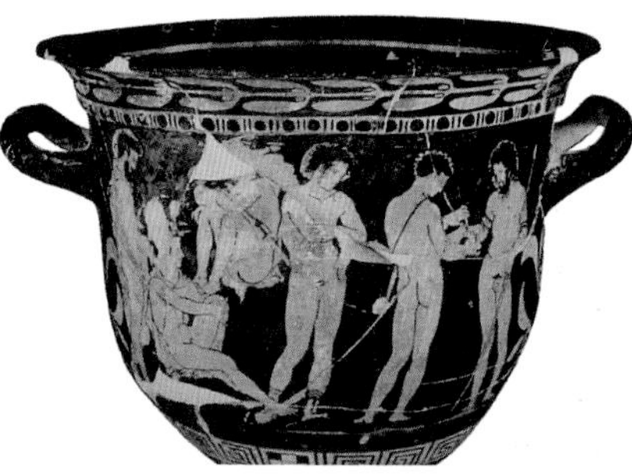

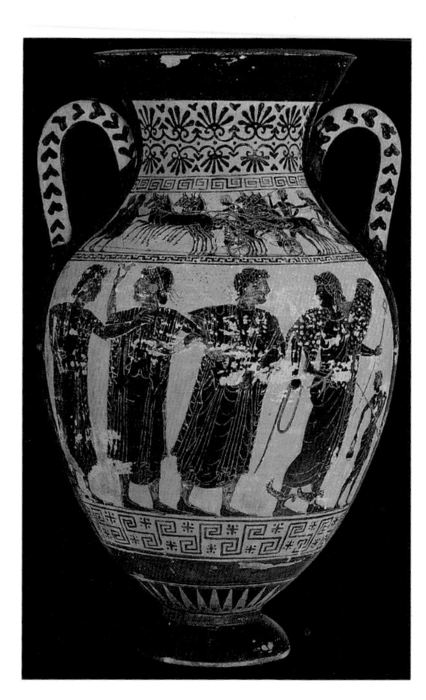

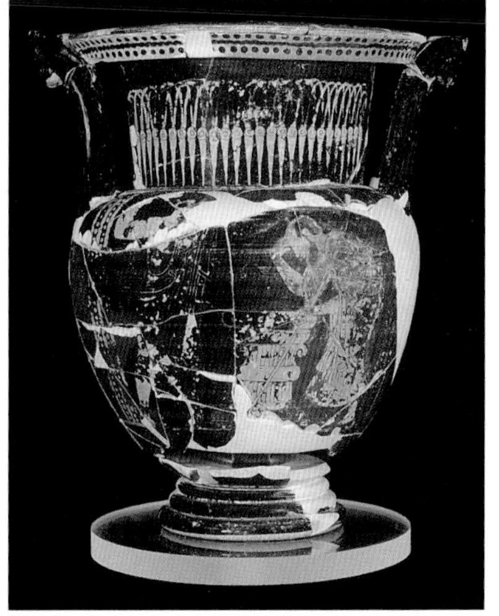

▲ The Bargagli Painter (attributed), a painted column-krater from a workshop of Chiusi, from the middle of the fifth century B.C. Chiusi, Museo Archeologico. The artist was a follower of the Vulcian Praxias. The krater shows obscure ritual scenes.

Currency and the City-States

Before the Classical period, commercial transactions along the Tyrrhenian coast were carried out without the use of money. Contact with the Greek community had the effect of introducing money as a theoretical principle, without there being an actual corresponding unit of currency. The earliest coinage has been located in two regions of Etruria: the metalliferous area of Populonia and the Vulcian region. Populonia, which played a significant role in trade on the Tyrrhenian Sea and was, beginning in 453 B.C., the target of Syracusan pirate raids, was forced to provide its own currency in order to pay for troops and garrisons. Vulci, on the other hand, needed money in order to carry out its commercial role as a center for receiving and sorting luxury goods. These first coin series had limited areas of circulation and scarce production, so much so that one theory, supported by legends leading back to the nobility, maintains that they were not truly national mints. Rather, their production was dictated by a politics of acquisition on the part of aristocrats, who represented themselves with heraldic images. The first public issue, intended to affirm a common political consciousness, was that of Populonia.

▼ Silver stater from Populonia. London, The British Museum. On the front of the coin is a Gorgon head; the reverse bears an X, which marks its worth, and a legend signifying the *Pupluna* and *Puplana* ethnic groups.

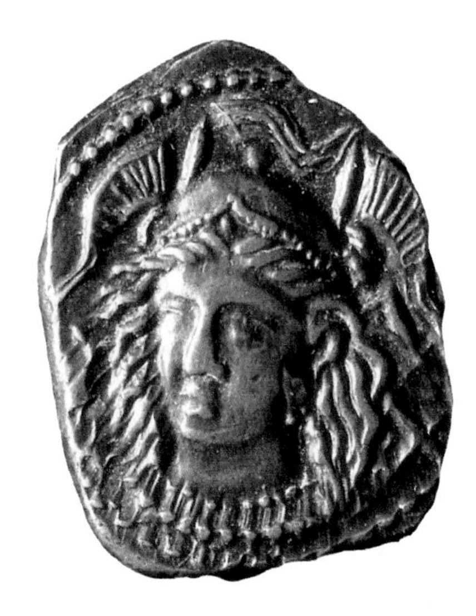

◀ Silver didrachma from Populonia. London, The British Museum. This silver coin series is attributed to the metalliferous area of Populonia. It featured a smooth back, and on the front, images of boars, Chimaerae, sea lions, and lion protomes. This example from the fourth century B.C. shows a three-quarter view of Athena and was part of a special issue of coins.

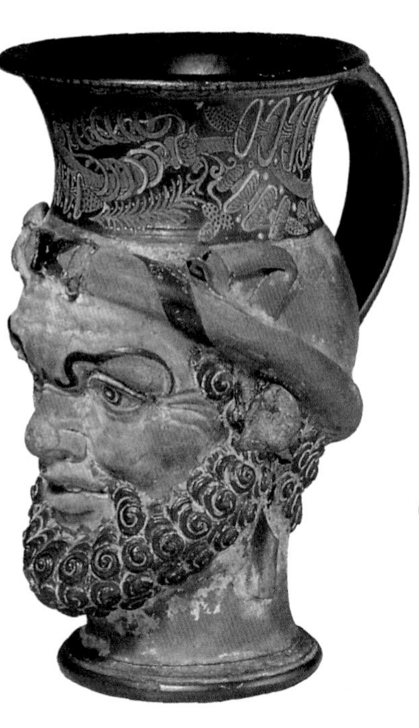

◀ Head-*kantharos,* a vase configured as a silenus, by the Montediano painter, 350 B.C. Paris, Musée du Petit Palais. Characteristic of Etruscan workshops was their specialization in particular vase shape.

▼ The Argonaut Painter, an Etruscan red-figure krater from Chiusi, from the second half of the fifth century B.C. Florence, Museo Archeologico. Italiot features are present in the nude masculine figures, which have been arranged in a cross pattern in the manner of the Protolucanian Amykos Painter.

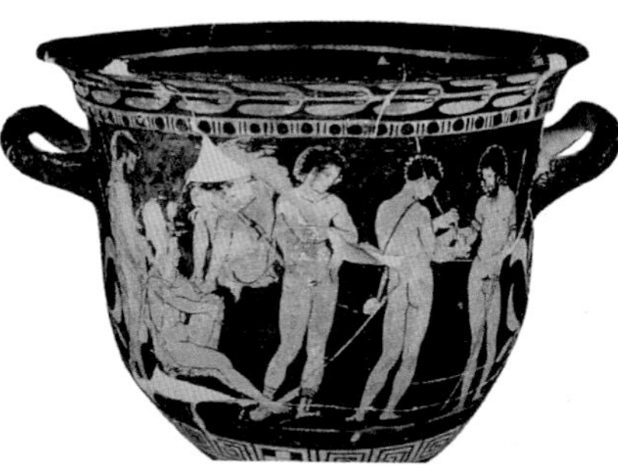

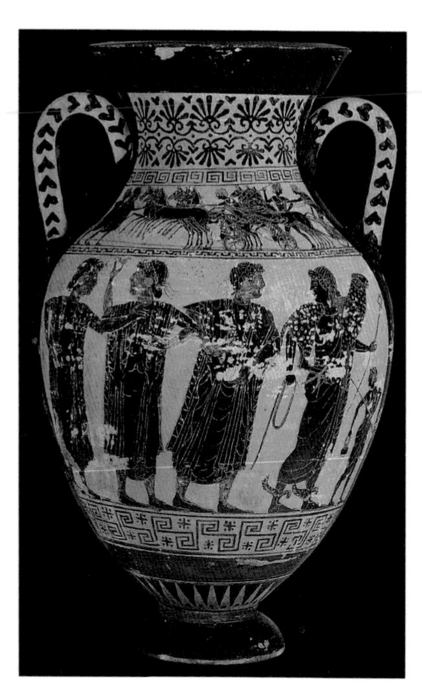

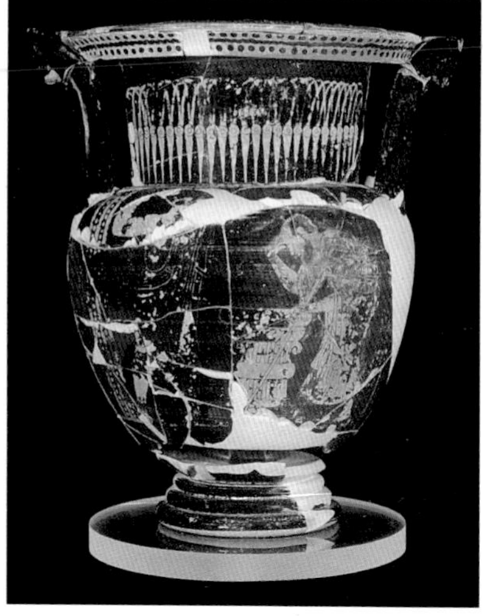

▲ The Bargagli Painter (attributed), a painted column-krater from a workshop of Chiusi, from the middle of the fifth century B.C. Chiusi, Museo Archeologico. The artist was a follower of the Vulcian Praxias. The krater shows obscure ritual scenes.

Gens and *Familia*

▶ Panel from the right wall of the François Tomb in Vulci, from the middle of the fourth century B.C. Rome, Museo Torlonia. Vel Saties, wearing a red toga, appears with a small servant named Arnza, who kneels on the ground wearing a light, bordered toga. The accumulation of wealth brought with it the possession of servants and slaves.

The power of the Etruscan aristocracy was mainly based on the economic and social structure of the *gens,* in which the acting head of the clan drew the highest earnings from the land. The structure of the nobility was initially made up via blood-ties; later it expanded to include "family" in the Latin sense of the word, that is, relations forged through private solidarity and patronage. Livy speaks of Etruscan *gentes* formed by *cognati*—blood relations—*sodales,* and *clientis.* The latter was a circle of people gravitating around a powerful patron, offering him services in return for protection, while *sodales* were the brothers-in-arms of the patron and his blood relations. The description of the *gens* supplied by the historian Dionysius of Halikarnassos is completely analogous. It is interesting to note how the Etruscan word for *sodales (etera),* which in texts sometimes appears connected to two titles of the military magistracy, derived from the Greek word *hetairos,* which is semantically linked to "youth" and "brother-in-arms." The solidarity of arms within the *gens* formed the basis of the Hoplite organization (from the Greek *oplon,* "arms," "armor"), an essential instrument for the consolidation of cities.

▼ Panels from the right wall of the François Tomb showing several violent confrontations, from Vulci, middle of the fourth century B.C. Rome, Museo Torlonia. Members of the Vibenna family, Caelius and Aulus, are present with their *sodalis* Mastarna, who has been identified through historic documents as Servius Tullius.

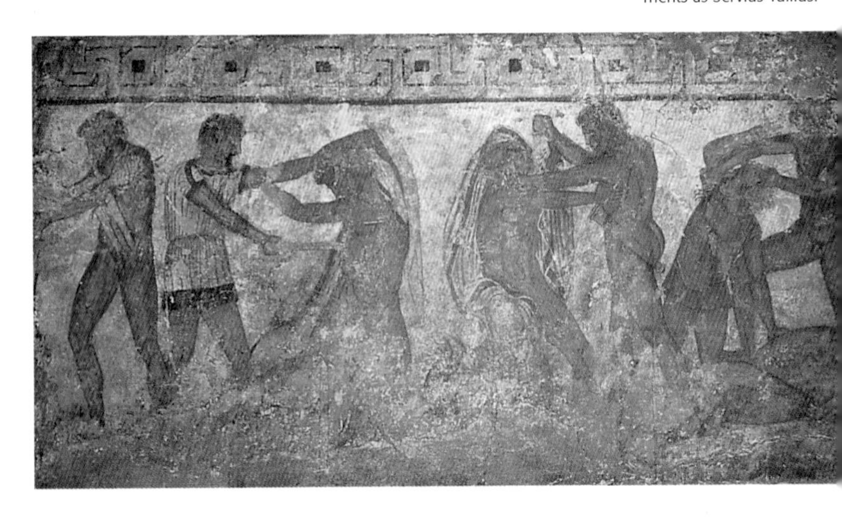

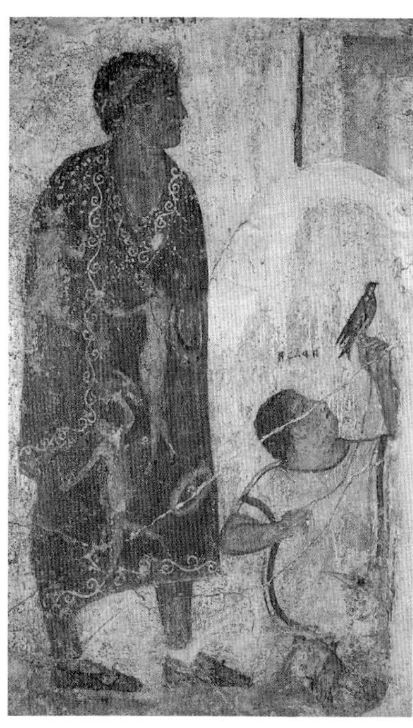

▼ Right wall of the Tomb of the Underworld I, a profile of Velia with a diadem, earrings, and a necklace, 350–325 B.C. Tarquinia. This impressive aristocratic sepulchral complex belonged to two interrelated families, the Spurinnas and the Velchas, whose founder, Velthur Spurinna, headed the contingent that aided Athens against Syracuse.

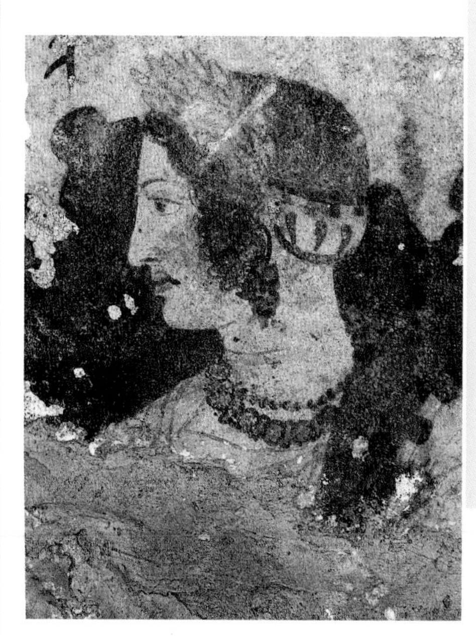

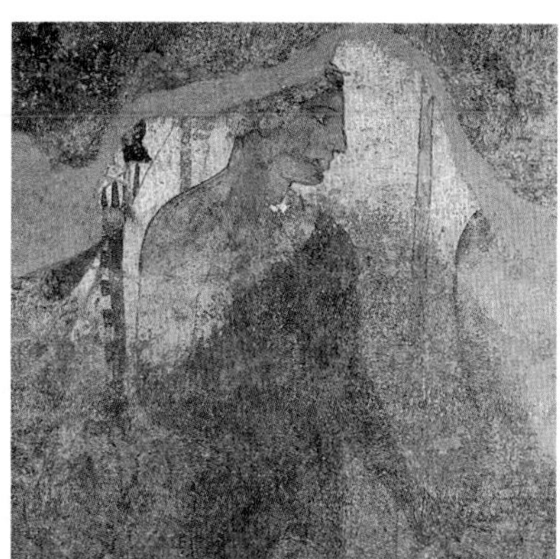

▲ Detail of the right wall of the Golini Tomb I, from the middle of the fourth century B.C. Orvieto, Museo Archeologico. The servant identified here by a written name confirms the relative freedom given to the servant class in Volsinii.

▶ Right wall of the Tomb of the Shields, 325–320 B.C. Tarquinia. A reclining bearded man wearing a crown places his hand on his wife's shoulder. This noble hypogeum contains many genealogical inscriptions.

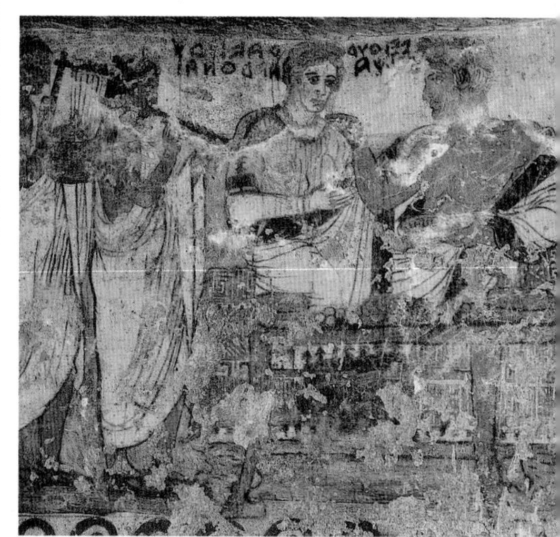

Currency and the City-States

Before the Classical period, commercial transactions along the Tyrrhenian coast were carried out without the use of money. Contact with the Greek community had the effect of introducing money as a theoretical principle, without there being an actual corresponding unit of currency. The earliest coinage has been located in two regions of Etruria: the metalliferous area of Populonia and the Vulcian region. Populonia, which played a significant role in trade on the Tyrrhenian Sea and was, beginning in 453 B.C., the target of Syracusan pirate raids, was forced to provide its own currency in order to pay for troops and garrisons. Vulci, on the other hand, needed money in order to carry out its commercial role as a center for receiving and sorting luxury goods. These first coin series had limited areas of circulation and scarce production, so much so that one theory, supported by legends leading back to the nobility, maintains that they were not truly national mints. Rather, their production was dictated by a politics of acquisition on the part of aristocrats, who represented themselves with heraldic images. The first public issue, intended to affirm a common political consciousness, was that of Populonia.

▼ Silver stater from Populonia. London, The British Museum. On the front of the coin is a Gorgon head; the reverse bears an X, which marks its worth, and a legend signifying the *Pupluna* and *Puplana* ethnic groups.

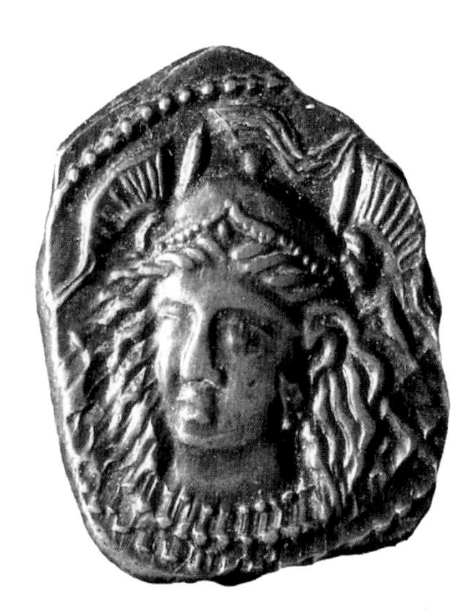

◀ Silver didrachma from Populonia. London, The British Museum. This silver coin series is attributed to the metalliferous area of Populonia. It featured a smooth back, and on the front, images of boars, Chimaerae, sea lions, and lion protomes. This example from the fourth century B.C. shows a three-quarter view of Athena and was part of a special issue of coins.

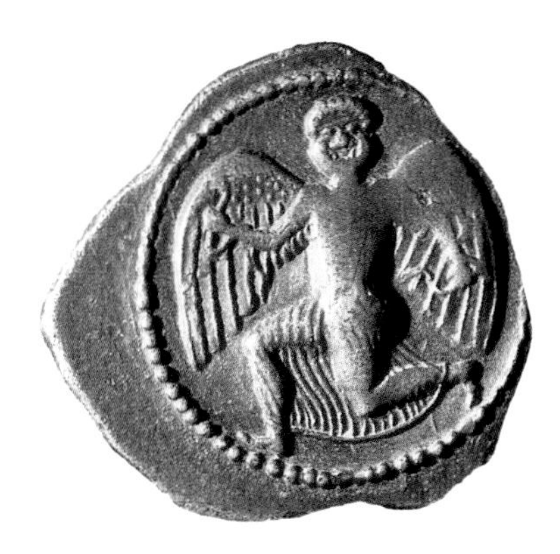

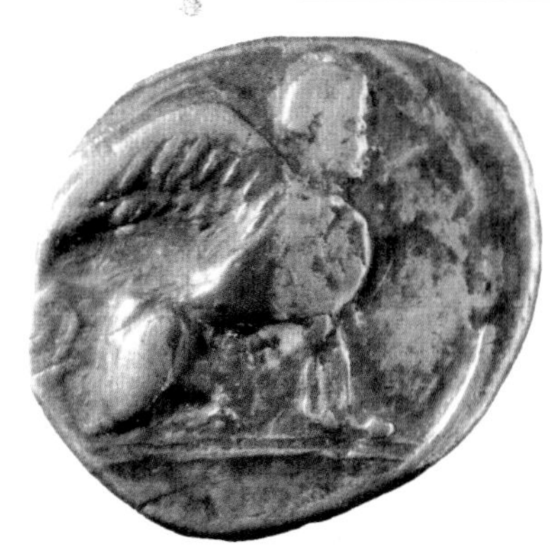

▲ A winged Gorgon running on the front of a Vulcian silver coin from the first half of the fifth century B.C. London, The British Museum. The name "Thezi" appears on the reverse.

▲ A sphinx on the front of a silver Vulcian coin from the middle of the fourth century B.C. Florence, Museo Archeologico. The reverse bears the inscription "Thezi," perhaps the name of the issue's maker or a representative of authority.

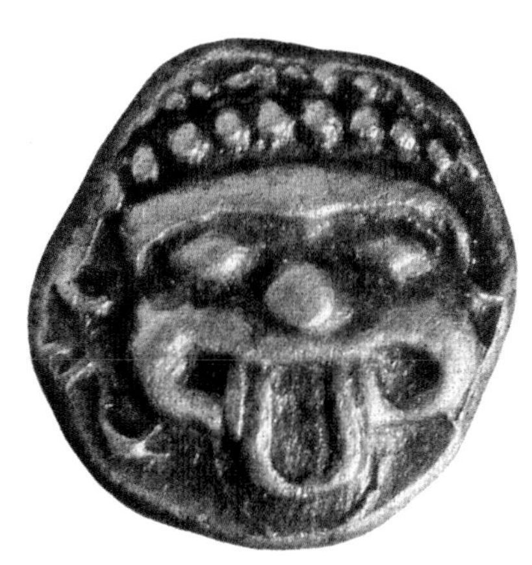

◀ An image of a Gorgon on a divisional silver coin from Volterra, first half of the fifth century B.C. Florence, Museo Archeologico. Weighing little more than half a gram, these coins must have been made for small market transactions.

▼ A nominal cast coin from Volterra showing the two-faced head of Culsu. Volterra, Museo Guarnacci. On the reverse is a club with the inscription "Velathri." This work coincided with the highest stage of craftsmanship in Volterra.

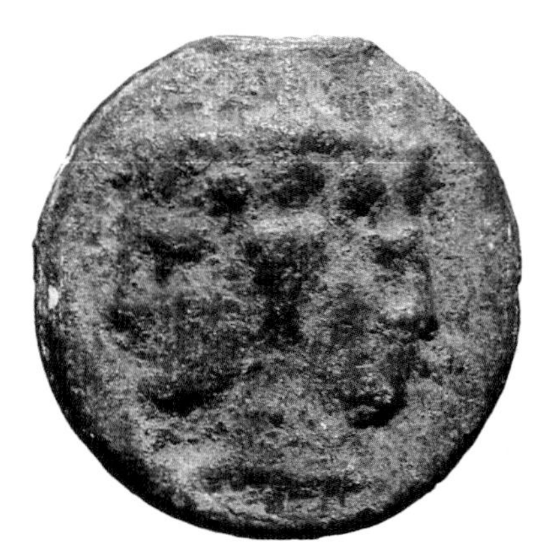

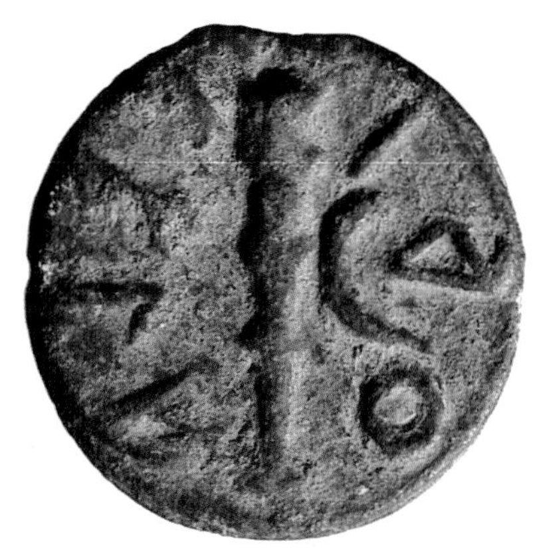

Funerary Crafts

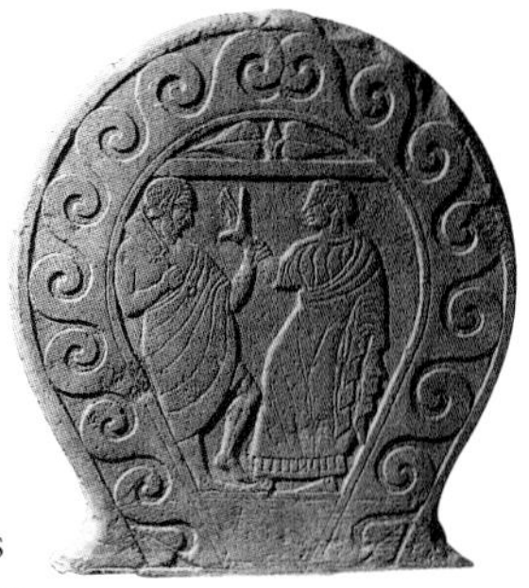

▲ Funerary stela from Bologna, 420–410 B.C. Bologna, Museo Civico Archeologico. A demon holds an oar, an allusion to ferrying, and halts the well-dressed deceased by the arm.

The concept of burial monuments that reflect the physical form of the deceased, even in those regions where the ritual of cremation endured, transformed cinerary urns from their vase shapes into containers with human features. It is no coincidence that in Chiusi, the end of the use of *cippi*—crowns or guards for the cinerary urns themselves—coincided with the progressive development of this new feature of funerary crafts. The ideological reaffirmation of lineage found its material expression in the great cinerary urns that, from the simple thrones of canopic urns, transformed under Hellenism's influence into figures of banqueters in *pietra fetida*. The declining population in the Chiusi countryside brought to light the archaic economic structures that had survived in those few locations where a class of magnates had persisted and continued to represent themselves through these high-quality monuments. In the northern regions, at Bologna, the tradition was perpetuated of funerary stelae in horseshoe-shaped stones decorated with flattened figures derived from the repertory of Attic potters after the middle of the fifth century B.C. Meanwhile, the production of stone sarcophagi in the district of Tarquinia continued.

▼ Cinerary statue in *pietra fetida* from Chianciano, 400 B.C. Florence, Museo Archeologico. Vanth sits on a *kline* next to the deceased, who wears a crown and reclines at a banquet.

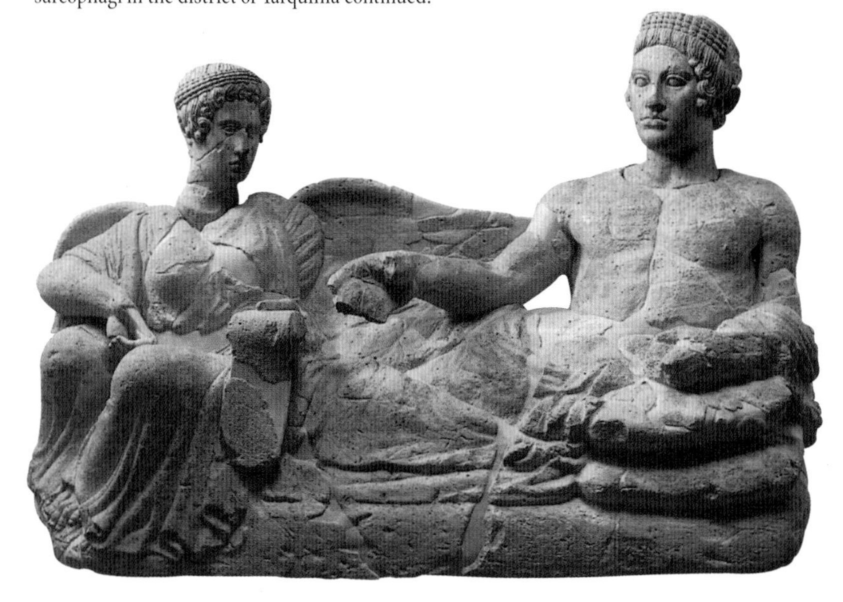

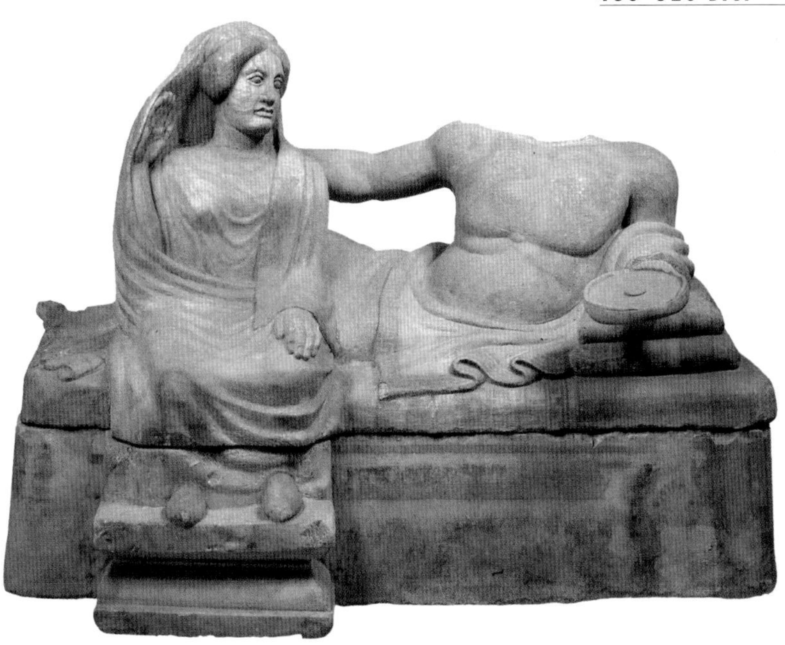

▲ Painted alabaster cinerary urn from Città della Pieve, first half of the fourth century B.C. Florence, Museo Archeologico. This is a late work of Chiusi funerary sculpture. The woman seated at the feet of the deceased, shown unveiling herself on their wedding night, is surely his wife and not a demon from the afterlife. The box has two chambers to accommodate the bodies of both spouses.

▼ Nenfro sarcophagus from Tuscania, 300 B.C. Florence, Museo Archeologico. The representation of the deceased man on the lid is partly recumbent; his folded cloak has been rendered in a mannerist fashion. This work was made by itinerant Tarquinian artisans.

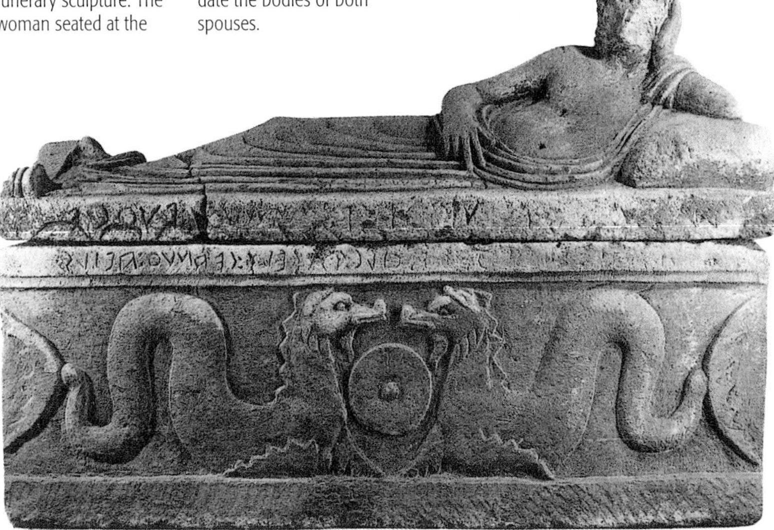

Rock Necropolises

The necropolises carved from living rocks located in the areas surrounding the great southern coastal cities, specifically in the territory of Cerveteri, Tarquinia, and Vulci, represent the most revealing artistic expressions of inland Etruria. The development of this type of sepulchre, which is distinguished from the Orientalizing or Archaic burial chamber by its articulated exteriors, was not continuous over time. Two distinct periods in two separate territorial areas stand out: In the Archaic period, the necropolises of San Giuliano and Blera featured cube tombs with sloped roofs and upper arcades; in the Hellenistic period the more northern areas of Castel d'Asso and Norchia had temple-like tombs. From a geographical and topographical point of view, the cities that adopted this type of sepulchre had certain consistent features: settlements situated on high plateaus of steeply sloped tufa with watercourses in the valley below, which provided excellent natural protection as well as guaranteeing a water supply. The economic strengthening of these regions was directly stimulated by crises in the urban areas from which they sprang. The movement toward the countryside demonstrates the continuous dialectic relationship between city and country.

▼ Cube tombs arranged on terraces facing the Pile trench, Norchia necropolis. *Below,* burial chambers detached from the rock and crowned with cornices of various shapes.

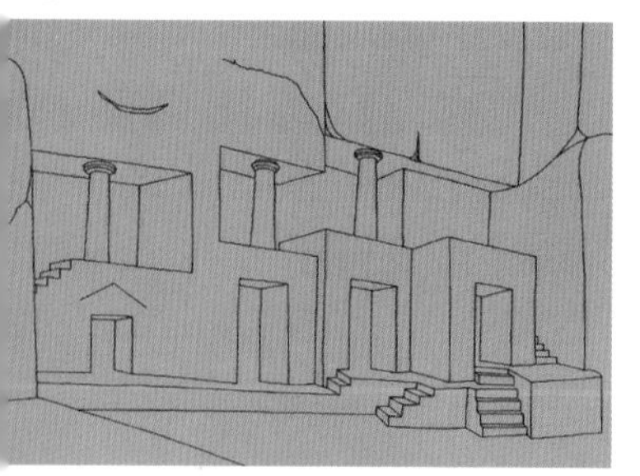

▲ A reconstruction of tombs with upper arcades from the necropolis of San Giuliano. They featured a facade with a funerary chamber, an upper opening with a single column, and external stairs.

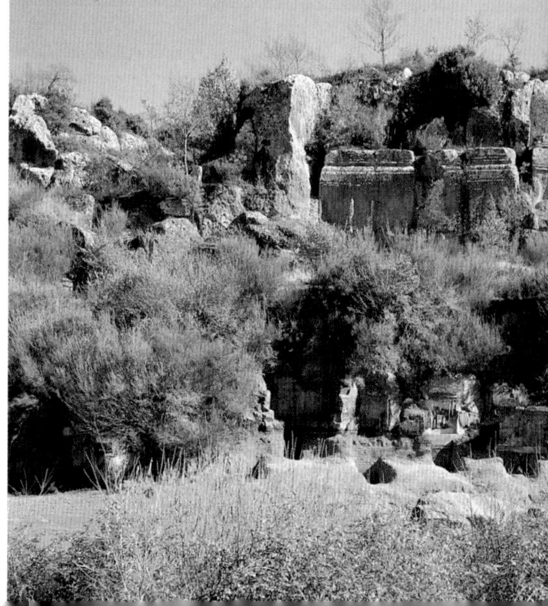

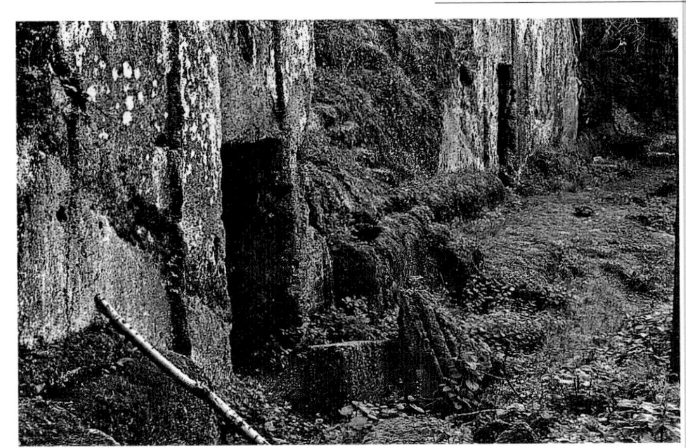

▶ Detail of the entrance to a burial chamber, San Giuliano necropolis. Situated within a block of tombs at road level, this design is typical of an earlier time. A later formula stipulated digging the burial chamber deeper and transforming the real entrance into a symbolic false door. The upper arcade was set aside for funerary rites.

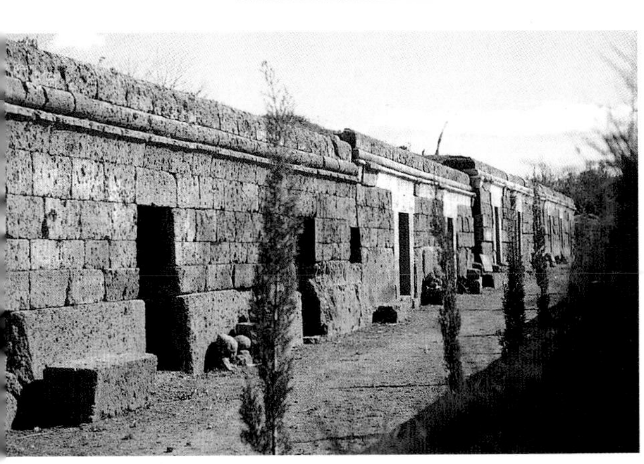

◀ Completed cube tombs at the Banditaccia necropolis, from the middle of the sixth century B.C., Cerveteri. Decorated with cornices and doorways, these were the forerunners of rock tombs.

▼ A double tomb with a partly assembled facade, from the end of the fourth century B.C., Cerveteri. There are false doors and what seems to be a false cube tomb.

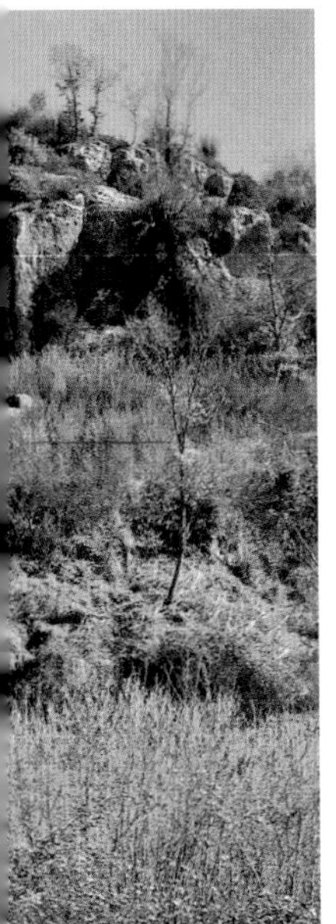

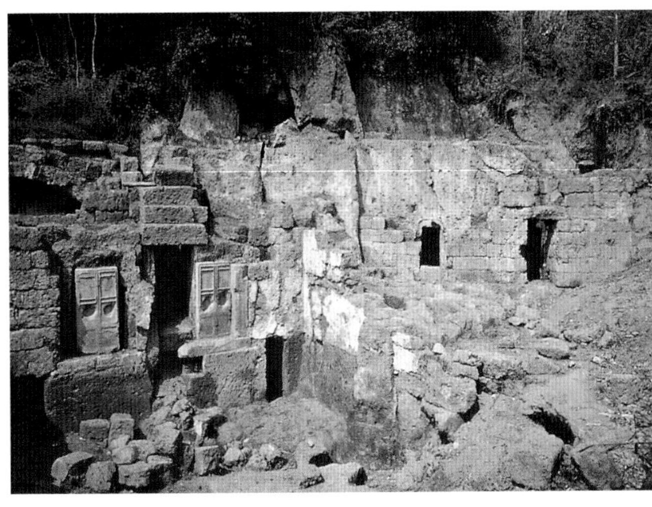

Toward Hellenism

The years between Veii first falling to Rome in 396 B.C. and the Roman destruction of Volsinii in 265 were peculiar, both for the evolution of social sensitivity toward the subordinate classes that preceded true Romanization and for the contextual spread of Hellenistic figurative types. The shift of patronage from the coastal metropolises at their apogee toward inland cities took place along trajectories from the heart of the region: east toward Perugia and south toward Volsinii, Falerii, and the territories of Lazio. Lazio was the closest to Rome, making that area the most prolific and paradigmatic artistically. The moderation of late Classicism shown in the Belvedere temple's pediments opened the way for a softening of interpretation that can be seen in terra-cotta high reliefs at Falerii. These are comparable to numerous fragments of pedimental figures that originated at a temple in Tivoli, the first examples of figurative decorations upon the architrave. Reminders of the great Greek sculptors Lysippus, Praxiteles, and Skopas animate these figures. Stone sculpture in the great marble sarcophagi of Tarquinia and Volsinii began to anticipate the most recurring leitmotives of Hellenistic art: closed compositions, contrasts of light and shade, and glimpses of shields and legs that emerge from an almost dissolved state in the background.

▶ Bronze statuette of a woman holding an offering, provenance unknown, dating to about 300 B.C. Florence, Museo Archeologico. The hairstyle has radial locks, and the soft and flexible movement of the body recalls works by Lysippus.

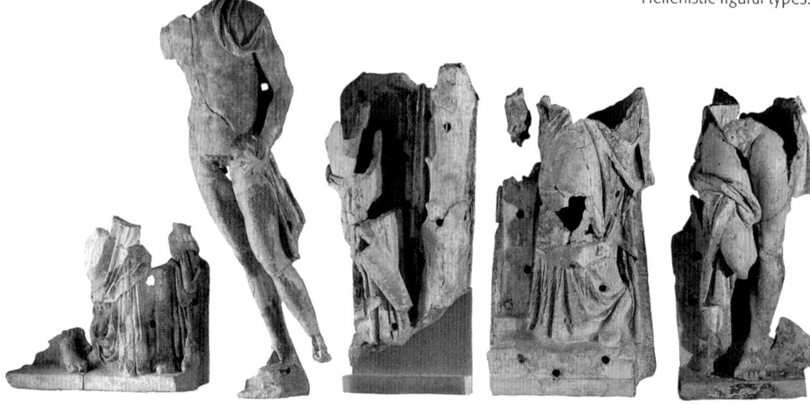

▼ High-relief figures from the pediment of a temple in Tivoli, middle of the fourth century B.C. Vatican City, Museo Gregoriano Etrusco. The clinging clothing, the construction of the bodies, and the free leg crossing over the supporting leg and resting on its toes all echo Hellenistic figural types.

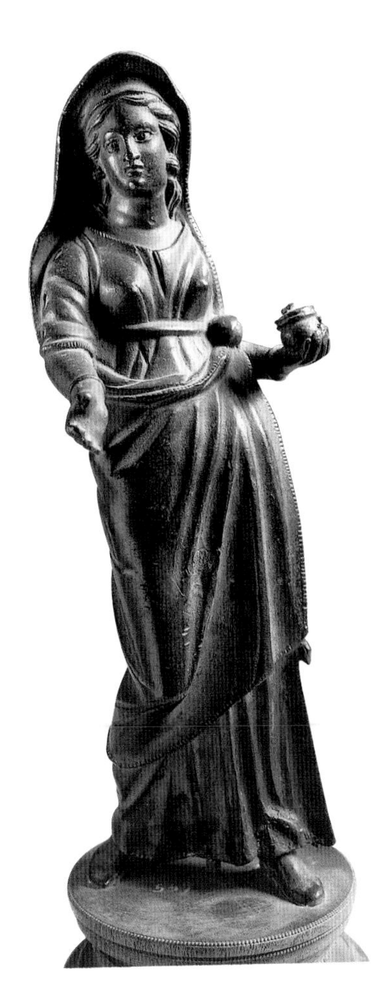

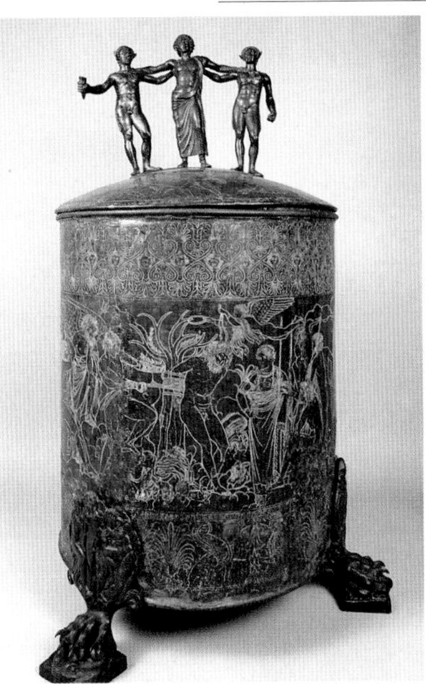

▲ The Ficoroni *cista,* in bronze, from Palestrina, middle of the fourth century B.C. Rome, Museo di Villa Giulia. The figure of Dionysus in its head and rendering of hair is comparable to the woman bringing an offering shown at the left.

▼ Marble sarcophagus showing the Amazonomachy, from Tarquinia, middle of the fourth century B.C. Florence, Museo Archeologico. The foreshortening and the fluidity of light and shade in this simple, closed composition were not received well by the client, who defaced it with a celebratory epigraph.

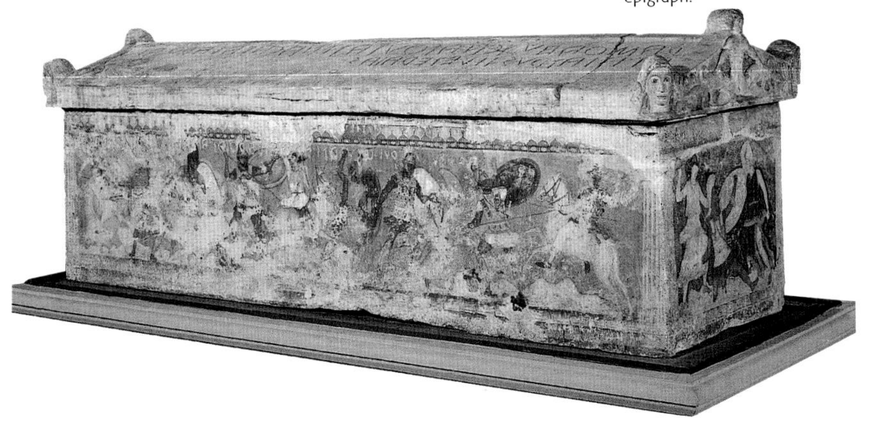

320–327 B.C.

The Tomba del Convegno at the Monterozzi necropolis, from the second half of the second century B.C., Tarquinia

Norchia and Temple Tombs

Temple tombs—typical of the Hellenistic period and displaying an openness to eastern Greek influences—implied great affluence on the part of the patron, relative to what was required for modest tombs with Classical facades. Norchia and Sovana are the sites that house the most celebrated examples of such architecture. The decorative qualities of the sacred Etruscan buildings were heightened by eastern Greek influences. The two fused together, giving life to theatrical structures that are quite suggestive and enriched with sculpted pediments, friezes, capitals, and fluted columns.

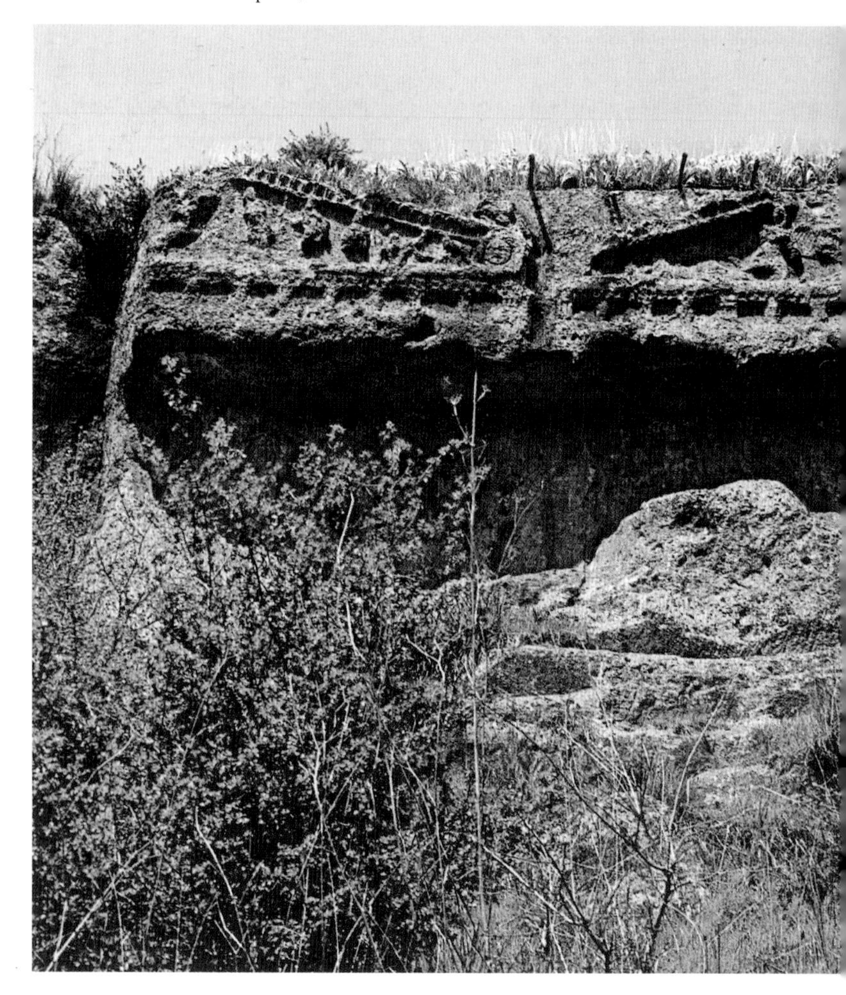

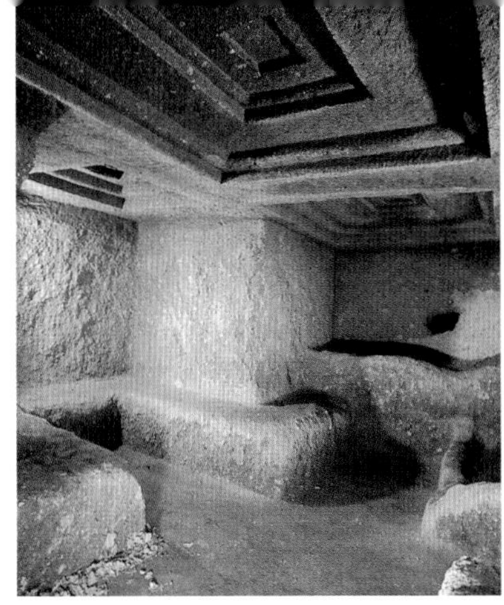

◀ Detail of the coffered ceiling in a burial chamber, Sovana, fourth century B.C. The realistic rendering of tomb interiors according to the canons of domestic architecture is typical of rock tombs from the late Archaic period, whose latest manifestations included gabled roofs.

These were surpassed in Sovana and Tarquinia with the introduction of flat roofs and coffered ceilings. The sepulcher's symbolic and commemorative values are expressed through the rich architecture of the facade, which celebrated the wealth of the deceased.

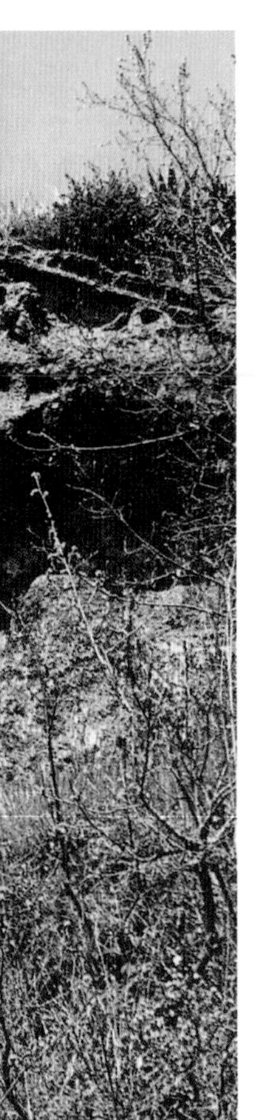

▶ The Hildebrand Tomb, Sovana, from the end of the fourth to the beginning of the third centuries B.C. Detail of a fluted Doric column with a capital and double torus base. This impressive monument, typical of Norchia, seems to imitate in its plan a peripteral temple without a posticum (rear portico). The burial chamber, which can be accessed through a long stairway carved from the rock, contained a series of sarcophagi.

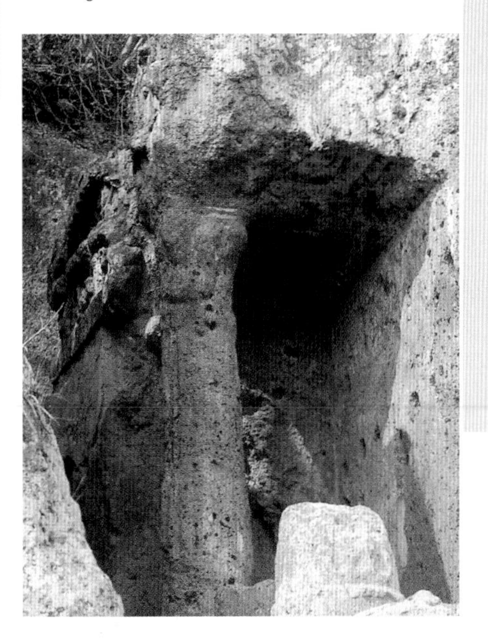

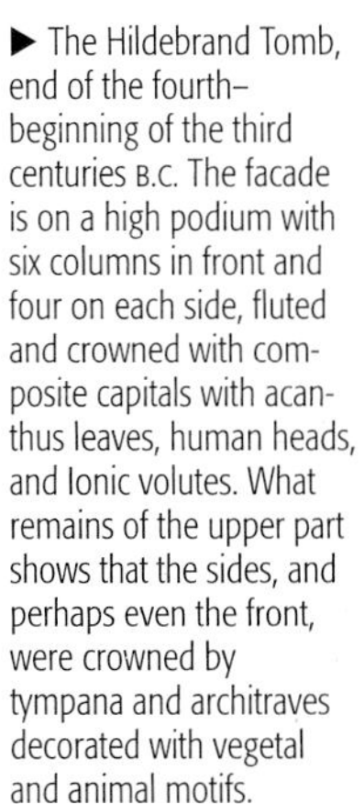

▶ The Hildebrand Tomb, end of the fourth–beginning of the third centuries B.C. The facade is on a high podium with six columns in front and four on each side, fluted and crowned with composite capitals with acanthus leaves, human heads, and Ionic volutes. What remains of the upper part shows that the sides, and perhaps even the front, were crowned by tympana and architraves decorated with vegetal and animal motifs.

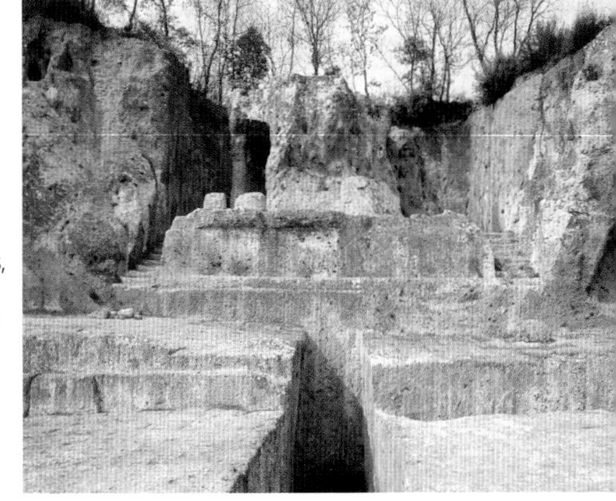

The Great Conflict and the "*Pax*" *Romana*

The Roman conquest of Veii in 396 B.C. was the first blow to Etruscan hegemony, leading to important repercussions within its sociopolitical order: the loss of the federal context that was the ancient polis, and the consolidation of rebel plebs in the heart of Etruria. In 358 the Tarquinian magistrate Aulus Spurinna reestablished forms of republican government and weakened prior agreements between Cerveteri and Rome, through which Cerveteri had become a Roman outpost against the Gauls. Tarquinia then became head of the confederation, guardian of the oligarchy, and enemy to Rome. Forty years of peace and treaties followed. In 311 it was the turn of Perugia and Volsinii to guide the politics of the league. Roman forays northward shattered Etruscan dominance on the peninsula; in 294 Roselle fell, Falerii in 293; Tarquinia was defeated in 283, Volsinii in 280, and Cerveteri in 273. The imposed *pax* radicalized the frontier cities to the north in the hands of small oligarchies, which in the second century would attempt reforms in independent cities in the south. These, however, would be consumed by class conflict, while the colonized areas enjoyed social peace.

▼ Etruscan mirror from the end of the fourth century B.C. Bloomington, Indiana University Art Museum. Sophisticated mythological scenes are illustrated with critical detachment, a sign of intermingling between the middle classes and more traditional higher ones.

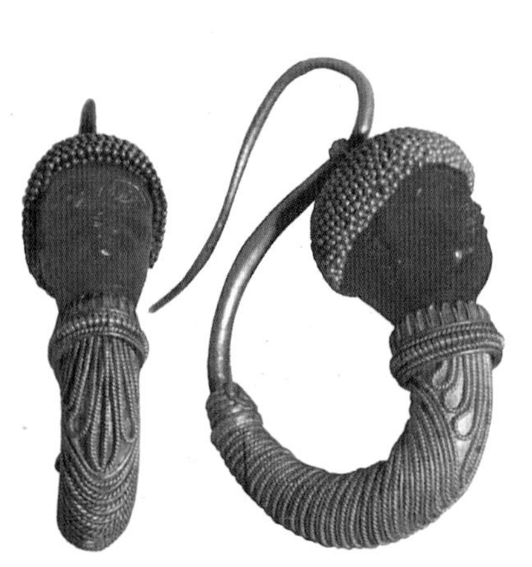

◀ Gold and amber earrings with the heads of Africans, third century B.C. Rome, Museo di Villa Giulia. The circular shape of the earring, with decorative motifs in granulation, was well known in the Macedonian areas. These objects were connected to the brief rebirth of the provincial aristocracy, which was sensitive to Hellenistic exoticism.

▶ Black-painted *hydria* from the Volterran workshop of Malacena, third century B.C. Volterra, Museo Guarnacci. This shop produced practical ceramics, although they were also pieces of great prestige, created according to typically Hellenistic technical and commercial tastes.

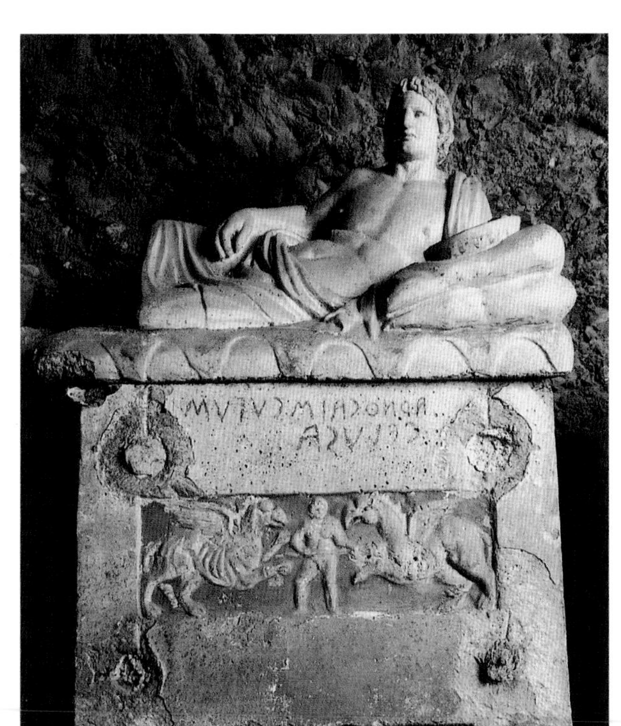

◀ The travertine urn of Arnth Cutu, from Monteluce, third century B.C. Perugia, Museo Archeologico. A naked, armed youth is shown at center, defending himself against two griffins. The Cutu were a family of freed servants who were recognized by the nobles of the city. This urn is from the same studio that produced that of the Volumnii.

▼ Volterran *kelebe* depicting a dwarf trumpeter, from the end of the fourth century B.C. Cole Val d'Elsa, Museo Archeologico. A factory that produced *kelebai* has been discovered in Volterra. Vessels of this type constitute one of the most consistent groups of Etruscan red-figure ceramics from the second half of the fourth century.

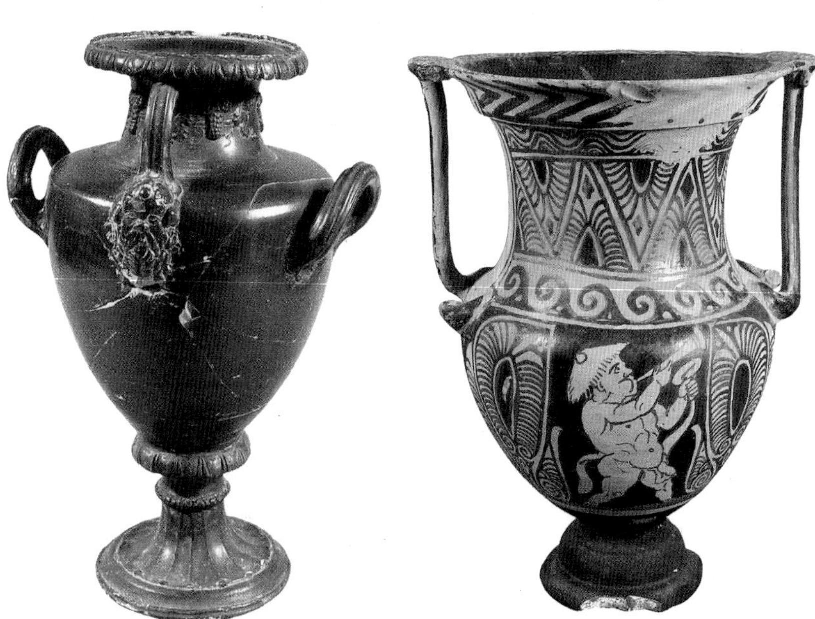

Defensive Architecture

The territory's diverse topography determined the choice of defensive techniques in Etruscan cities. The poleis of the southern regions, founded on plateaus, took advantage of the natural bulwark of the tufaceous valleys at the feet of their strongholds and for a long time did not need true boundary walls. Cities in the northern and inland regions, however, needed to equip themselves with boundary walls built of a variety of local materials: in the north, limestone, travertine, sandstone, and unfired bricks; in the south, tufa. The political situation of the fifth century B.C., and increasingly in the fourth, made the fortification of cities necessary. In the fifth century Tarquinia and Veii constructed boundary walls that were almost seven kilometers (4 miles) long, pierced by up to ten gates. In the third century Rome's impending threat brought an expansion of *opus quadratum*—walls composed of parallelepiped tufa blocks—in Tarquinia, Roselle, Vetulonia, Populonia, and Volterra and the construction of new walls for Vulci, Cerveteri, Perugia, and Bolsena. Sometimes an *agger* (earthwork) was connected to the rampart. The walls of Arezzo, made of unfired bricks, represent an exception to the norm.

▶ The Arco di Augusto, third to second centuries B.C. Perugia. Flanked by two trapezoidal towers, the gate has two levels that are divided by a frieze, with Ionic pilasters and shields framing a blind arch as wide as the gate itself.

▶ The Porta di Giove, third century B.C. Falerii Novi. The walls of regular tufa blocks measure two meters (6.5 ft.) wide by five meters (16 ft.) deep, with a perimeter of two kilometers (1.2 miles). Lookout towers, fifty in all, guarded the most exposed areas.

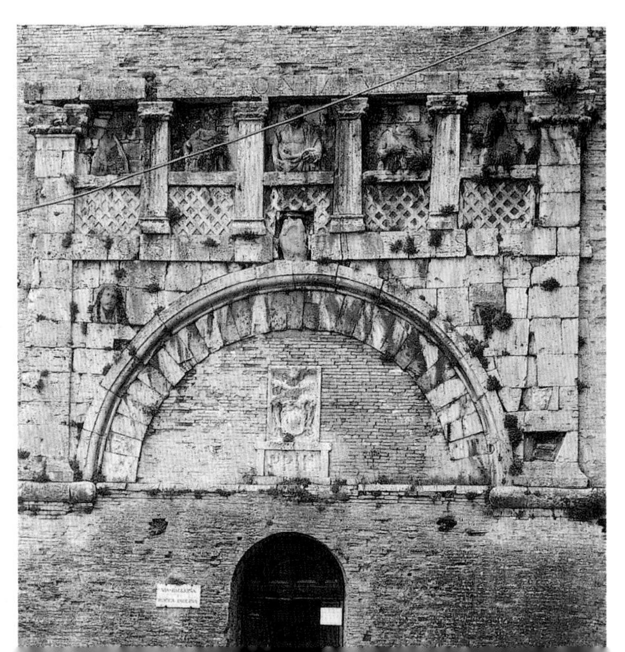

◀ Porta Marzia, third century B.C. Perugia. An arch is surmounted by an ashlar lunette enclosed by an arched lintel and inserted within a two-tiered facade. Two Corinthian pilasters frame a cordoned false loggia divided by four smaller pilasters, between which Jupiter, the Dioscuri, and their steeds look out.

▼ Detail of a stretch of walls in Bolsena, from the middle of the third century B.C. The regular blocks are marked with letters or groups of letters. These walls reinforce others built in the fifth century. They represent a vain attempt to resist Rome before they were destroyed in 264.

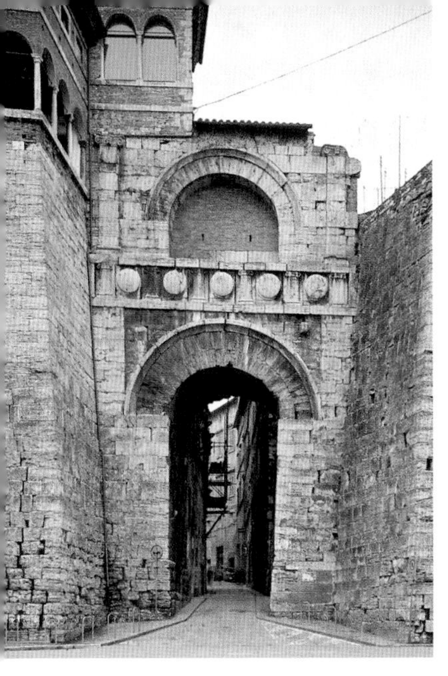

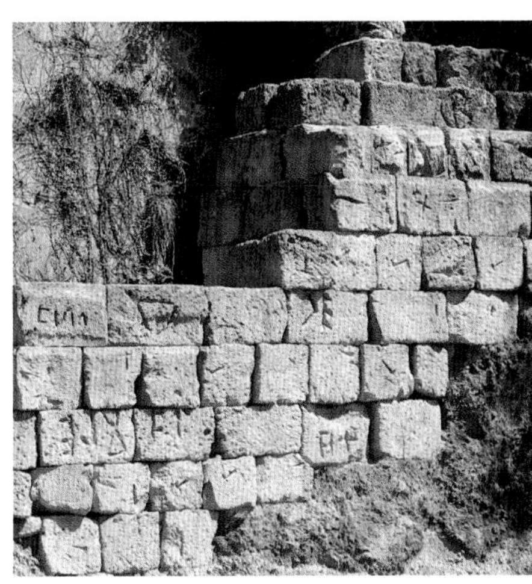

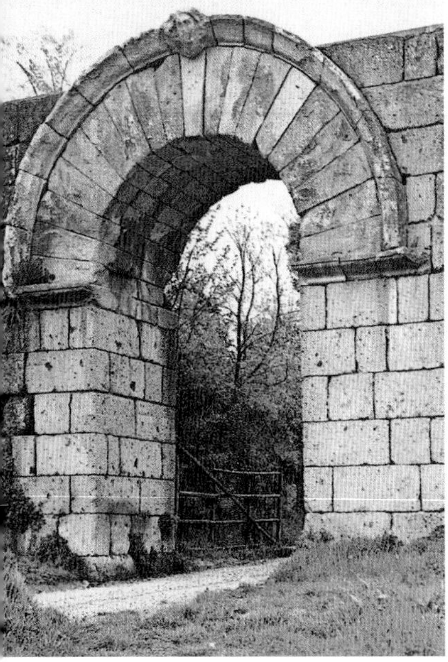

▶ The Porta all'Arco, from the middle of the fourth to the third centuries B.C., Volterra. The inner chamber, which was originally covered with wood, was eventually given a travertine vault. On the exterior, three heads of divinities have been sculpted in a Hellenistic manner upon capitals at the arch's imposts and keystone.

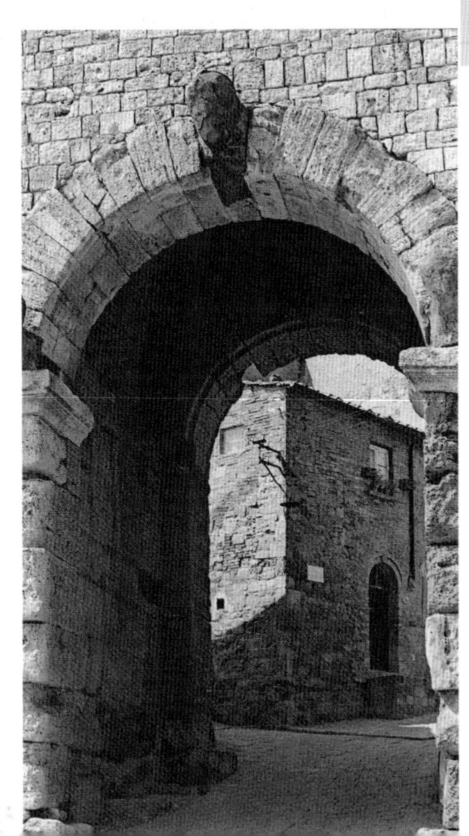

The *Tabula Cortonensis*

This recent discovery is a rectangular bronze panel that in ancient times was intentionally broken into eight parts, one of which is missing. Overall, it comprises a text of 206 words and is one of the "long texts" of the Etruscan *corpus*. A juridical record dating to between the end of the third and the beginning of the second centuries B.C., it deals with a land transaction, probably the division of a large estate.

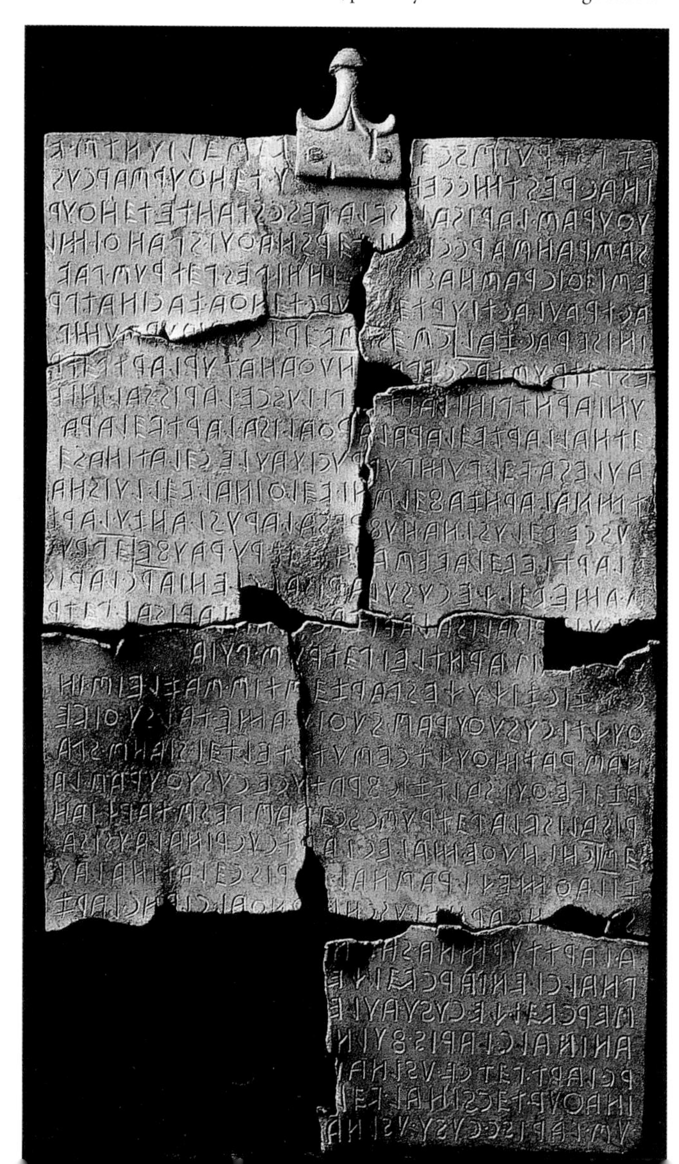

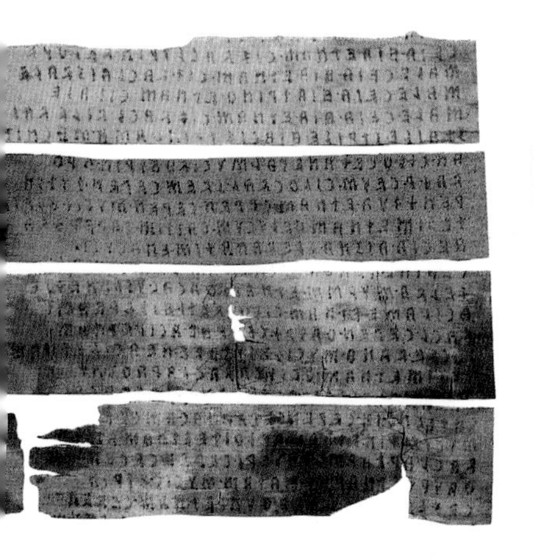

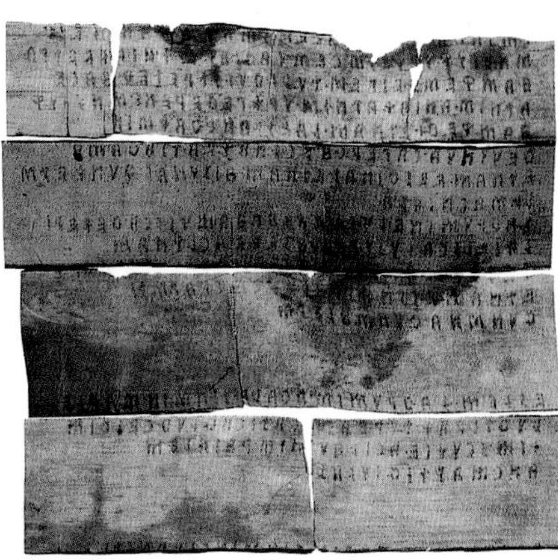

▲ A linen book (*liber linteus*) from the second century B.C. Zagreb, National Museum. A religious calendar written in the Cortona or Perugia region, it was cut up and used as bandages to wrap an Egyptian mummy. A reconstructive theory holds that the book consisted of a single strip that was folded like an accordion, which could be consulted as a codex of twelve pages.

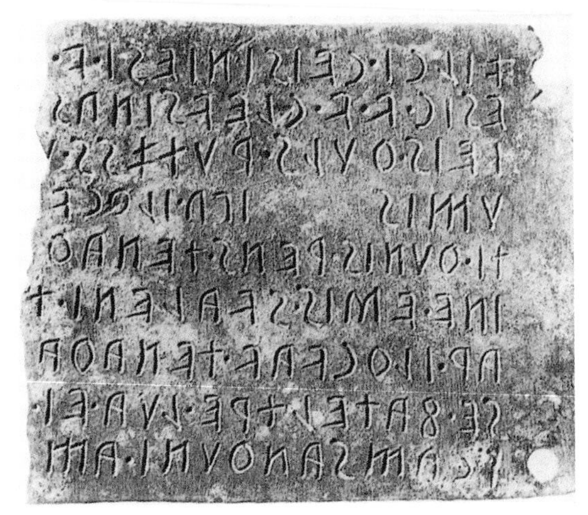

▲ A rectangular bronze tablet from Tarquinia, from the end of the third to the beginning of the second centuries B.C. Tarquinia, Museo Archeologico. The only portion of a larger work to have survived, it has holes at the right for hanging. It contains the names of two supreme magistrates who ruled over Tarquinia and supplies information regarding the names of political posts.

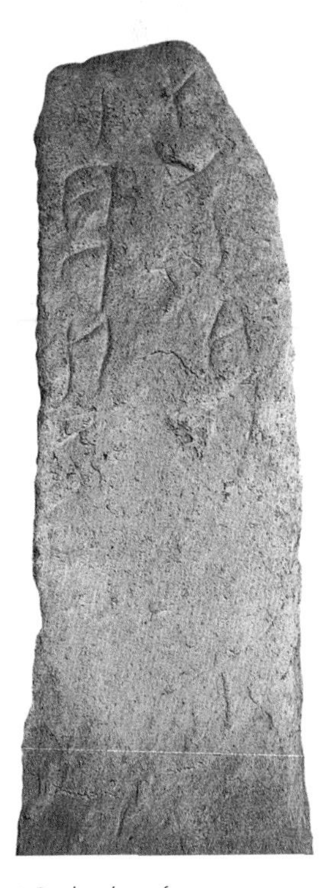

▲ Border *cippus* from the late third to the early second centuries B.C. Bettona, Museo Civico. The inscription reads from right to left and bears the word *tularlarna; tular* is equivalent to the Latin *fines,* "border."

The Birth of Portraiture

The veneration of ancestors' images was typical in the Etruscan and Roman worlds and was linked to the aristocratic structure of society and the memory of forebears. The practice led to portraiture, representing family members who were distinguished for political or military achievements. In the Hellenistic period, this inclination toward naturalistic portrait-painting received a boost from Greece. The roots of portraiture in central Italy can be found in the tradition of the poleis of Magna Graecia, with which the Etruscans shared territorial contiguity and cultural affinity. Realistic portraiture absorbed and overcame a partiality for the old Italic and Etruscan ideal forms, establishing the basis for Roman portraiture. The chronological evolution of types passed from the post-Classical or Protohellenistic forms of veiled heads, which were common from the middle of the fourth century through the third century, to characters from late Hellenism. These forms evoked the art of Praxiteles for female portraits and Lysippus for male examples.

▼ Male head in multicolored clay, from the Manganello Temple in Cerveteri, third century B.C. Rome, Museo di Villa Giulia. Modeled by hand with strong physical characterization, this portrait combines Hellenistic realism with a more local selectivity regarding significant details.

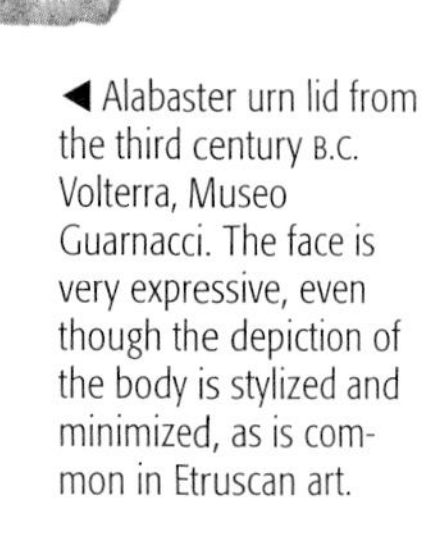

◀ Alabaster urn lid from the third century B.C. Volterra, Museo Guarnacci. The face is very expressive, even though the depiction of the body is stylized and minimized, as is common in Etruscan art.

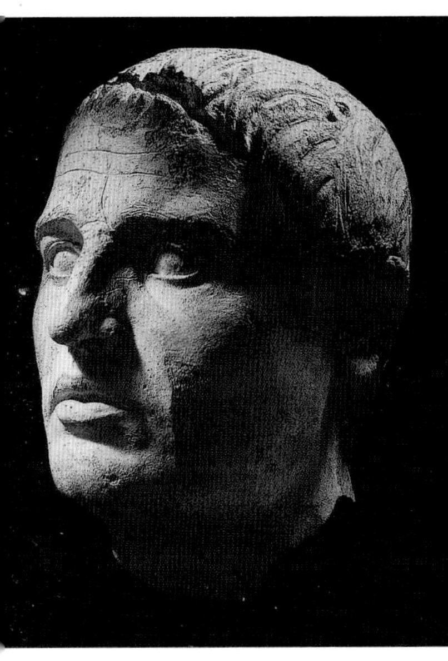

◀ Male votive head in terra-cotta, from the end of the third or the beginning of the second century B.C. Tarquinia, Museo Archeologico. Traces of reddish paint have survived. The short hair parted into locks, the large forehead with engraved wrinkles, the eyes with raised eyelids, the parted lips, and the square jaw show it to be an example of portraiture from central Italy.

▼ Bronze statuette of a man in prayer, from the first half of the third century B.C. Los Angeles, The J. Paul Getty Museum. The arrangement of the facial features and the hairstyle are close to types by Lysippus. The deepened eye sockets and melancholy expression, the fleshy lips, and the movement of the body are elements that recall Hellenistic models.

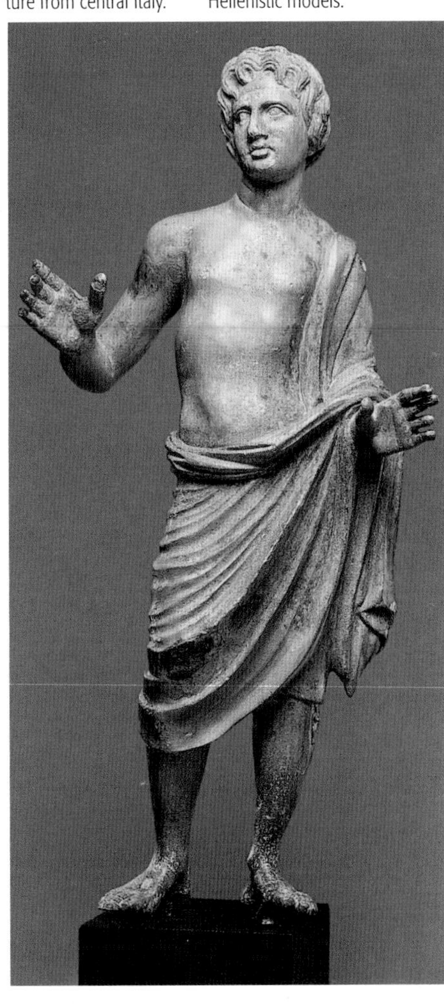

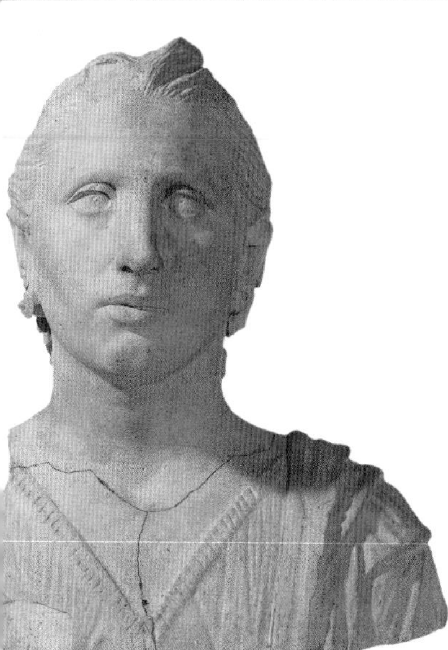

▲ Female portrait in terra-cotta from Cerveteri, from the fourth to the third centuries B.C. Vatican City, Museo Gregorian Etrusco. The prominent locks of hair on the forehead recall the influence of Alexander the Great's portraits, while more individualized features are the evenness of the face, the hollow cheeks, and the high cheekbones.

The Orator

This statue was a votive offering at a sanctuary near Perugia, which became a Roman municipality in 88 B.C. Cast in seven different pieces that were soldered together, the work depicts a mature man in the act of raising his right arm to request silence before delivering a speech (*silentium manu facere*).

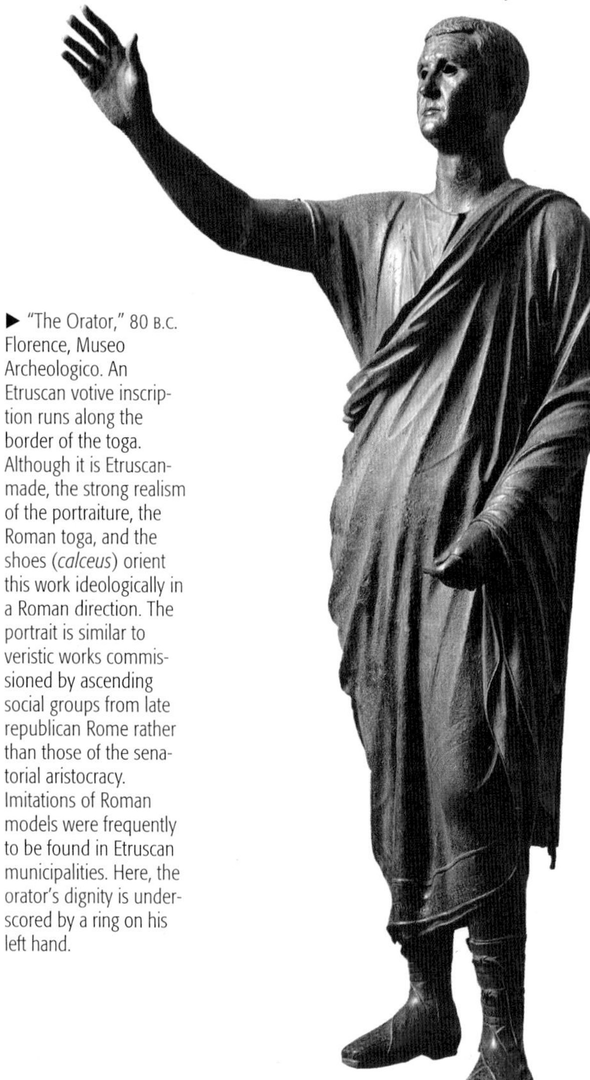

▶ "The Orator," 80 B.C. Florence, Museo Archeologico. An Etruscan votive inscription runs along the border of the toga. Although it is Etruscan-made, the strong realism of the portraiture, the Roman toga, and the shoes (*calceus*) orient this work ideologically in a Roman direction. The portrait is similar to veristic works commissioned by ascending social groups from late republican Rome rather than those of the senatorial aristocracy. Imitations of Roman models were frequently to be found in Etruscan municipalities. Here, the orator's dignity is underscored by a ring on his left hand.

▶ Detail of a portrait from the third century B.C. Perugia, Tomb of the Volumnii. One of the richest expressions of funerary art, this work is emblematic of the provincial aristocratic classes that were able to sail upon the prevailing winds of Romanization. The face is shown in profile with its gaze partly turned upward, in keeping with the striving for a celebratory self-image. The style, while mediated by Rome, did not abandon Hellenistic embellishments or the use of traditional noble references.

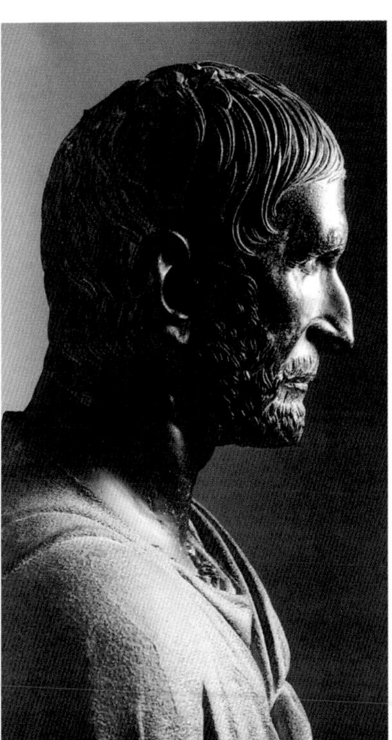

◀ The "Capitoline Brutus," from the middle of the third century B.C. Rome, Musei Capitolini. It depicts a mature man with small eyes, an aquiline nose, and thin, closed lips: an emblem of the republican nobility's self-image.

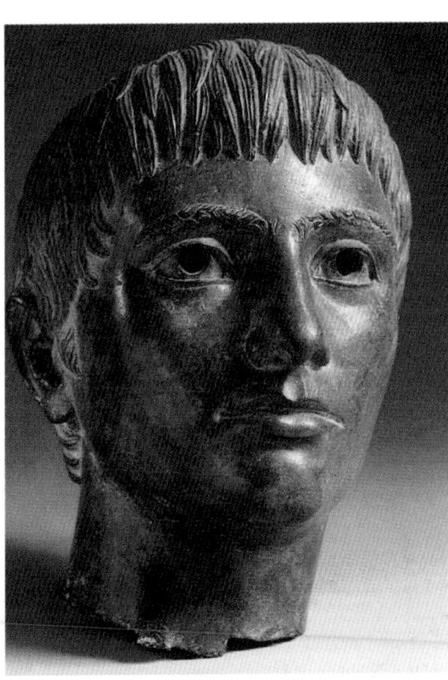

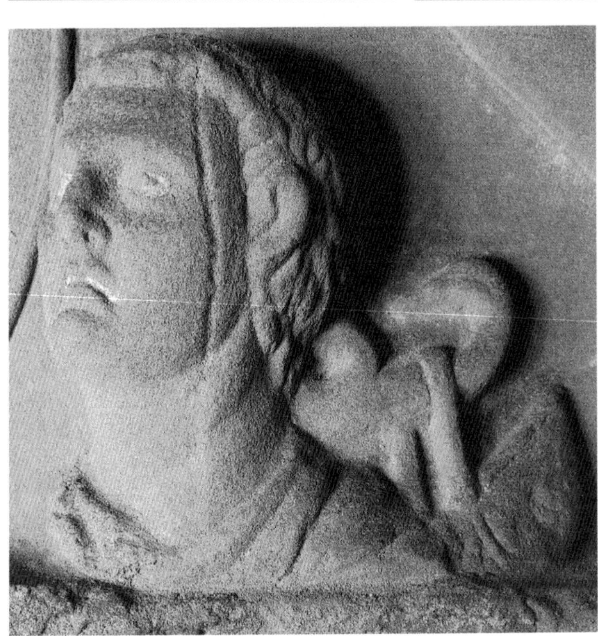

▲ Bronze head from a statue of a young man, from the middle of the third century B.C. Florence, Museo Archeologico. It demonstrates the spread of the central Italic style of portraiture in Etruria. The style is poorer and only approximates that of the "Capitoline Brutus," despite the rendering of the eyebrows in a braided motif and the hairstyle of short bangs along the forehead with locks of different lengths, combed out from the center. Although it is an idealized face, this head represents a model type for male physiognomy.

The Temple of Talamone

The return of public patronage during the years of Roman integration caused the most indigenous of Etruscan crafts—works in terra-cotta—to flourish, especially in northern cities. The majestic pediment from the Temple of Talamone is an eloquent example.

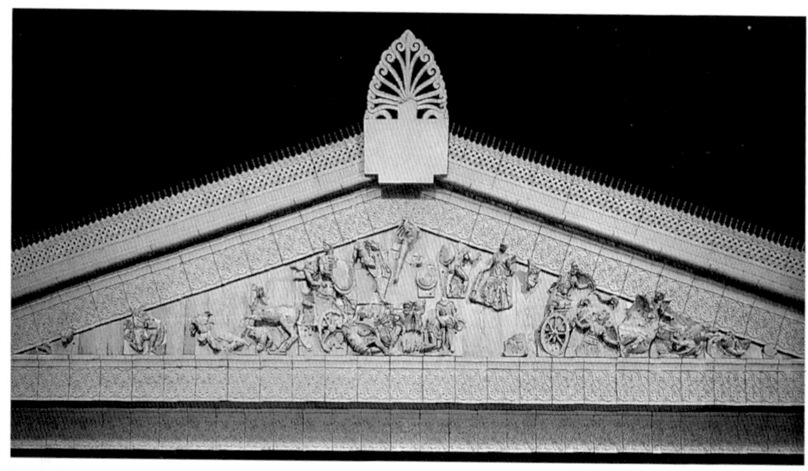

▲ Rear pediment of the temple, with scenes taken from the mythological saga *Seven against Thebes,* from Talamone, second century B.C. Florence, Museo Archeologico. The group of Oedipus with the lifeless bodies of his sons occupies a central position in the pediment, forming a focus toward which the composition turns. Models that were more sculptural than pictorial inspired the design.

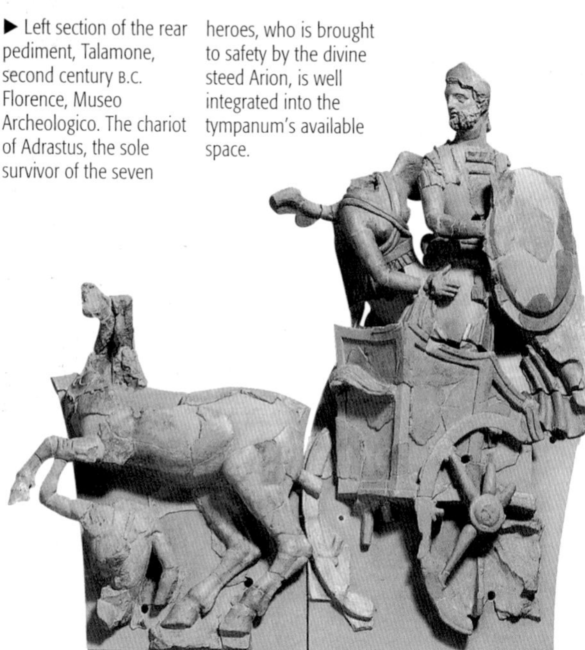

▶ Left section of the rear pediment, Talamone, second century B.C. Florence, Museo Archeologico. The chariot of Adrastus, the sole survivor of the seven heroes, who is brought to safety by the divine steed Arion, is well integrated into the tympanum's available space.

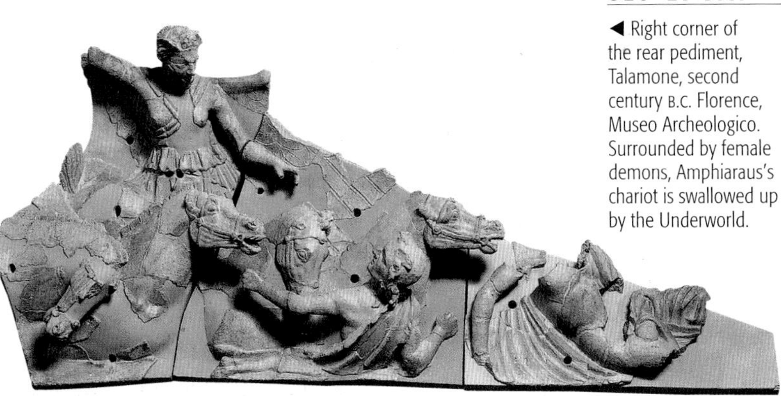

◀ Right corner of the rear pediment, Talamone, second century B.C. Florence, Museo Archeologico. Surrounded by female demons, Amphiaraus's chariot is swallowed up by the Underworld.

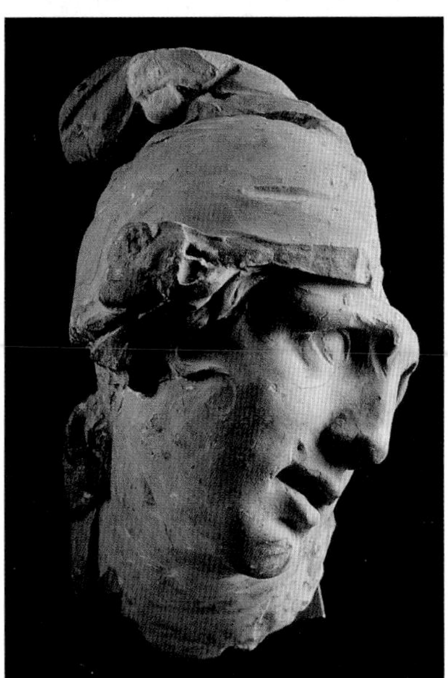

◀ Female head belonging to a pediment decoration from La Catona, early second century B.C. Arezzo, Museo Archeologico. This figure, possibly an Amazon, is portrayed in three-quarter and turning toward her left shoulder, with a Phrygian cap, furrowed brow, and half-open mouth. The pathos of the figure is inherited from the world of Asia Minor.

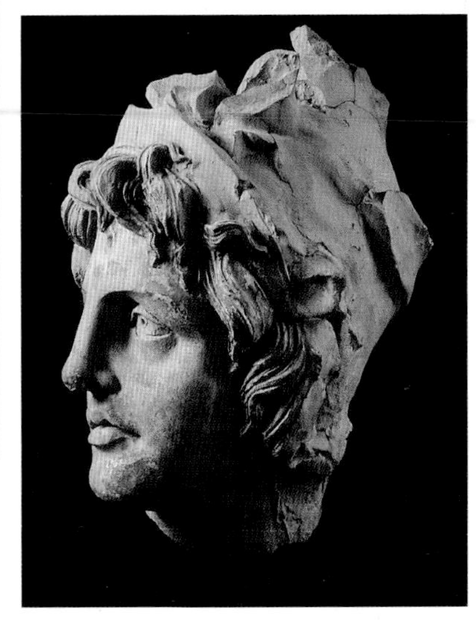

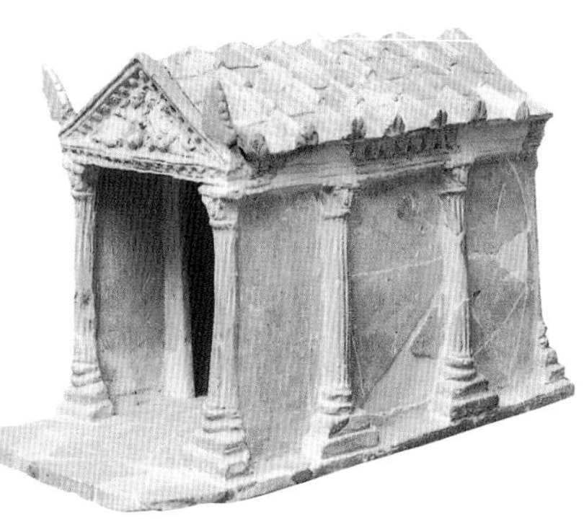

◀ Temple model of the late Hellenistic period from Vulci. Rome, Museo di Villa Giulia. The pronaos is enclosed, the pediment decorated in high relief, and the corner acroteria of palmettes allude to the Corinthian order.

▲ Male head from La Catona, from the first quarter of the second century B.C. Arezzo, Museo Archeologico. The youth wears a Phrygian cap from which locks of long, wavy hair poke out.

Mass-Produced Pottery

A general trait of Hellenism was the standardization that affected all crafts, from embossed metalwork to sculpture, from pottery decoration to the production of sarcophagi. As in previous eras, ceramic studios began to pop up in every district, but this time local specialization became pedantic, as seen in its radical thematic and morphological impoverishment. The vast repertory of vase variants was reduced to a few recurring forms of cups or plates. The iconography froze into stereotypes that were increasingly less structured, with isolated figures that were anatomically reduced. Overpainting began to be used as a decorative shortcut. A new relationship began between the artisan industry and buyers from the emerging middle classes, which also corresponded to changes in funerary rituals that were no longer linked to the message conveyed by the objects, but only to their quantity. Faliscan manufacturers, who were active exporters during the fourth century B.C., were transplanted to Cerveteri, which as a new member of the Roman federation was enjoying a renewed commercial bliss. Volterra would continue its production of *kelebai,* vases featuring a repertory of funerary images, until the beginning of the third century. Meanwhile, the self-aggrandizement of Vulci's elite could be found in late Classical accents in the red-figure pottery of the Hague Painter.

▼ Overpainted *oinochoe* with a scroll-like spout, a specialty of the Cervetaran shops, by the Phantom group, from Tarquinia, late fourth century B.C. Tarquinia, Museo Archeologico. The cloaked figure shown in profile and the decorative vegetal elements are recurrent themes.

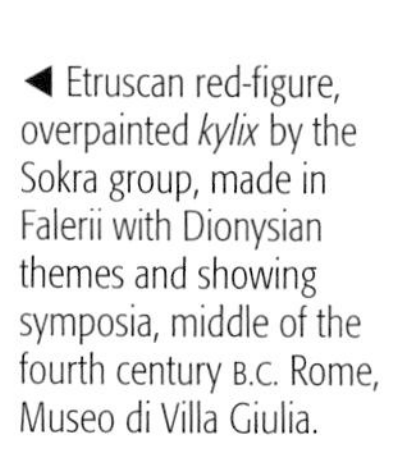

◀ Etruscan red-figure, overpainted *kylix* by the Sokra group, made in Falerii with Dionysian themes and showing symposia, middle of the fourth century B.C. Rome, Museo di Villa Giulia.

▼ Genucilia plate, a variation on the one with a female head below, from the late fourth century B.C. Bassano del Grappa, Museo Civico. Genucilia plates owe their name to one signed example at the Rhode Island School of Design Museum. They spread throughout the Mediterranean basin and coincided with Roman expansion.

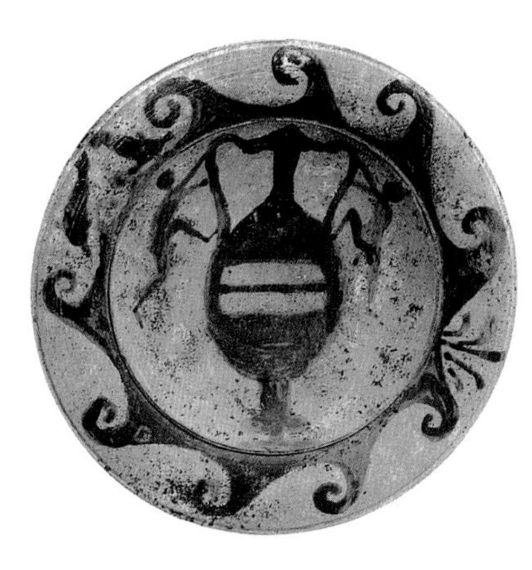

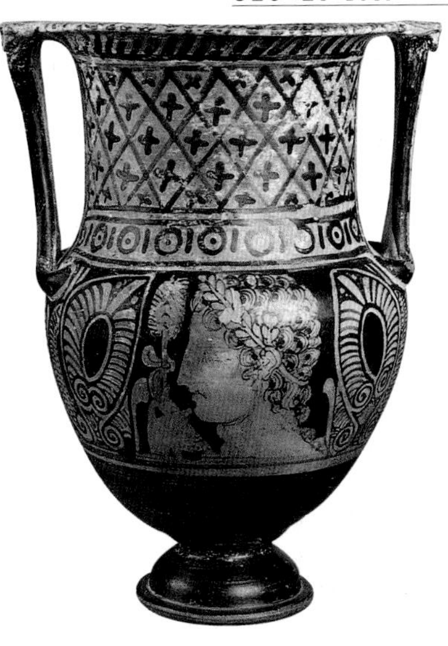

▲ Red-figure *kelebe* from the beginning of the third century B.C. Florence, Museo Archeologico. This vase may be by Aison, one of the major ceramic decorators. On one side is the head of a youth in profile with a crown and a *thyrsus* (Bacchic staff) in hand. The neck features a diamond pattern with tiny crosses. The Volterran *kelebai* are linked to Faliscan pottery ornamentation in their subjects and motifs.

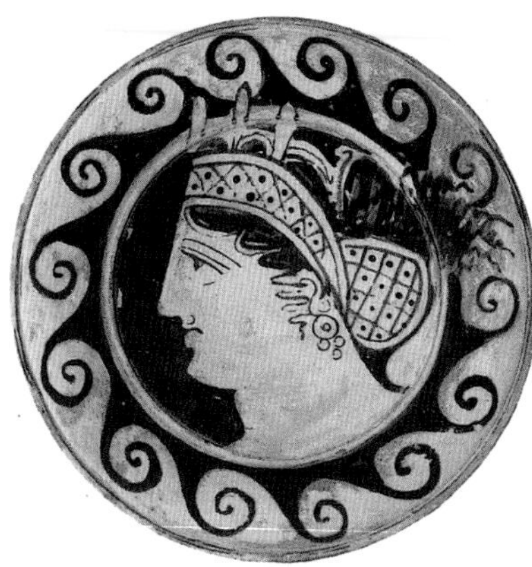

▲ Genucilia plate with a woman's head in profile, circled by a repeating motif of breaking waves, from the end of the fourth century B.C. Rome, Museo di Villa Giulia. On her head are a diadem and a *sakkos,* which ties back her hair. A variant with star motifs has also been found.

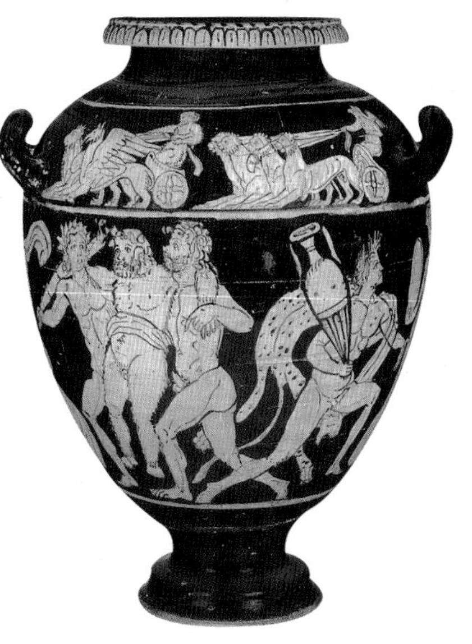

▶ The Hague Painter, a *stamnos* with a frieze of a Dionysian orgy, 290 B.C., from Vulci. Paris, Musée du Louvre. This painter's works feature rich iconography with intense content full of religious symbolism.

Cinerary Urns at Chiusi and Volterra

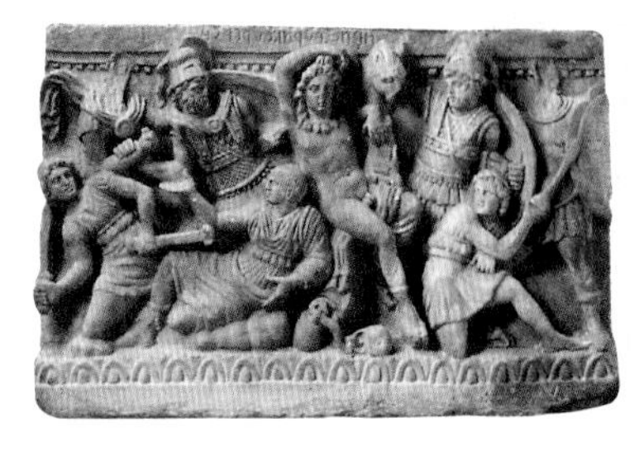

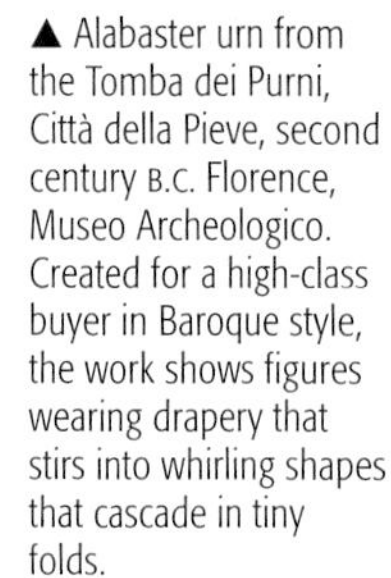

▲ Alabaster urn from the Tomba dei Purni, Città della Pieve, second century B.C. Florence, Museo Archeologico. Created for a high-class buyer in Baroque style, the work shows figures wearing drapery that stirs into whirling shapes that cascade in tiny folds.

Funerary crafts in the regions of Chiusi and Volterra developed distinctive tendencies, articulating their production in diverse ways from city to city, according to the various socioeconomic factors and an unequal absorption of figurative models from the Hellenistic world. In the second century B.C. in the Chiusi countryside, the urns of the middle classes, who were benefiting from newly granted political rights, show a standardization of production featuring recurring figurative subjects that alluded to reconciled social tensions. Meanwhile the aristocracy continued to recall the heroic ideology through works in clay, favoring handmade works over mass-produced ones. The cultural dynamics of Volterra can be clearly read in the production of its stone urns. Hellenistic tastes permeated the objects with emotional overtones and accentuated anatomy. These qualities, manifested in the mass-produced works, had emerged following Roman exploits in Macedonia, and local aristocracies now used them to proclaim their cultural alignment with Rome. During the final years of the second century, until a more immediately recognizable class distinction was delineated, the customers of different classes demanded different uses of materials and representations of decorative themes: alabaster and heroic mythology for the aristocracy; tufa and scenes linked to the funerary world, or ones that exalted status, for the middle class.

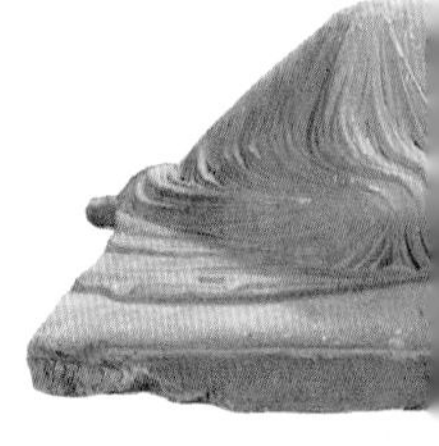

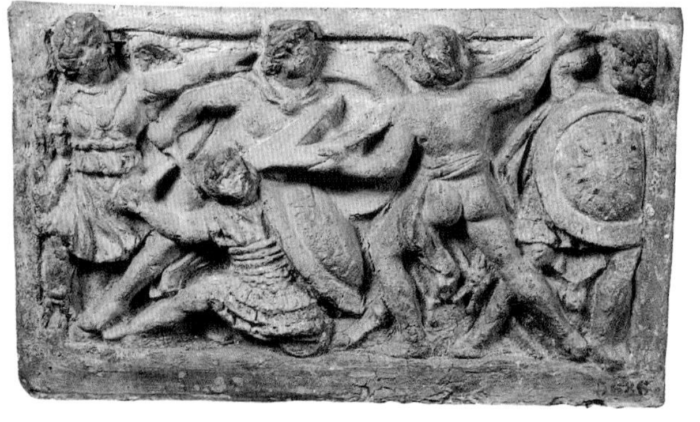

◀ Earthenware cinerary urn from the region of Chiusi, 130–110 B.C. Florence, Museo Archeologico. The decoration presents a hero with a quiver battling against three warriors. In Chiusi this subject alternated with the Theban duel and fratricide, which reflected the social struggles of the era.

▶ A small earthenware cinerary urn from Santa Mustiola. Chiusi, Museo Archeologico. The deceased is portrayed on the lid in a tunic and cloak, while Polynices and Eteocles appear on the front. Alabaster ceded to terra-cotta at the end of the second century B.C., in order to meet the needs of a class with less disposable income.

▼ Alabaster cinerary urn lid, 190–170 B.C. Volterra, Museo Guarnacci. The long inscription and the ring worn by the man lead the viewer to suppose that the subject was an important figure among the aristocracy of Volterra.

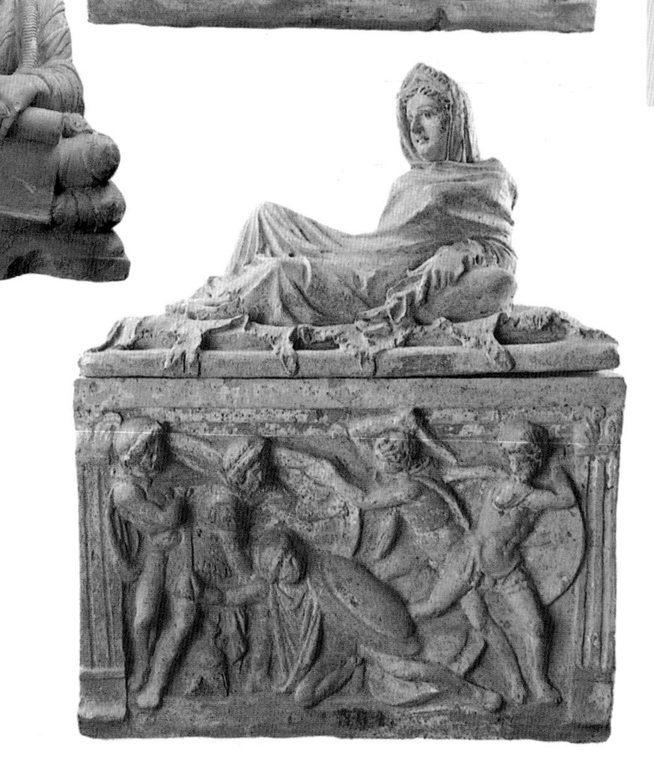

▶ Earthenware cinerary urn from the country around Chiusi, second century B.C. Chiusi, Museo Archeologico. The lid, modeled with a flat instrument, is decorated with a partially reclining female figure. She wears a diadem and is completely enfolded in a cloak. On the urn is a standardized version of a battle scene.

The Manufacture of Ex-Votos

If monumental terra-cotta techniques reveal the religious mindset of aristocratic buyers, the devotional forms linked to popular religiosity are no less eloquent. Vaguely utilitarian and functional, ex-votos were dedicated at numerous sanctuaries. The archaeological record shows that most ex-votos were humble offerings, expressions of the lower classes, comparable to those that filled the federal sanctuary of Volsinii and were brought to Rome when that city was destroyed in 264 B.C. The grand bronze *anathemata*—the Chimaera, the Mars from Todi, and the Orator—are the exceptions that prove the rule. From a religious standpoint, ex-votos sought to protect the most elemental aspects of life, such as health and reproduction. This religiosity becomes tangible through offerings of objects in base materials such as terra-cotta and pottery that reproduce heads, figures of infants, or individual parts of the body. The practice of offering ex-votos began in Veii and Falerii in the fifth century B.C., following the growing prestige of the medical cult of Asclepius. It then spread in the fourth century and, more intensely, in the Hellenistic period in Tarquinia, Vulci, and Volsinii, from whence it firmly set down roots in Lazio.

▼ Terra-cotta foot, an anatomical ex-voto, symbol of a received healing, discovered at a sanctuary near the Ara della Regina temple, third century B.C. Tarquinia, Museo Archeologico. Numerous ex-votos, anatomical and figurative, have been found in Tarquinia, revealing a series of works that were mechanical and increasingly shoddy as time wore on.

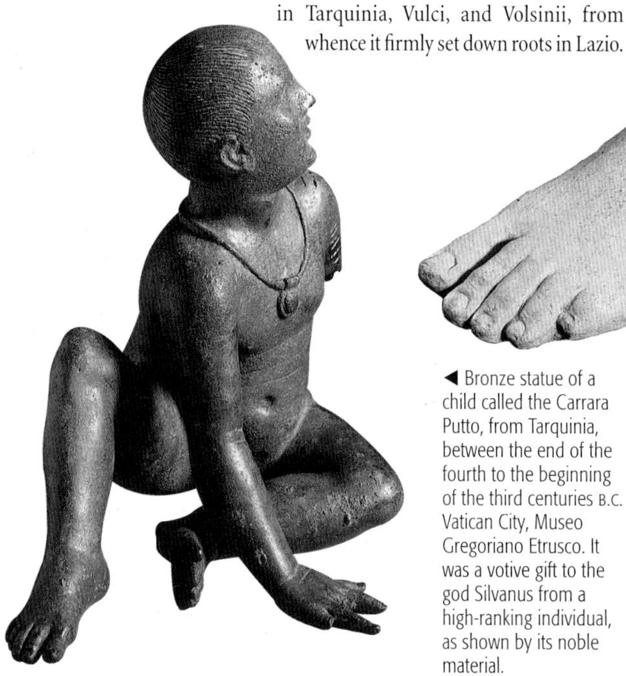

◀ Bronze statue of a child called the Carrara Putto, from Tarquinia, between the end of the fourth to the beginning of the third centuries B.C. Vatican City, Museo Gregoriano Etrusco. It was a votive gift to the god Silvanus from a high-ranking individual, as shown by its noble material.

▶ Male votive head from the sanctuary of Diana at Nemi, third century B.C. Florence, Museo Archeologico. The head is covered, and has a curly beard, short hair with a central part, and a mustache that ends in spirals.

▼ Male votive head in terra-cotta from Cerveteri, third to second centuries B.C. Vatican City, Museo Gregoriano Etrusco. The short, disordered hair recalls a portrait of Alexander the Great.

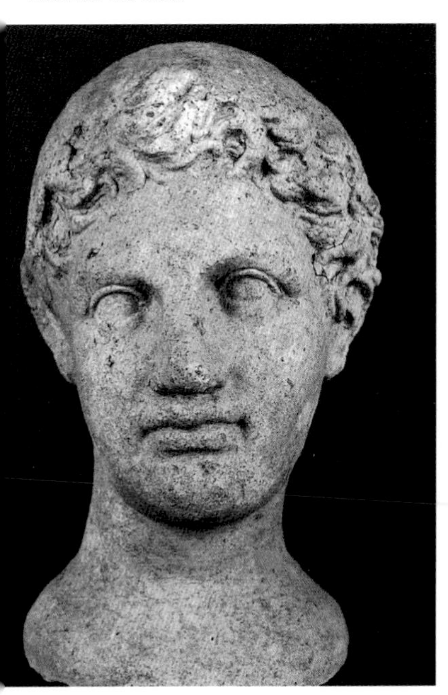

▶ Female votive head, covered, from the sanctuary of Diana at Nemi, third century B.C. Florence, Museo Archeologico. Her untied hair is parted in the middle, with side ringlets.

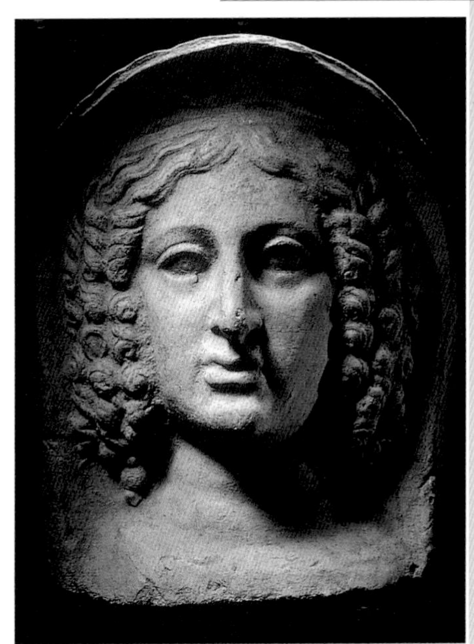

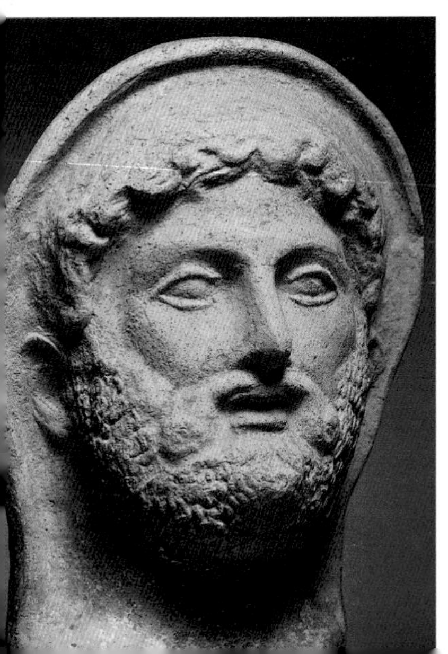

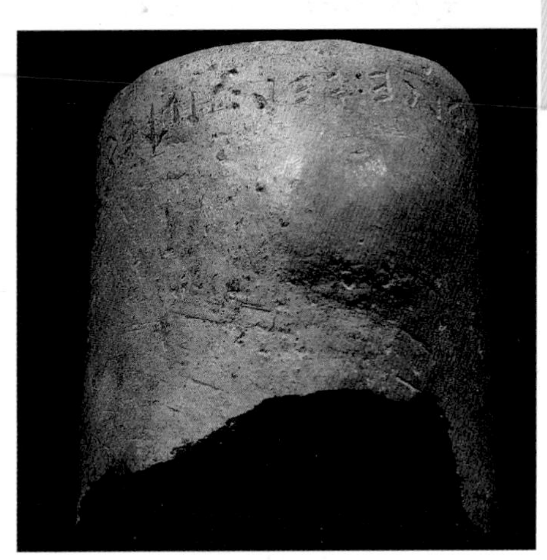

▲ Anatomical ex-voto in the shape of a leg from the votive deposit at the Ara della Regina temple, Tarquinia, second century B.C. Tarquinia, Museo Archeologico. Made of brown clay, this leg ends just above the knee. An inscription, *alce vel tiples,* was engraved before firing, indicating that the gift came from someone who was of servile origins. The noble name *Tiples* is of Greek derivation. This devotional piece was intended to safeguard health.

The Corsini Throne

An epilogue to the aristocratic pride of a people who had been integrated into the Roman state, yet were still vitally attached to their lineage, this Roman copy of an Etruscan throne was created to celebrate the royalty of the Etruscan *gens* of Urgulania, who were related to the Plautii Laterani, new patricians of Augustus. Uncovered at the villa of Plautius Lateranus, where it was displayed among images of ancestors (*imagines maiorum*) in a genealogical self-glorification, the throne must have emphasized that the origins of the *gens* went back to the ancient *principes* of the most prestigious pre-Roman people.

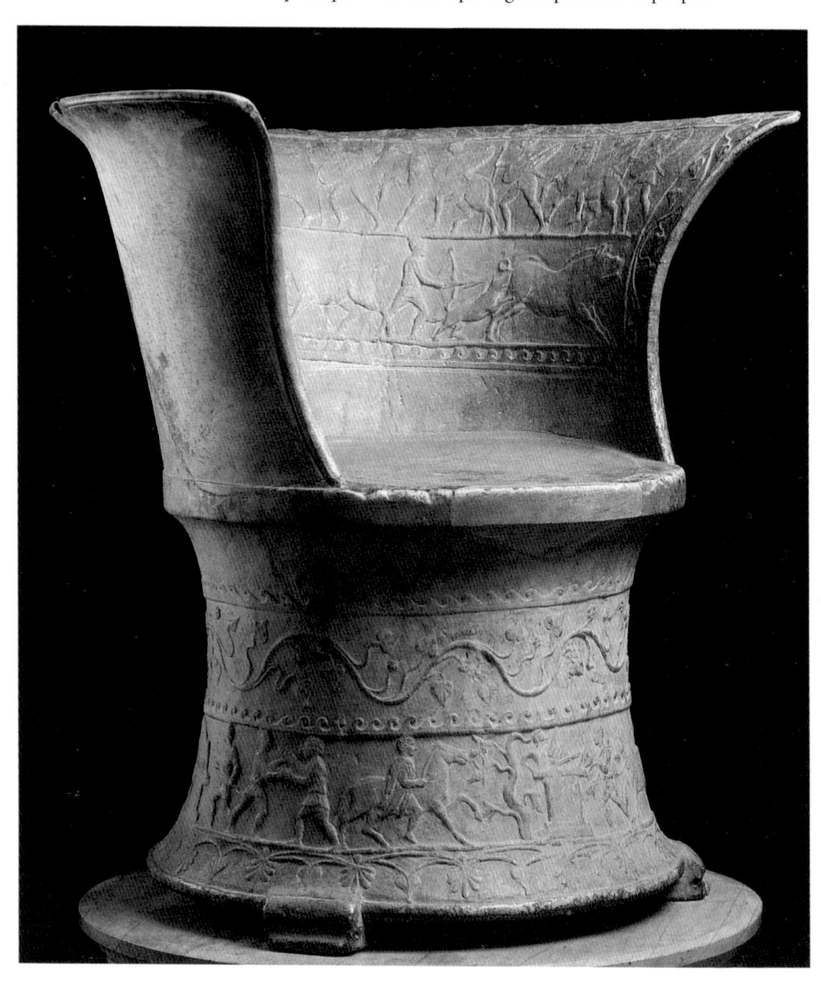

▼ Bronze throne from a royal tomb in Palestrina, 675–650 B.C. Rome, Museo di Villa Giulia. Its similarity in type to the Corsini Throne is immediately obvious.

▶ Wooden throne with a curved back and cylindrical base, like one from Palestrina, mid-seventh century B.C. Verucchio, Museo Archeologico.

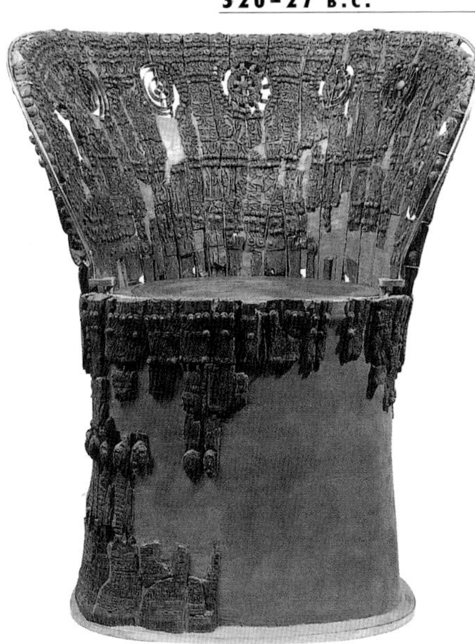

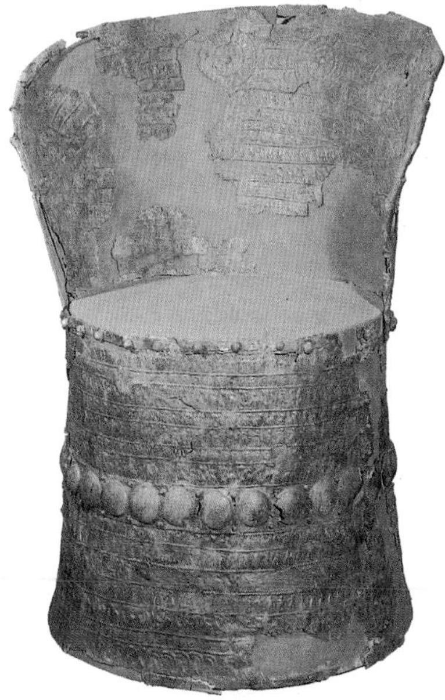

▶ Female terra-cotta figure from Ariccia, fourth century B.C. Rome, Museo Nazionale Romano. The figure is seated upon a throne that is comparable to the Corsini Throne, but much less richly decorated.

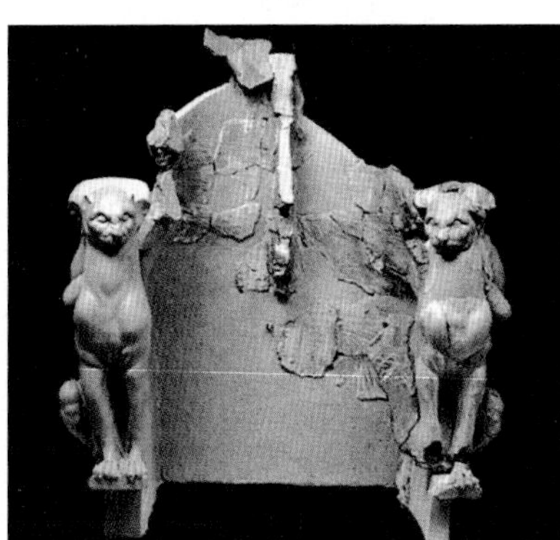

▲ The "Panther Throne," in terra-cotta. Bolsena, Museo Rocca Monaldeschi della Cervara. The throne is made up of a square plinth that supports the seat and a vegetal and zoomorphic back. The sides are decorated with panthers with putti on their backs. It is an example of a throne linked to Dionysian cults.

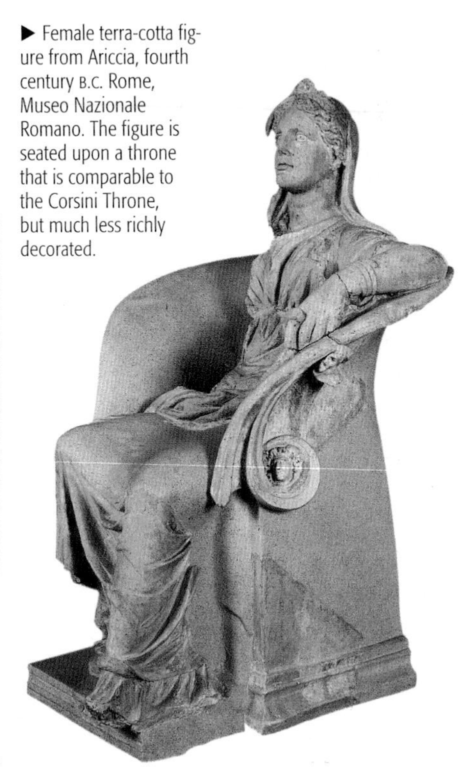

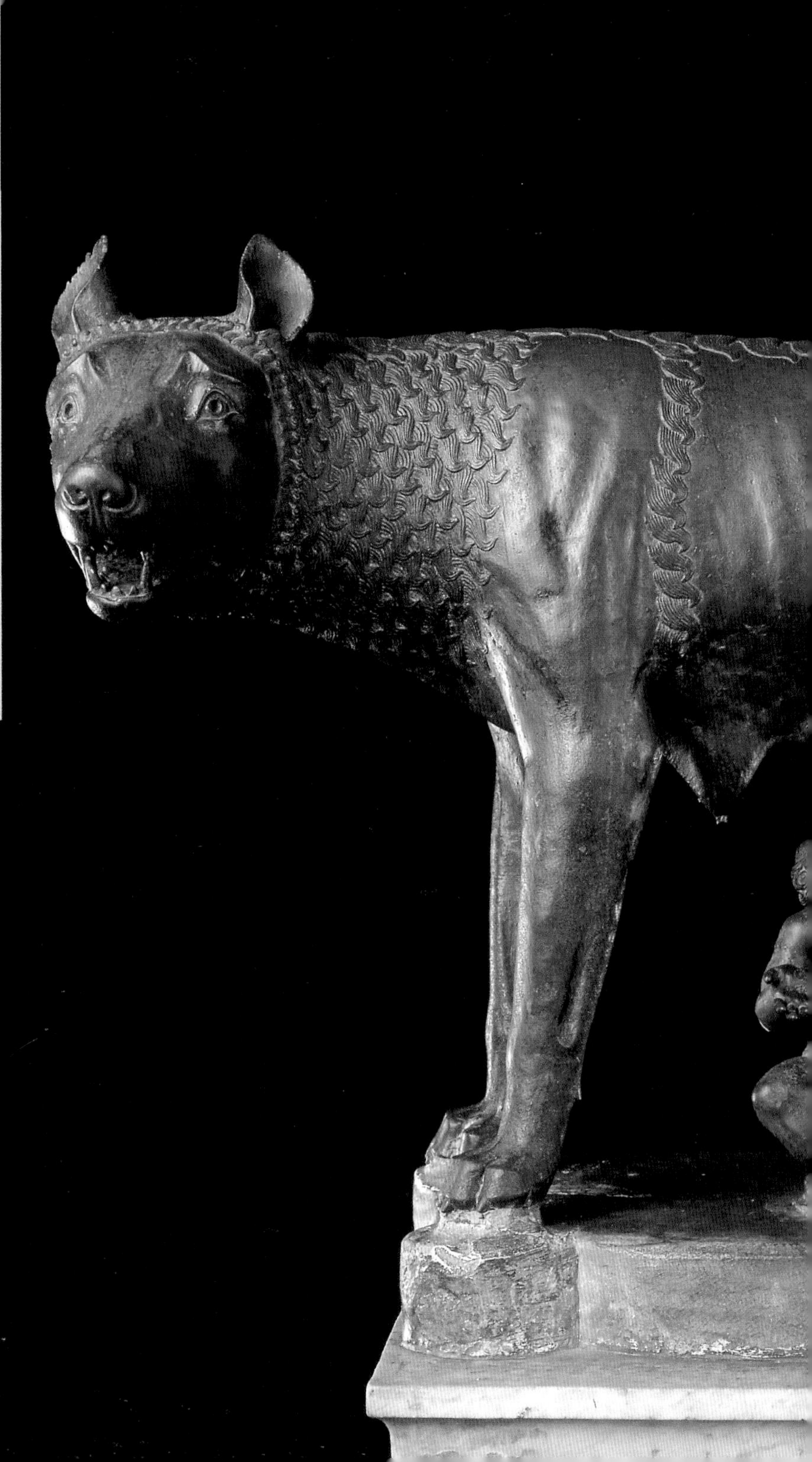

The Capitoline She-Wolf, 450–430 B.C. Rome, Musei Capitolini

Appendixes

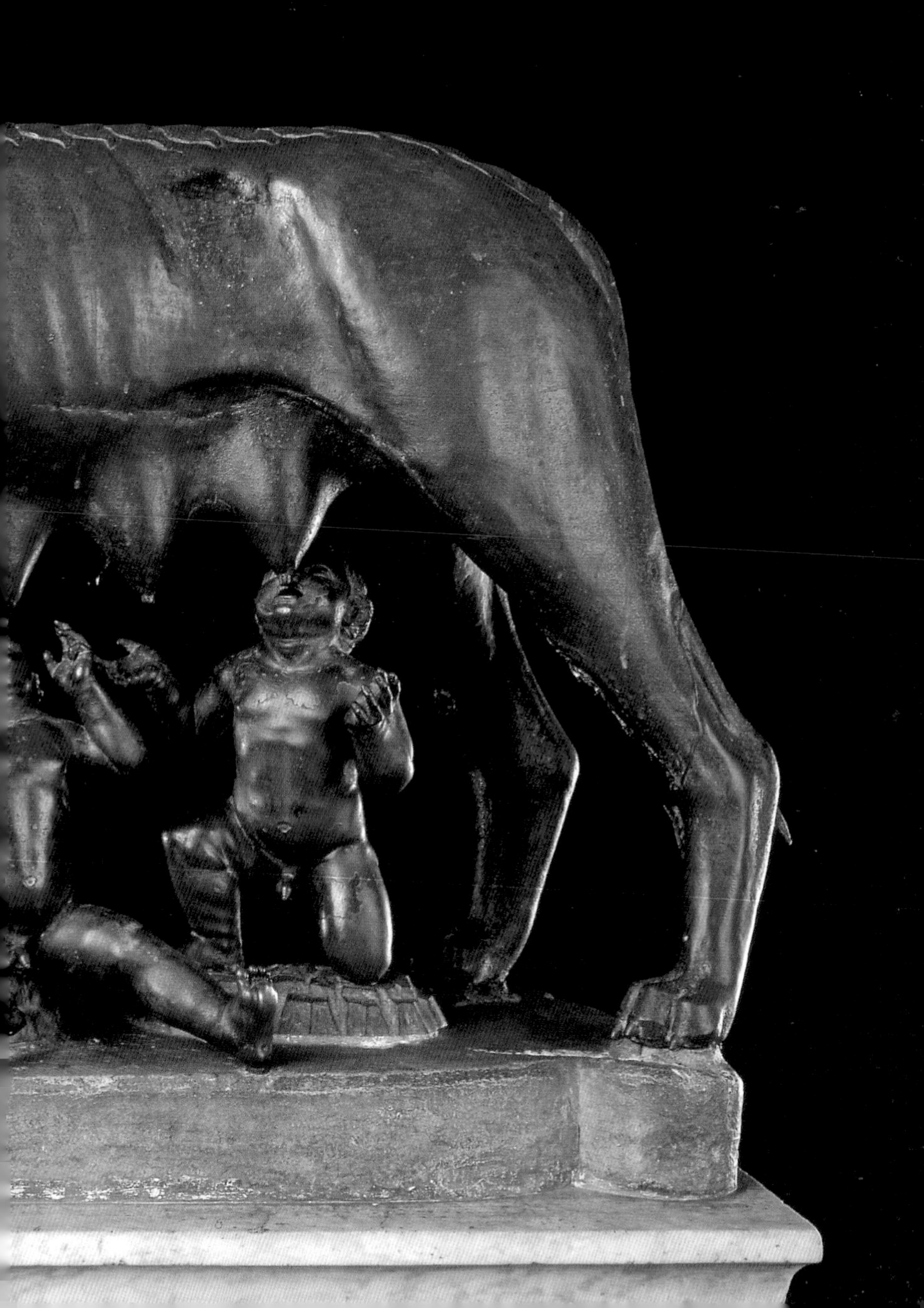

The Etruscans in Pre-Roman Italy

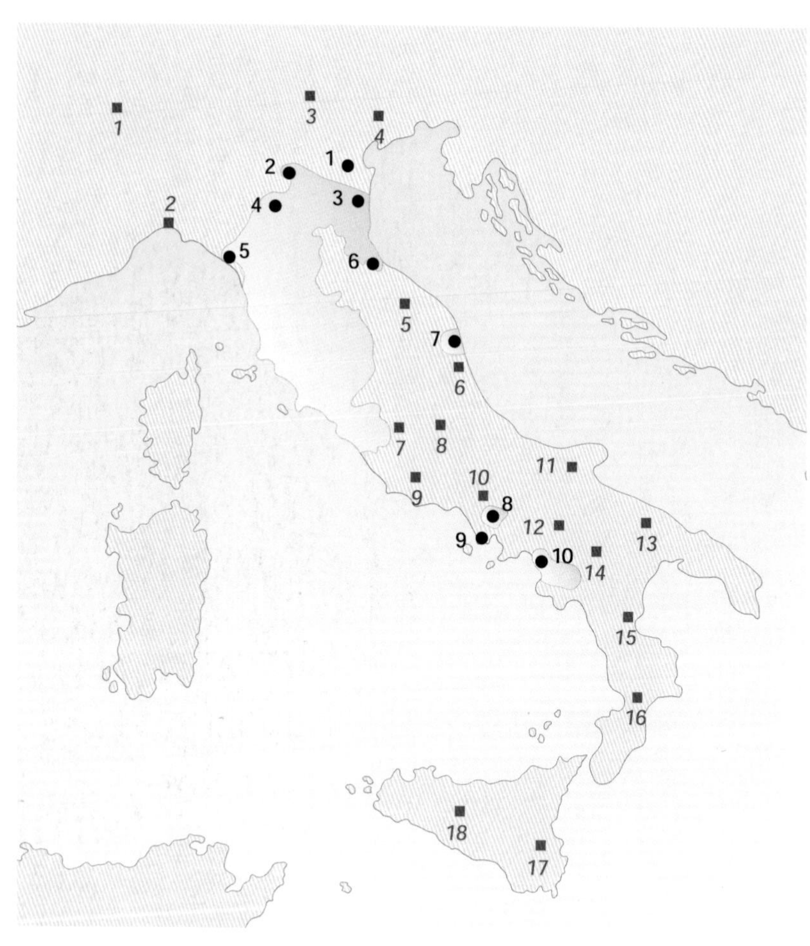

Peoples (in red)
1. Celts
2. Ligurians
3. Raeti
4. Veneti
5. Umbrians
6. Picentes
7. Faliscans
8. Sabines
9. Latins
10. Volsci
11. Samnites
12. Campanians
13. Apuli
14. Lucani
15. Oenotrii
16. Bruttii
17. Siculi
18. Sicani

Cities (in black)
1. Este (Ateste)
2. Mantua
3. Adria
4. Bologna (Felsina)
5. Luni (Luna)
6. Verucchio
7. Fermo (Firmum Picenum)
8. Capua
9. Cumae
10. Pontecagnano

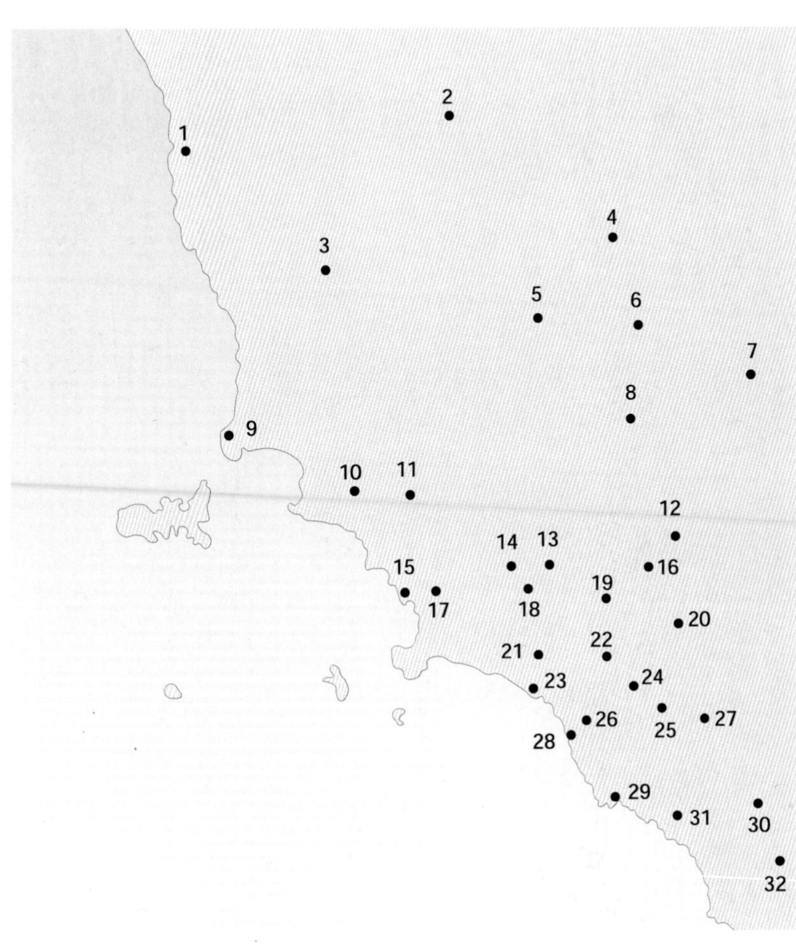

Cities

1. Pisa (Pisae)
2. Fiesole (Faesulae)
3. Volterra (Volaterrae)
4. Arezzo (Arretium)
5. Poggio Civitate (Murlo)
6. Cortona
7. Perugia (Perusia)
8. Chiusi (Clusium)
9. Populonia
10. Vetulonia
11. Roselle (Rusellae)
12. Orvieto
13. Sovana (Suana)
14. Saturnia
15. Talamone (Telamon)
16. Bolsena (Volsinii)
17. Heba
18. Statonia
19. Bisenzio (Visentum)
20. Acquarossa
21. Vulci
22. Tuscania
23. Regisvilla (Regae)
24. Norchia
25. Blera
26. Tarquinia (Tarquinii)
27. Sutri (Sutrium)
28. Gravisca
29. Pyrgi
30. Veii
31. Cerveteri (Caere)
32. Rome (Roma)

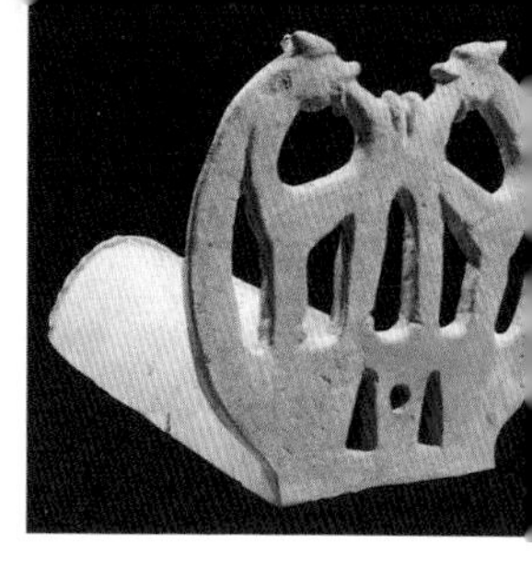

▶ Central acroteria decorated with perforations from the houses of Acquarossa, late seventh century B.C. Viterbo, Deposito di Palazzo San Pietro.

Acroterion (-a, pl.), a modeled figurative decoration placed on top of a pediment

Agger, a fortification made up of an earthwork connected to a trench

Anathema (-ata, pl.), an offering, often hung in a temple

Antefix, a modeled terra-cotta decoration masking the ends of semicircular roof tiles

Antepagmentum (-a, pl.), a terra-cotta slab, painted or marked in relief, that decorates a doorway or window

Architrave, the lowest architectural element of the entablature resting above the columns

Aryballos, a small jar for ointment

Atrium, a central domestic area with rooms opening onto it

Biga, a two-horse chariot or cart

Calceus, a closed shoe

Canopic jar, a vessel, originally from Egypt, designed to contain the remains of the deceased; its lid took the shape of a human or animal head

Caryatid, a statue-column portraying a woman, a support for trabeation

Cella, a room or chamber, sometimes within a temple

Chiton, a tunic

Cippus, a large stone grave marker of elliptical shape with a crested top

Cista, a decorated cylindrical metal container with three legs, a lid, and incised decoration

Clientes, a class of persons who provided goods and services to a patron in return for protection

Columen, the central beam of a pitched roof

Compluvium, a square opening at the center of the atrium roof

Cymatium (-a, pl.), the decorated upper part of a candelabra; also a crown molding

Dinos (-oi, pl.), a large mixing bowl for wine and water

Dioscuri, in Greek mythology, the twins Castor and Pollux (Polydeuces), brothers of Helen

Embossing, a technique for making figures in relief on sheet metal or another material

Faience, earthenware covered with glazed enamel

Flabellum, a luxurious fan with a decorated handle

Griffin, an imaginary animal with an eagle's beak and claws and the hind parts of a lion

Himation, a cloak

Hoplite, a citizen-soldier who bought his own armor, including helmet, cuirass, greaves, shield, spear, and sword

Hydria, a vessel for water, with a rounded shape and three handles

Hypogeum, an underground space for rituals or burials

Impluvium, the open-air space of an interior courtyard

Insula, a block of houses delineated by intersecting roads

Kantharos, a drinking cup with high, looped handles

Kelebe, a vessel with an ample mouth used for funerary purposes

Kline (-ai, pl.), a bed or couch used for dining or celebrating symposia

Kore (-ai, pl.), a statue of a clothed woman

Kotyle (-ai, pl.), a high-walled cup with horizontal handles

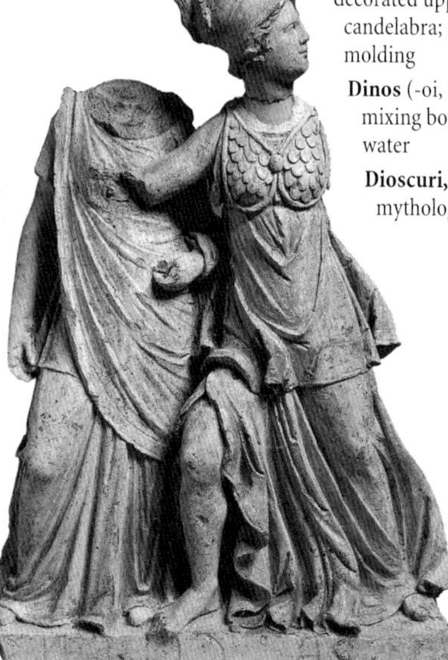

◀ Earthenware antefix portraying two female deities, Mera and Cilens, from Bolsena. Florence, Museo Archeologico.

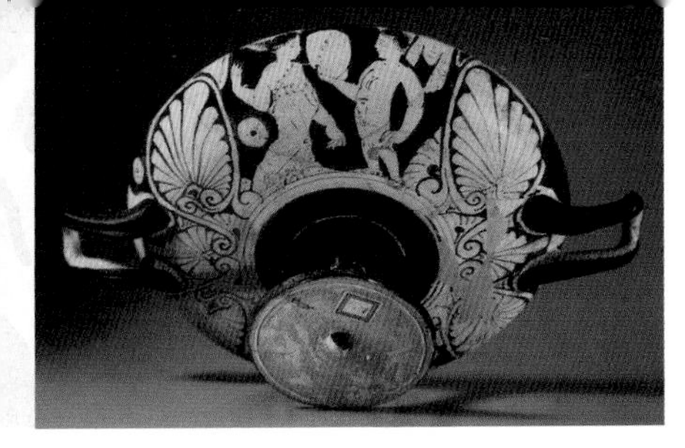

◀ *Kylix* from Civita Castellana, 350 B.C. Rome, Museo di Villa Giulia.

Kouros (-oi, pl.), a statue of a naked young man

Kyathos, a vessel for drawing liquids

Kylix, a wide, shallow drinking cup

Lebes, a bronze container with embossed or fused handles, supported on a tripod

Lituus, a curved staff marking priestly or political status

Maenad, a follower of the orgiastic cult of Dionysus

Mutule, a flat block on the underside of a cornice

Naiskos, a small shrine

Nenfro, a pink volcanic stone quarried in Etruria

Nimbus, in art, a decorative halo or disc that surrounds the head of a divinity

Oinochoe, a spherical pitcher with a long neck and three-lobed mouth

Olpe, a vase similar to an *oinochoe*

Opaion, a hole in a roof tile to allow smoke to escape

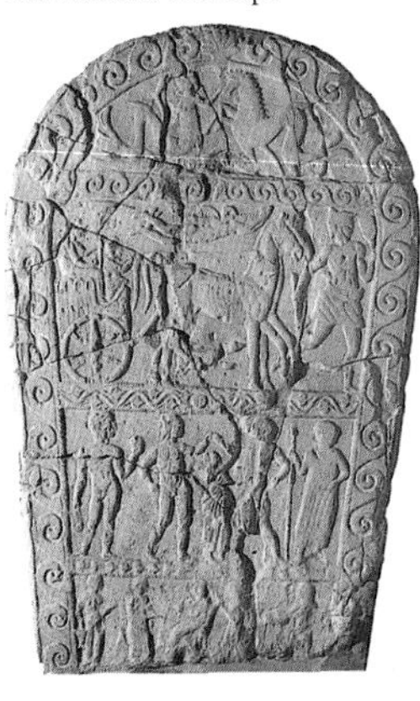

Pediment, the triangle at the top of a temple's short sides

Peripteral, surrounded by a single line of columns around all sides

Pileus, a felt hat

Platea, a broad passageway or street

Posticum, the rear half of a temple occupied by the *cella*

Pronaos, a front portico of a building

Prothesis, the ritual display of the deceased

Protome, a decoration in the shape of an animal or human head

Pyxis, a box-shaped container with a lid

Sakkos, a net used to tie back the hair

Schnabelkanne, a bronze or ceramic vessel with a long sloping lip

Silenus (-i, pl.), companion of Dionysus, celebrated by followers of his cult

Situla, a container for liquids made of embossed sheet-metal

Stamnos, a vase with horizontal handles

Stela (-e, pl.), a slab of stone, either inscribed or decorated, fixed in the ground as a funerary monument

Strigil, a bronze object that athletes used to clean sweat and dirt from their bodies

◀ Stela from Felsina showing the journey to the Underworld. Bologna, Museo Civico Archeologico.

Symposium, a drinking ceremony

Syrinx, a shepherd's reed instrument, also known as panpipes

Tablinum, an area between an atrium and a garden used to receive guests

Tholos, a circular building

Tintinnabulum, a sonorous, bell-like pendant, probably used for religious purposes

Torus, a convex molding with a smooth, oval, or fluted profile

Tutulus, a cone-shaped wool headdress

Tympanum, the triangular space enclosed by a pediment

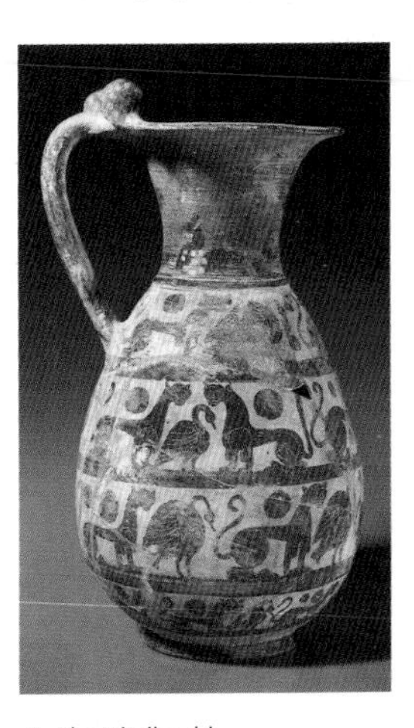

▲ The Vitelleschi Painter, a banded *olpe*, presumably from Tarquinia, 590–570 B.C. Tarquinia, Museo Archeologico.

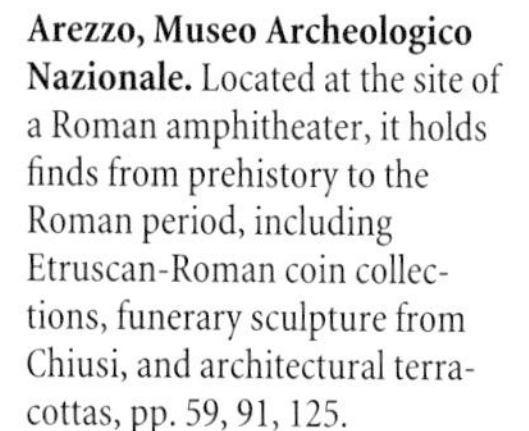

▶ Ring from Chiusi, first quarter of the fifth century B.C. London, The British Museum.

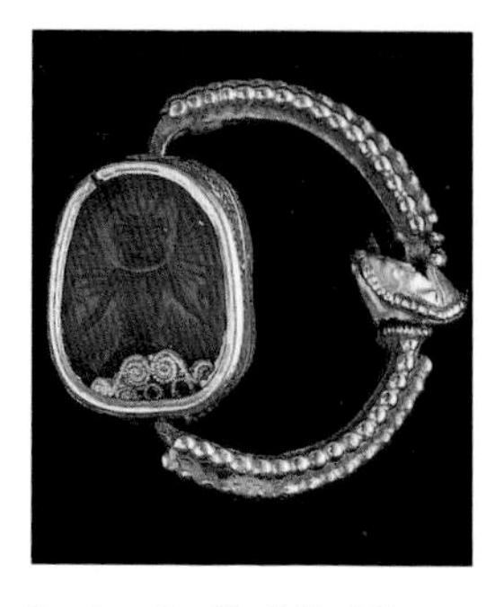

Arezzo, Museo Archeologico Nazionale. Located at the site of a Roman amphitheater, it holds finds from prehistory to the Roman period, including Etruscan-Roman coin collections, funerary sculpture from Chiusi, and architectural terra-cottas, pp. 59, 91, 125.

Bologna, Museo Civico Archeologico. Preserves important finds from the Etruscan civilization from the ninth to the fourth centuries B.C., plus discoveries from excavations in Bologna and the surrounding areas, pp. 18, 56, 67, 104, 139.

Chiusi, Museo Archeologico Nazionale. Exhibits of funerary urns, bucchero vases, and other finds from tombs in the area, pp. 29, 79, 99, 128–29.

Cortona, Museo dell'Accademia Etrusca. Holds Etruscan and Roman material, the most famous being a bronze Etruscan lamp; there are also works in bucchero, bronze, and a rich collection of coins, p. 92.

Este, Museo Nazionale Atestino. Hosts discoveries from necropolises, residences, and sanctuaries, especially ex-votos, inscriptions, and rich grave goods, p. 67.

Florence, Museo Archeologico Nazionale. Housing an important collection of Etruscan, Greek, and Roman art, the museum preserves masterpieces of Etruscan bronzework such as the Chimaera and the Orator, pp. 7, 14–15, 19, 21–23, 28, 31, 47, 55, 60–61, 67, 69, 77, 79, 88, 90, 93, 95, 99, 103–5, 108–9, 122–25, 127–28, 130–31, 138, 140.

Grosseto, Museo Archeologico e d'Arte della Maremma. Besides a section dedicated to the city of Roselle, the Orientalizing tombs of Vetulonia and Marsiliana d'Albegna stand out, pp. 19, 23, 32.

London, The British Museum. The section dedicated to classical antiquity houses noteworthy collections of Etruscan finds, such as the grave goods from the Tomb of Isis in Vulci, pp. 12–13, 56, 78, 89, 102–3, 140.

Los Angeles, The J. Paul Getty Museum. The museum houses important Etruscan, Greek, and Roman collections. Etruscan bronzes and figured pottery from Cerveteri are also preserved there, as well as examples of architectural terra-cottas, among which is a painted tile, pp. 51, 121, 141.

Marzabotto, Museo Nazionale Etrusco Pompeo Aria. The museum gathers numerous finds from Etruscan residences: sculpture, inscriptions, weapons, coins, architectural fragments, and grave goods from the fifth and fourth centuries B.C., pp. 86–87.

Orvieto, Museo Archeologico. Holds original frescoes from the Golini Tombs I and II from the second half of the fourth century B.C., as well as materials from the necropolises of Crocifisso del Tufo and Cannicella, p. 101.

Orvieto, Museo Claudio Faina. Among the Etruscan, Greek, and Roman material are terra-cottas from the Belvedere temple and Via San Leonardo, pp. 74–75, 88, 141.

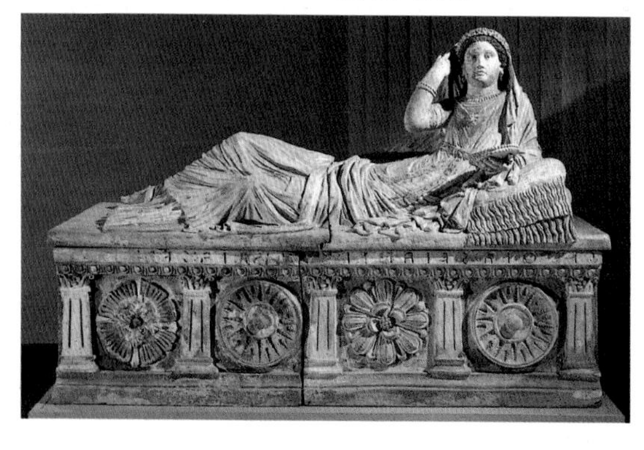

◀ The Sarcophagus of Larthia Seianti, the woman luxuriously clothed and adorned with jewels, from Chiusi, first half of the second century B.C. Florence, Museo Archeologico.

Paris, Musée du Louvre. The section on Etruscan antiquity includes vases, paintings, jewels, and sarcophagi, among which is the Sarcophagus of the Married Couple from Cerveteri, pp. 21, 32, 72, 78, 127.

Perugia, Museo Archeologico Nazionale. Among a variety of material from local artisans, the Etruscan-Roman section houses the cippus from Perugia and the famous intact tomb of Arnth Cai Cutu, pp. 59, 81, 115.

Populonia, Museo Archeologico del Territorio di Populonia. Inaugurated in 2001, it retraces the history of the city and the surrounding area through materials dating from prehistory to the late Roman period.

Rome, Musei Capitolini. Among the noteworthy Etruscan and Roman works of art, the museum preserves the famous bronzes of the Capitoline She-Wolf and Capitoline Brutus, pp. 92, 123, 134.

Rome, Museo Nazionale di Villa Giulia. The villa, destined for more than a century to absorb the collection of the Museo Etrusco, houses a number of private collections and numerous discoveries from the territory around Rome. Among the most famous pieces, the Sarcophagus of the Married Couple, the gold laminae from Pyrgi, the rich Orientalizing grave goods from Palestrina, the Castellani goldwork, and the Apollo from Veii stand apart, pp. 7, 9–10, 13–18, 24, 31, 33, 41, 43–44, 49, 50–52, 55, 68, 75, 78, 81, 83, 90, 98, 109, 114, 120, 125–27, 133, 139.

Siena, Museo Archeologico Nazionale. Holds various classes of Etruscan materials from the Siena and Chiusi areas.

Tarquinia, Museo Archeologico Nazionale. The Palazzo Vitelleschi here houses materials that were discovered at necropolises and excavations in the area, including a number of the principal wall paintings that have been removed from the tombs. In addition, numerous sarcophagi and the majestic winged horses from the Ara della Regina are on exhibit, pp. 6, 9, 13, 15, 17, 34, 38–39, 48–49, 51, 70, 73, 77, 83, 96, 119, 121, 126, 130–31, 139.

Vatican City, Museo Gregoriano Etrusco. In this important collection of Etruscan discoveries, the precious gold from the Regolini-Galassi Tomb of Cerveteri and the bronze statue of the Mars from Todi deserve mention, pp. 12, 17, 25, 33, 69, 77, 93, 108, 121, 130–31.

Viterbo, Museo Archeologico Nazionale. Preserves objects that were excavated at the most important Etruscan sites of Acquarossa, San Giovenale, and Ferento, pp. 37, 54, 87.

Volterra, Museo Etrusco Guarnacci. A collection of about six hundred Etruscan cinerary urns in alabaster, decorated with bas-reliefs from the Hellenistic period, pp. 54, 103, 114, 120, 129.

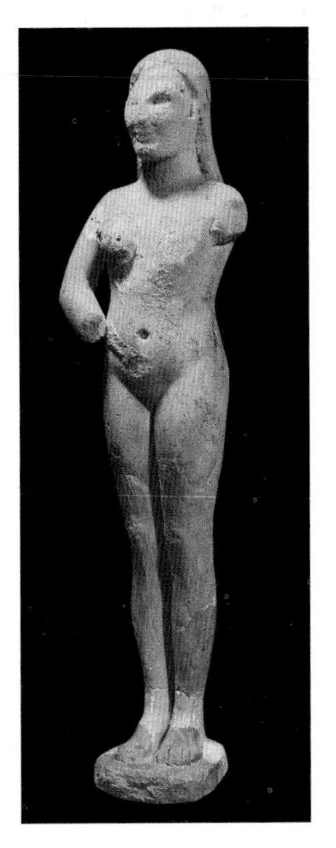

▼ Statue of a female divinity from the Cannicella necropolis, second half of the sixth century B.C. Orvieto, Museo Claudio Faina.

◀ Statuette of a bearded man, perhaps Tinia, from Populonia, about 480 B.C. Los Angeles, J. Paul Getty Museum.

▶ Aerial view of the site of Gravisca, Viterbo.

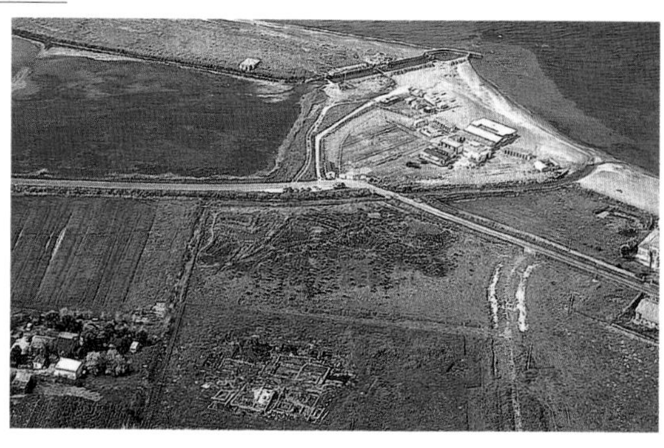

Acquarossa. Not far from Ferento, in the Acquarossa area, are traces of one of the few surviving Etruscan cities. There are remains of residences and a large complex that has been identified as the residence of a prince.

Blera. Famous for the monumental cube tombs of the Pian del Vescovo necropolis, carved into the tufa.

Castel d'Asso. Cube tombs preserved here have been dated between the fourth and second centuries B.C.

Cerveteri. Despite being one of the most important Etruscan cities, few traces remain of the inhabited city. Quite well preserved, however, are the necropolises of Banditaccia, Sorbo, and Monte Abetone, which have yielded extraordinary grave goods.

Cortona. Archaeological evidence relating to this important Etruscan city is scarce, but outside the city, which is enclosed by a fifth century B.C. wall, are tumulus tombs of great interest.

Fiesole. The Etruscan city, situated on Colle San Francesco, was enclosed by a wall that still borders an archaeological site. It includes an Etruscan temple from the Hellenistic period, a necropolis, a theater from the Flavian period, and Roman thermal baths.

Gravisca. This important archaeological area corresponds to the ancient port of Tarquinia.

Lago dell'Accesa. The archaeological park of Lago dell'Accesa was opened in 2001 in the area that yielded the remains of an Etruscan mining village active between the seventh and sixth centuries B.C., along with a number of necropolises.

Marzabotto. The orthogonal urban framework of the Etruscan city is easily visible, with roads, blocks, and the remains of residences.

Norchia. While traces of residences are scarce, the rock necropolises with temple tombs, dating between the fourth and third centuries B.C., are notably important.

Orvieto. The remains of the Etruscan city consist of some stretches of walls, the archaeological area under the church of Sant'Andrea, and the Belvedere temple. Interesting evidence also comes from the Crocifisso del Tufo and Cannicella necropolises.

Perugia. Besides the architectural remains of the Etruscan city, the necropolis of Palazzone, with the scenic burial chamber of the Volumnii, can be visited.

Poggio Civitate. This site is in the Siena area, in the territory of Murlo. A royal residence in use between the seventh and sixth centuries B.C. has been identified here.

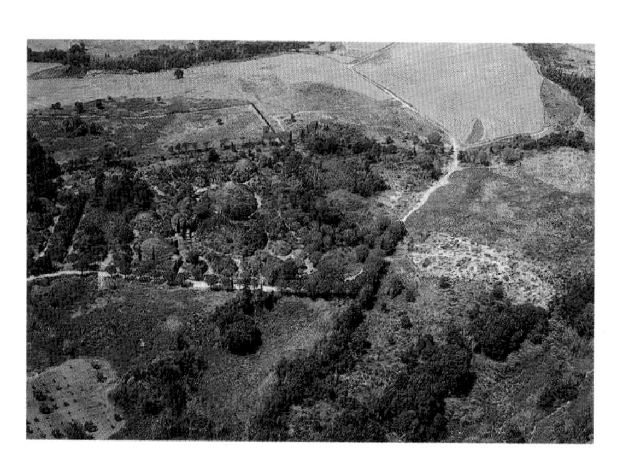

◀ Aerial view of the necropolis at Cerveteri.

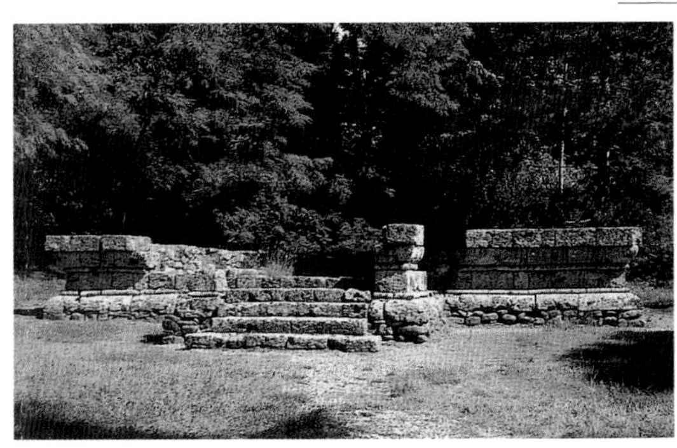

◀ view of the acropolis at Marzabotto.

Populonia. The only Etruscan city founded on the sea. The remains of the acropolis can be seen, with a temple from the late Hellenistic period and necropolises with tombs of different kinds.

Pyrgi. The commercial port of Cerveteri.

Roselle. The remains of the Etruscan city, founded in the seventh century B.C. and developed until the Roman era, are preserved here. Numerous tombs have been uncovered outside the city walls.

San Giovenale. The Etruscan residential area, which goes back to the Bronze age, rose up on a tufaceous plateau, where traces of the wall and the defense trench are still visible, together with ruins of the homes. The necropolises occupy the slopes of the hills.

Sovana. Here the ancient Etruscan city has been incorporated into the modern one. The necropolises that were carved into the tufa remain, of which the Hildebrand Tomb from the fourth century B.C. is the most significant.

Talamone. Excavations at Poggio di Talamonaccio brought to light parts of a Hellenistic temple.

Tarquinia. The ancient Etruscan city extended onto the Civita plateau, where the remains of the Ara della Regina and an older sacred area are visible. Necropolises with the famous painted tombs of the Archaic period can be found in the surrounding territory.

Veii. Only the walls and acropolis of this important Etruscan city remain, located in Piazza d'Armi. Outside the city at Portonaccio,

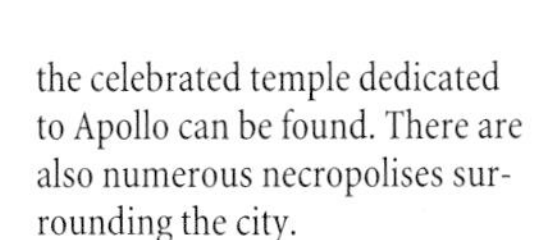

the celebrated temple dedicated to Apollo can be found. There are also numerous necropolises surrounding the city.

Vetulonia. This Etruscan city is known for its collection of Orientalizing tombs and rich grave goods.

Vulci. Monumental tombs and the remains of the Etruscan city, which flourished between the seventh and sixth centuries B.C., can be seen within the naturalistic archaeological park. The François Tomb, from the middle of the fourth century, is of particular importance. The medieval bridge of Abbadia, still spanning the river Fiora, was erected over a previous Etruscan bridge.

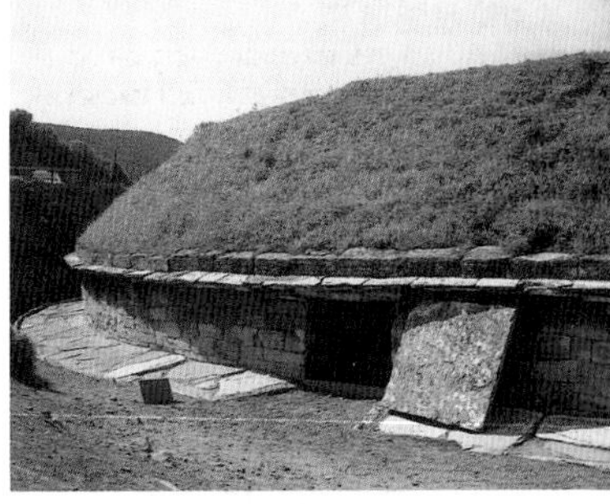

▲ The wagon entrance to the tumulus and its corresponding closing slab at the necropolis at Populonia.

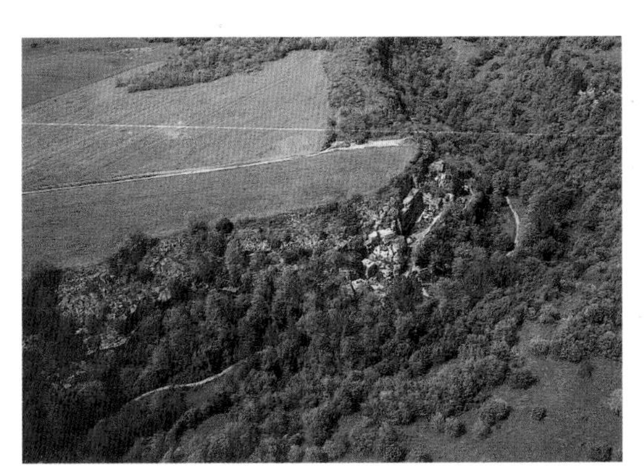

◀ Aerial view of the necropolis at Norchia.

First published in the United States of America in 2004 by
Getty Publications
1200 Getty Center Drive, Suite 500
Los Angeles, California 90049-1682
www.getty.edu

Christopher Hudson, *Publisher*
Mark Greenberg, *Editor in Chief*
Mollie Holtman, *Editor*
Robin H. Ray, *Copy Editor*
Pamela Heath, *Production Coordinator*
Thomas Michael Hartmann, *Translator*
Hespenheide Design, *Compositor and Designer*

Library of Congress Cataloging-in-Publication Data

Borrelli, Federica.
[Etruschi. English]
The Etruscans : art, architecture, and history / Federica Borrelli, Maria Cristina Targia ; edited by Stefano Peccatori and Stefano Zuffi ; translated by Thomas Michael Hartmann.
p. cm.
ISBN 0-89236-753-9 (hardcover)
1. Art, Etruscan. I. Targia, Maria Cristina. II. Peccatori, Stefano. III. Zuffi, Stefano, 1961– IV. Title.
N5750.B6513 2004
937'.0049994—dc22

2003023714

Printed and bound in Italy

Photo Credits

Sergio Anelli, Milan
Archivio Electa, Milan
Archivio Scala Group, Antella (Florence)
RCS Libri S.p.A./Andrea Baguzzi
Soprintendenza ai Beni Archeologici per l'Etruria Meridionale

Special thanks to the museums and photographic archives who kindly furnished the images for this book.